WOMEN IN CIVIL SOCIETY

WOMEN IN CIVIL SOCIETY

THE STATE, ISLAMISM, AND NETWORKS IN THE UAE

Wanda Krause

palgrave
macmillan

First published in 2008 by PALGRAVE MACMILLAN® in the US -
a division of St. Martin's Press LLC, 175 Fifth Avenue, New York,
NY 10010.

Where this book is distributed in the UK, Europe and the rest of the
world, this is by Palgrave Macmillan, a division of Macmillan Publishers Limited, registered in England, company number 785998, of
Houndmills, Basingstoke, Hampshire RG21 6XS.

Palgrave Macmillan is the global academic imprint of the above companies and has companies and representatives throughout the world.

Palgrave® and Macmillan® are registered trademarks in the United
States, the United Kingdom, Europe and other countries.

ISBN-13: 978-0-230-60956-3
ISBN-10: 0-230-60956-2

Library of Congress Cataloguing-in-Publication data

Krause, Wanda.
    Women in civil society : the state, Islamism, and networks in the
UAE / Wanda Krause.
       p. cm.
    Includes bibliographical references and index.
    ISBN 0-230-60956-2
    1. Women—United Arab Emirates—Social conditions.   2. Muslim
women—United Arab Emirates—Social conditions.   3. Women in
Islam—United Arab Emirates.   4. Sex role—United Arab Emirates—
History.   5. United Arab Emirates—Social conditions.   I. Title.
HQ1731.5.K73 2008
305.48'697095357—dc22   2008017987

A catalogue record of the book is available from the British Library.

Design by Westchester Book Group.

First Edition: October 2008

10 9 8 7 6 5 4 3 2 1

Printed in the United States of America.

CONTENTS

ACKNOWLEDGMENTS

This book would not have been possible without the generous help of several people in its preparation and writing. I am most grateful to the women and men who allowed me to interview them and their trust and faith in my work. In various ways, people allowed me into their own personal lives. Such an invitation and acceptance enabled me to be immersed in the struggles, desires, aspirations, and worldviews. It is my hope that this work adequately exposes what they struggle to achieve.

My appreciation is extended to all experts and informants, academic and nonacademic, some of whom are not mentioned, due to sensitivities, but who, nonetheless, equally provided me with insights, suggestions, and links. I am grateful to several faculty members at the United Arab Emirates University who guided me at the initial stage of this project. Faculty members at the American University of Sharjah were also helpful. Of those who offered continuous support, I would like to thank especially Sharla Musaibeh (winner of the 2007 National Women's Day Award), Maitha al-Shamsi, Amna al-Shamsi, Mariam al-Naymi, Maryam Yamani, Dr. Mona al-Bahr, Dr. Abdulkhaleq Abdullah, and finally, Dr. Suaad al-Oraimi.

This book is developed out of my Ph.D. work. I owe the development of the ideas to Dr. Salwa Ismail and thank her for patience and continued encouragement. I am grateful to Dr. Kamil Mahdi and Dr. Sami Zubaida for their generous feedback. I am also indebted to Dr. Christopher Davidson for providing feedback and sharing his extensive knowledge on the UAE. I thank an anonymous reviewer for insightful commentary. I extend my gratitude to two of my earlier professors who played an important role in directing my path culminating in this work—Dr. Roger Epp and Dr. Thomas Bateman, and also in my academic journey for playing a big role in developing my ideas—Dr. Janine Clark.

I would like to thank, firstly, Lindy Ayubi for her editing and for proofreading through parts or drafts also Michele Moore, Jennifer Moore, Naomi Khan, Melissa Finn, and Marsena Hydes. Among those who helped ease the difficult moments of the research by providing their friendship and encouragement, I would also like to thank Naomi, Hawwa, Mari, Bushra, Jen (also for freely sharing her experience and expert knowledge), and especially Lobna and Melissa for their ear whenever I needed to talk. A few I opt not to mention by name as they were also activists in the field who dealt with highly sensitive issues, but I hope they will know their friendship and help is greatly valued. Deep appreciation goes to my parents, Werner Krause and Pam Herdes, for their wisdom, direction, and practical help. Most important in my gratitude is Jasser Auda. His immense patience, support, and encouragement brought me through the most intense stages of this experience to the completion of this book. Finally, I thank Radwa, Omar, Ahmed, and Sarah Auda for all they endured throughout this process.

CHAPTER 1

WOMEN IN CIVIL SOCIETY: KEY ISSUES IN THE MIDDLE EAST

BASIC GOALS

This book investigates how indigenous forms of interaction and participation can assist in reaching a broader conception of civil society and also addresses inadequacies and biases in the application of the civil society concept. It studies the participation of women as a major sector of the population that until recently has remained unaccounted for in mainstream political science. In applying a civil society framework focused on UAE women, the book seeks to incorporate a gendered perspective of marginalized groups essential to the comprehensive understanding of politics and change. Thus, the question: Does UAE women's activism play a significant role in the development of civil society? If so, what does this mean for the civil society concept in explaining this process?

As such, this book focuses on the role of women in UAE civil society. Literature on civil society (usually translated as *mujtama madani* among Arab intellectuals) in the Middle East and the rentier state conclude that independent groups in the Gulf are unimportant, associational life is weak, and public space between the family and state is sparsely populated. The UAE represents one of the most comprehensive and enduring examples of a rentier state consisting of a tribal elite. The state's use of its institutions to confine wider public participation in the political process, referred to as corporatist politics, does play a role in frustrating civil society efforts but not always in ways that one might expect when political practice is analyzed beyond state structures. Thus, it was necessary to investigate the mechanisms through which the state seeks to circumscribe civil society outside the entity called the "state." As such, it chooses a region that is under-researched to nuance understandings and challenges of civil societies. It chooses to include women's Islamic activism as a category often viewed as problematic to the secular liberal normative project of civil society and a force little understood and underestimated within Islamist politics. It, furthermore, focuses on networks of women in the UAE that implement various strategies to pursue their interests and prove to spearhead the struggle against human rights abuses. The fieldwork, conducted from 2001 until 2005, demonstrated various processes within civil society that have been hardly taken into account. One major facet of the investigation was how women ardently pursue a variety of interests and engage others with competing views in a region thought to be void of civil society.

SIGNIFICANCE OF PROJECT

As the subject of this project is theoretically complex, its contribution lies in several areas. First, since identities, goals, and desires form complex sites of struggle, I seek to rethink the narrow and often dichotomous frameworks that obscure a more thorough understanding of state-society relations and civil society struggle. In this vein, one construct is found within what is termed the state as an entity completely separated from society in composition and formation. The state is not a concrete entity; such a distinction wrongly produces the idea of a self-contained unit.[1] As such, some have sought to deconstruct the "state."[2] This work adds to such works through analyzing the role of government-run associations, such as the UAE women's societies, in extending the functions of the state to the realm of civil society. Another dichotomous construct is found in the way a power struggle against a dominant force is categorized as either resistance- or compliance-oriented. Its obstruction is found by way of an analysis of multiple forms of agency. The agency of women in the Middle East cannot be explained merely by delineating repression by men or by the state. Women's capacities and modes of being, that is, the kinds of selves they are inspired to be with the proclivities and qualities they are motivated to unconsciously desire and embody, we will refer to as their subjectivities, are also constituted through religious, social, and political negotiations that are part of particular discursive traditions. Tribe, social class, or ideology form some of the forces underlying the goals and interests of women. Thus, the subject pursues a variety of interests, many that are privately oriented, that have an effect on the public. Therefore, the significance of this work is in broadening the civil society concept so that it theoretically allows for the study of actions excluded from mainstream scholarship. As such, it searches for modalities of action otherwise missed through narrow lenses.

Second, the book focuses on female actors as a significant part in civil society activism in contrast with civil society studies that focus on male actors. Focus on male actors occurs in works on civil society and on social movements that include actors in democratic transitions, Islamist movements and groups, and a conglomeration of nongovernmental organizations (NGOs). The civil society concept is not gender neutral. Jude Howell suggests that civil society is discussed as though gender is irrelevant and warns that such neglect implicitly reinforces the idea of there being naturally a public realm for men and a private realm for women.[3] By offering a clearer picture of women's actions and influences through its case study on women in the Emirates, this book contributes to the growing number of studies on women's struggles in developing countries. It examines actions that are often privately oriented in order to uncover various modes of action marginalized in civil society literature, and through its more specific analyzing of civil society from a gender perspective, it addresses largely ignored dimensions of civil society. The current civil society concept is not gender neutral.

Third, scholars have proposed numerous theories as to why Middle Eastern states cannot sustain civil societies. A body of literature has developed as a reaction to such hypotheses and assumptions. As part of that literature, this study discusses conceptual frameworks through which it has been argued that the region is void of civil societies. In the post-9/11 era, such an endeavor is especially crucial, since Islamic identities are being politically defined and correspondingly constructed as antithetical to civic values. As such, the study revisits values ascribed to Islam, as well Islamic discourse and modes of action among civil society actors, and investigates why these or other variables may be seen to impede civil society growth. The case study contributes to a clearer understanding of civil society expansion constituted through actors deemed ill-suited to such a project.

Fourth, with an example of a rentier state influenced from the bottom up or within civil society, the research simultaneously nuances rentier state theory. Because it focuses squarely on state action, rentier state theory cannot account for change produced within civil society. Hence, after probing the idea of a concrete state, I attempt to interrogate the dominant paradigm applied to the Gulf region to explain political processes.

CIVIL SOCIETY: THEORETICAL PROBLEMS

This section surveys major works and significant contributions concerning the issue of women in civil society. The aim is to try and expose the limitations and biases confounding rigorous analysis of the Middle Eastern region, in particular the Arab Gulf, as well as to identify existing developments toward this goal already in place. I shall do this by outlining arguments for the various manifestations of civil society activism—principally women's contributions—in the Middle East.

The Definition of Civil Society

Mainstream scholarship focusing on the Middle East approaches the question of civil society by asking if there is, indeed, a civil society in the region, only to conclude that it is profoundly absent. It is helped by the definitions used for a civil society concept, which reflect rigid, narrow, and context-specific usage. Such definitions have been developed in response to specific historical events and, therefore, cannot account for societal and state-society interaction born out of wholly different backgrounds. The resulting hermeneutic problems are acute in the civil society application to the Middle East. Defining civil society in a manner that excludes important action groups and local expressions of basic values obscures our understanding of political processes, influences, and change.[4] Exclusions are often due to biases in which action groups can be considered significant, civil, modern, or sufficiently progressive to be included in the civil society definition.

Civil society literature on the Middle East often excludes certain women's action groups. This is because women's actions are theoretically confined to the private sphere and are, thus, deemed irrelevant to studies on the public and political spheres. There is a bias in the literature on searching for politically relevant action through studying formal political institutions. The fact that the exercise of power in privately oriented activities could be more important to some outside a Western trajectory is a completely ignored dimension. Because women occupy scarcely any positions in government, their actions are already excluded. The problem is indeed much the same in studies focusing on civil society. As in the Athenian *polis* or Roman republic, the Western construct of "citizen," which means a contract-making individual, has referred to a property owner who could only be a male citizen. As such, the social contract is a fraternal pact from which civil society has developed.[5] When an academic discipline is not gendered through the analysis of women's movements and activities, the struggles, desires, goals, and everyday activities of such women become trivialized, or more accurately, invisible.

The inclusion or exclusion of Islamic groups or associations as civil society institutions has, for example, also been a matter of considerable disagreement. While many argue that Islamic groups or associations fall outside the realm of civil society, scholars, such as Janine Clark, Koenraad Verhagen, Nilüfer Göle, and Amani Kandil, assert that religious organizations have an important function in civil society. Clark shows that a danger in analyses has been the blurring between the minority of violent Islamist groups and the majority of nonviolent Islamist groups, in which Islamic associations are characterized as instruments of the undemocratic and extremist Islamic groups.[6] As Verhagen notes, the contribution of religious organizations is in terms of the value systems they furnish and also of the catalyst for social transformation they often become. Göle, in fact, in her study on Turkey, speaks of the creation of an autonomous sphere in society due to Islamic values and the Islamicization of politics.[7] Kandil recognizes that religion plays a key role as a motivating factor for women's voluntary initiatives since it encourages them to volunteer time and give charity and, thus, enables them to assume a profound role in civil society.[8] Yet it is not unusual to find that Islamic organizations are thought to be "non-civil," and hence outside the scope of any study on civil society. Excluding Islamic organizations and *halaqas* (religious study circles) merely because their missions and agendas are guided by ideology means ignoring the fact that, as well as contributing to "civility," they can be the most effective means for responding to the needs of citizens.[9]

Civil society is utilized as both an analytical and a normative tool, and its progressive teleology embraces secular liberal politics. Thus, the behaviors, norms, and practices that run against secular liberal politics are seen as incongruous with the project of civil society. While groups that are at war with civility are excluded from a civil society definition, groups that simply run against the dominant Western worldview of modernity and progress must not be excluded. As Marlies Glasius argues, "[C]ivil society is not the exclusive domain of 'progressive' human rights, environmental, social justice and women's rights activists, it is a space co-inhabited by conservatives, anti-abortionists, and religious fundamentalists."[10] Such groups are equally relevant to the sphere in which dominant discourses are challenged and competing views are put forward.[11] As such, "civil society can be an arena where gendered behaviours, norms and practises are acted out and reproduced."[12] It is also important to recognize that a "common good" is a contested domain. As political scientist Thomas Carothers explains, "struggles over public interest are not between civil society on the one hand and bad guys on the other but within civil society itself."[13]

In its mainstream definition, civil society is cast as an entity that operates separately from the state. Many scholars have recognized that civil society cannot occupy a space entirely distinct from the state, but rather that it is a sector that intermingles fluidly with the state.[14] This is a key factor in understanding how civil society activism can produce change in a context in which political society is absent. If peaceful and durable change is to occur, it will probably happen through the incremental effects of civil society sectors. Where a multiparty parliamentary system finds no place in the state apparatus and conflict cannot find expression in and through political parties or unions, demands for change must be made elsewhere. In the UAE, overt political organizations (especially political parties and unions) and Islamist groups are banned, though professional associations are tolerated. Thus, as some researchers confirm, activities that might have political impact must find expression in NGOs, including women's associations.[15]

However, an authoritarian state is often so intrusive that NGOs can be handicapped in providing an autonomous space for activity. As such, it is pertinent that informal types of collaboration be included. In fact, as Sayyid Hurreiz states, "there are various social and religious occasions which provide informal avenues for meetings of political significance."[16] Perceiving how the various forms of collaboration respond to state goals or how they place demands on state officials will illuminate the fluid boundaries between state and civil society. Explaining the interaction between state and civil society will, thus, expose civil society actions that are otherwise missed in studies that focus on civil society and cast the state as an impermeable entity.

Nevertheless, many of these studies risk overemphasizing civil society actions in relation to the actions of state actors. Thus, some scholars have argued for "bringing the state back in" for a comprehensive picture.[17] This book applies a civil society framework precisely because the state remains the focus for political action in oil-rich countries. However, it also maintains that excluding the state would also result in incorrect and incomplete conclusions. It is "meaningless to speak of civil society in absence of the state."[18]

Scholars, such as political science professors Nazih Ayubi and Khaldun al-Naqib, have added greater insight into state-society relations through the study of corporatist politics. Political scientist Philippe Schmitter defines corporatism as,

a system of interest representation in which the constituent units are organized into a limited number of singular, compulsory, non competitive, hierarchically ordered and functionally differentiated categories, recognized or licensed (if not created) by the state and granted a deliberate representational monopoly within their respective categories in exchange for observing certain controls on their selection of leaders and articulation of demands and supports.[19]

The corporatist framework helps identify the modes of action and means of control used by the state to circumscribe civil society, and it also clarifies the rather fluid boundaries between the state and civil society, often conceived to be neatly separated entities. Thus, while it does not explain how civil society actors circumscribe and undermine state modes of control, or how civil society actors can pressure the state into concessions and bargaining, it does at least lay the groundwork for studying patron-client modes of interaction and modalities of "governmentality."

I aim to expand the civil society concept to recognize networking as a core mode of action for the expansion of civil society, especially in authoritarian environments. As Thomas Carothers argues, "it is a mistake to equate civil society with NGOs; in many countries. . . . NGOs are outweighed by more traditional parts of civil society."[20] Networkers are most able to place their demands on state actors through their vertical relationships. The intention is to illustrate the modes of action utilized by networkers to evade obstacles, and to show how power can be exercised from the bottom up through the patron-client networks. I will also demonstrate the way in which actors can assist the state in its objectives of civil society control.

As such, when discussing the boundaries of the state in relation to civil society, the state should not be construed as a "preconstituted and coherent actor."[21] Rather, states represent "powerful sites of symbolic and cultural production that are themselves always culturally represented and understood in particular ways."[22] One needs to investigate how the state is produced through bureaucratic practices, interaction between state and societal actors, and public cultural representations. Literature on governmentality helps in this objective.

Governmentality was first introduced by Michel Foucault to describe how government regulates the conduct of others or oneself,[23] or in other words, "the conduct of conduct."[24] It is concerned with the different mentalities of government and the various ways in which human conduct is directed by calculated means. Importantly, governmentality is not characterized only by discipline and regulation; rather it emphasizes a productive dimension. This means that instead of punishment and direct coercive measures, the state can use various other mechanisms of control, such as the entitlements and welfare allocations typically found within a rentier state. I use the concept to signify the diffusion of modes of governance, such as state feminism, beyond the boundaries of the state and the "imbrication of all kinds of social actors such as GONGOs in the project of rule."[25]

More recently, "governmentality" has been used to describe a process of neoliberalism in which a transfer of government operations to nonstate entities occurs. This is achieved by devolving responsibility to subjects who are thereby increasingly empowered to discipline themselves. The process of governmentality, however, will look different in contexts outside the West.[26] The book will look critically at the case of the UAE with regard to the "techne of government," as in the "means, mechanisms, procedures, instruments, tactics, techniques, technologies and vocabularies" through which authority is constituted.[27] As Mitchell Dean attests, programs of empowerment are particularly clear examples of neoliberal governmentality that seek to operationalize a decentralization of power.[28] Thus, how do the government organized nongovernmental organizations (GONGO) associations of this study function as institutions that assist government?

If civil society is to be a useful heuristic tool in deciphering participatory action toward the common good in the Arab Gulf, then it has to be conceptualized in a way that avoids excluding action groups while differentiating the civil society sphere from other realms of interaction that are dominated by other functions. Sociologist Edward Shils provides a basic working definition for civil society:

The idea of civil society is the idea of a part of society which has a life of its own, which is distinctly different from the state, and which is largely in autonomy from it. Civil society lies beyond the boundaries of the family and clan and beyond the locality; it lies short of the state.[29]

Building on this basic framework, civil society will be understood as the realm loosely located between the family and the state, in which individuals participate through structures of independent voluntary associations, networks, or discursive space. Within these, (1) the values of trust, tolerance, cooperation, and reciprocity are fostered; (2) individuals attempt to empower themselves through identifying notions that will lead to their personal and societal development, happiness, and satisfaction; and (3) individuals pursue their interests, engage others in contesting discourses, and compete over notions of the common good or "truth."

While this broad definition will be used here, the boundaries around the civil society sphere require clarification. As the Centre for the Study of Civil Society explains, "In theory, its institutional forms are distinct from those of the state, family and market, though in practice, the boundaries between state, civil society, family and market are often complex, blurred and negotiated."[30] Following the traditions of Gramsci and Tocqueville, I exclude the economy and political society (not to mention the fact that there are no political parties in the UAE), since I regard these two as essentially separate realms, while I acknowledge that these spheres will overlap in various ways.

Nonetheless, I maintain that one must simultaneously remain sensitive to the fact that historically, the civil society concept in classical theory included the business sector, which, in fact, was dominant in the traditions of Hegel and Marx. Essentially, the business sector pursues self-serving interests that are usually not in the interest of the common good. As sociologist Christopher Bryant points out, the economic sphere "affords possibilities of concerted action and social self-organization."[31] Marx's characterization of the economic sphere was insensitive to the notion of an inclusive citizenship,[32] and he uncritically adopted Hegel's notion that the working class was a class excluded from civil society.[33] When adopting concepts one must be critical of the historic contexts out of which they emerged. The exclusion of the working class occurs among numerous theorists because of particular historical circumstances; that is, during certain periods, the working class stood in a contradictory state to civil society and the state.[34] Political scientist Krishan Kumar laments the keenness of modern theorists to cling to what he calls a "bankrupt tradition."[35] Weighing up Marx's notion of civil society, sociology professor Alvin Gouldner stresses its aspect of civility—referring to this component as a sociological notion of civil society.[36] Again, this book also views civility as a crucial indicator for the assessment of a civil society.

Closer scrutiny of civil society's boundaries with the political is also required. Here the concept is defined in relation to the realm of government, or, in our case, the monarchic state. Civil society is viewed as occupying a space in which actions that can have consequences within the realm of the political take place. As the actions studied involve power relations, they cannot be viewed as entirely apolitical in nature. Normatively, strategies for solidarity and networking for mutual aid and benefit are predominant in such actions. As such, comprehending the nature of authority and politics is essential in understanding the point at which civil society and political society become separated.[37] This space is differentiated from institutional politics and is marked by the making and entrenchment of laws, policies governing society at large, and competition for power. This distinction is important in the study of a rentier state, where the ruling class attempts to inculcate and manipulate a rentier mentality to absorb civil society activism.

The feminist goal—as found in Western scholarship—to dismantle the theoretical distinction between the private and the public (state, civil society, and market) by deconstructing the boundary between the family and the civil society spheres is intended to reveal various actions that take place in private and that are political. Others have sought to deconstruct this distinction in an attempt to uncover certain actions within the tribe and the clan, arguing that these can serve a common good.[38] In my view, however, this move is largely unnecessary. The multitude of privately oriented actions that affect the public sphere can be included as civil society activities by virtue of their effect, without encompassing the structure of the family within the public sphere. Similarly, as Christopher Bryant explains, "Notwithstanding the part played by the family and the socialization of the citizen, the household is private whereas civil society is public."[39] Importantly, in the context where family, clan and tribal interests spread through the political and economic systems of society to the exclusion of other group formations and solidarities, familial collaboration is problematic for a working definition of civil society. As political science professor Sami Zubaida warns, both state and primordial groups represent spheres of authority and coercion that may violate individual and human rights.[40]

Is There a Civil Society in the Middle East?

In applying Western-developed civil society approaches to the Middle East, relatively few scholars would agree that the Middle East in general has a civil society. Indeed, while a plethora of literature exists on political participation, civil society, and prospects for democratization in Eastern Europe and, to a greater extent, Latin America, scholars are quick to assume that no evidence for civil society growth and democratic development can be sighted in the Middle East. Political science professor John Entelis comments: "Compared to other Third World regions, the Middle East and North Africa have lagged significantly in providing theoretical insight and empirical evidence for explaining the origin and development of state-society relations."[41] Jeff Haynes links the lack of democracy directly to "the virtual absence of civil societies in the Middle East,"[42] and in his argument goes as far as to affront Middle Eastern women in comparing them to Latin American and Indian women. While he grants women's movements the distinction of frequently being at the "cutting edge of democratization,"[43] he repeatedly expresses doubt about the ability of Middle Eastern women to fulfill any such role.[44]

The main approach of such skeptics focuses on the structural relationship between state and society. Many argue that it is within this framework that sectors of civil society—NGOs or particularly women—are so repressed. Some even argue that civil society associations must necessarily be government organized in order for them to be civil. And now that much evidence demonstrates ever-growing grassroots organizations in the developing world, it is argued that they are so buffeted by corporatist pressures, so insignificant in their capacity to influence, or so "little-institutionalized" that they barely constitute civil society.[45]

The second approach focuses on a Middle Eastern essentialism that is explained by culture and religion. The arguments seem to have originated from the orientalist approach that has now been widely criticized for its erroneous assumptions about Middle Eastern culture and religion. Essentialists argue that deep religiosity and Arab culture are absolute impediments to the development of civic values and institutions that are, by definition, secular. Ernest Gellner views civil society as absent in the Islamic world because of the Islamic religion and customs.[46] Middle East political scientist Mehran Kamrava explains that "Islam . . . in its current militant form poses an immovable obstacle to social and cultural democratization."[47] Indeed, he rightfully points out (growing) militant influences that threaten civility, but Islamic practice in the Middle East is so much richer. He also mentions that his views are backed by those of Elie Kedourie, Bernard Lewis, Albert Hourani, and Samuel Huntington, remarking that, "Thus there would seem to be hardly any room for yet another rehash of old arguments so meticulously presented by giants of the discipline."[48]

However, having dispensed with the orientalist propositions, a whole body of scholarship has developed to describe forms of activism and resistance in Muslim and Middle Eastern society. Scholars such as Augustus Richard Norton, Saad Eddin Ibrahim, Nilüfer Göle, Amani Kandil, Jillian Schwedler, and Sheila Carapico take the view that the Middle East, or parts thereof, has some level of a civil society. They

implicitly link the functioning of civil society to cultivating democratic principles and paving the way for political openings, thereby
acknowledging the complexity of civil society and the problems associated with the region's ability to liberalize politically and to sustain
democracy.

In reply to those (Western) researchers who contend that there is
no civil society in the Middle East, political scientist and human rights
activist Saad Eddin Ibrahim notes how often they have forgotten their
own long, arduous, and even bloody march toward a civil society and
democratization.[49] He also points out that civil society existed in the
Middle East long before the term was even developed, and describes
the mélange of earlier times' civil society forms.[50] Anthropologist
Richard Antoun maintains that such gross oversight in the literature
of various forms of interaction continues to result from the limitations
of what constitutes "civil institutions." In his case study on Jordan
and clanship, he addresses the problem of how civil society literature
has "discounted important action arenas of civil society [and has] thus
obscured a significant process that has contributed to civil society in
the Middle East for generations."[51] Mohammed Salim al-Awwa, professor of Law, explains that civil society also flourishes in Islamic societies, and that one must recognize that the institutions that represent
civil society simply take different forms in every society according to
context and time.[52] Looking beyond "cultural" explanations, these
scholars are pointing to a wide variety of civil society sectors to illustrate that civil society not only exists in the Middle East but is frequently vibrant.

In the application of the civil society concept to the Arab world—a
region composed of sometimes vastly different experiences—scholars
often fail to consider the connotations and historical background associated with the term. The yardstick has always been the West.
Richard Norton rightly warns of the tendency to idealize civil society.
He states, "At times, civil society is described in such rarefied, ideal-
typical terms that 'sightings' of civil society are dismissed as spurious.
Often, one has the sense that civil society is so pristinely defined that
it could not possibly exist anywhere."[53]

Christopher Hann, professor of Anthropology, asserts that Western scholars are propagating an ideal of social organization which, in
fact, bears little relation to current realities within their own countries
and furthermore, has developed in historical conditions that cannot
be replicated elsewhere.[54] Moreover, according to Kumi Naidoo and
Rajesh Tandon, "Our greatest enemy is arrogance and the notion
that a strong civil society is an end in itself rather than the means by

which peoples express their civic side in the collective enterprise we all share."[55] The question asked has traditionally been set strictly in terms of whether or not a certain country has a civil society, and the conclusion arrived at is that regions, mainly the Middle East, are devoid of a civil society. The problems concerning civil society in the Middle East are complex; thus, one cannot question in strict terms whether civil society exists.

Robert Hefner, professor of Anthropology, explains that scholars who follow a "culturalist" line of analysis base their conclusions on the belief that what he terms a "civil democracy" (or participation, equality, freedom, and tolerance) rests upon a constellation of values and institutions unique to the West. Linking civil society's function to forming a basis for democratization, he criticizes the notion that the Middle East can only become truly democratic if "the tiger can somehow change its stripes to a Western dress,"[56] which according to the scholars who share this view cannot happen because of a lack of this heritage.[57] Islamist thinker and political scientist Rached Ghannouchi cautions that the civil society concept has been situated as oppositional to a religious society through French cultural history, which witnessed a violent conflict between the church and the French revolution. The result of this conflict was the idea that religion and civility cannot be one. When scholars apply the idea of civil society in the Arab world, they fail to consider the connotations associated with the term.[58]

Ghannouchi's argument is set within a debate among intellectuals in the Arab world as to whether or not concepts such as "civil society" or "democracy," because of their Western connotations and "non-Islamic" philosophical basis, are unique to and belong to the West alone. While he does not explicitly attempt to find a replacement for these terms, many following the same line of analysis do so.[59] Clark, however, warns that even though the term *civil society* undoubtedly carries Western "connotational 'baggage'" with it, exchanging that term for another will not necessarily add accuracy; rather it will increase confusion in "a theoretical field already plagued with different understandings of this term."[60] And as Hefner points out to the (Western) culturalists (his comments being equally relevant to the above group), even though such ideals may have been influenced by the West, they are ideals that are not exclusively "Western," and at times may need "reelaboration" in their own contexts.[61]

In his case study on Egypt, Mustapha Kamel al-Sayyid, professor of Political Science, sets out three prerequisites to help in assessing the existence of civil society:

the presence of formal organizations of various types among different social groups and classes; an ethic of tolerance and acceptance by the majority of minority legitimate rights, no matter how such minorities are defined; and limitations on arbitrary exercise of state authority.[62]

He also warns that, in making such an assessment, no society will fully meet all three criteria.[63] He lists the statistics for a growing number of associations in Egypt to demonstrate that the first indicator has been met.[64] Focusing on Islamist groups, that is, groups asserting a political agenda using Islamic rhetoric (rather than Islamic voluntary organizations, referring to forms of organization based upon ideals that are claimed to be part of the religion Islam—or any other, for that matter), he concludes that the other two indicators "are lacking."[65] Apart from noting the contribution of greatly needed services to various communities, he makes no attempt to analyze the actual activities of these growing organizations to understand what function they might play in contributing to civil society.

Sheila Carapico argues that, in order to transcend biases in the study of civil society in the Middle East and to fully recognize the force of these actions vis-à-vis the state, actions need to be looked at within a political environment.[66] She considers that a civil society in the Middle East

> may more closely resemble what Jean François Bayart described as the process whereby society seeks to "breach" or counteract "totalization" by the state, or, in Henri Lefebvre's term, "an autonomous space of mass expression," than formal organizations cooperating within legal guarantees conceded in advance.[67]

In other words, by including the struggles of informal associations against the state in the political environment, a growth of civil society may be observed. To understand civil society processes, Jillian Schwedler asks the question: "How do citizens and communities address their interests or grievances vis-à-vis government policies?"[68] She argues that framing the question in this manner highlights a range of social interactions that might otherwise be dismissed as insignificant.[69]

Despite a broadening of the civil society sphere in the arguments put forward by Carapico and Schwedler, the government remains the focus of attention for observing the expansion of civil society. There is an overriding assumption in the literature that the greatest purpose of civil society is to stand in stark opposition to an incompetent and predatory state. However, power is exercised not only by the state, but also within civil society.[70] The actions of civil society actors are not merely reactions to state authoritarianism or policies, but are also initiations for a wide range of interests. Power, as described by Foucault, cannot be understood merely within the framework of domination, as something possessed and used by persons or states over others. Rather, it permeates life and produces new forms of desires, objects, relations, and discourses.[71] Civil society actors must be recognized as the initiators of a wide range of interests. Jean Cohen and Andrew Arato suggest that civil society is much more than just a safeguard against state authority and power, asserting that the "civic" behavior of members in their dealings with one another is central to civil society.[72]

To articulate the crisis of the civil society concept, some of these authors, among growing numbers who criticize the concept, point to further indicators of civil society dynamism beyond the conceptualized structure. Thus, whether intentionally or otherwise, they invariably challenge assumptions about what groups or values should and should not be included within the civil society concept. Chris Hann believes it is the responsibility of all human communities to seek and create a version of civil society, and that the "burden of scholarship" is to investigate these different versions.[73] But in order to compare these versions, scholars must then "shift the debates about civil society away from formal structures and organizations and towards an investigation of beliefs, values and everyday practices."[74] In this way, collaboration that accrues social capital can be highlighted. Robert Putnam, professor of Public Policy, refers to *social capital* as those "features of social organization such as networks, norms, and social trust that facilitate coordination and cooperation for mutual benefit."[75] Schwedler emphasizes the need to look for civil society by focusing on the function, rather than the structures, of civil society, "be they familial, professional, tribal, religious, or clan-based."[76] Looking specifically at the possibility for democratic transition, Putnam emphasizes that civic associations help democracy grow by fostering reciprocity, facilitating information flow, reducing opportunism, and heightening people's trust in each other.[77] Civil society associations educate individuals in the values of collective action, which also include participation in both organizational decision making and leadership selection. All authors in the volume edited by Hann and Elizabeth Dunn propose investigation of the diverse ideas and moralities that inspire cohesion and trust.[78]

Because values such as mutual trust and respect, tolerance, reciprocity, and cooperation are characteristic of communal life, the function of civil society rests upon the cultivation and practice of civility. Thus, since the UAE has a communal society, the search for a civil society in the UAE must encompass and emphasize the component values of civil society as inscribed in practices, interactions, networking, and other structures of participation. Naidoo and Tandon assert that the principal role of civil society is its contribution to the creation of a healthy public life.[79] Correspondingly, the search for civil society must include activism that empowers members of communities, while the inclusion of the notions, practices, and symbols that are regarded as conducive to better well-being, happiness, and satisfaction, is important for any analysis of the processes of empowerment. As a whole, scholars such as those cited above add valuable dimensions to the identification of a civil society, and in doing so, are enabling a broader picture of its possibilities and function.

WOMEN'S ACTIVISM IN THE MIDDLE EAST—MARGINALIZATION?

The literature is strewn with misconceptions about the Middle East and women's participation that effectively limit inquiries about the actions that may constitute civil society activism and political change. In fact, it is only since the late 1980s that the question "where are the women in world politics?" has been asked. Pioneering studies by Enloe, a liberal feminist, discovered that women were not only there but were playing central roles, and that the conventional picture painted in the literature regarded their activities as less important than the actions of statesmen.[80] At the same time, however, women in the Middle East have continued to be viewed as so oppressed and passive as to be unable to defend and claim their rights. As Parvin Paider, professor of Gender Studies, states:

One widespread assumption is the only political and economic domains worth studying in Muslim societies are the formal ones, and Muslim women are unimportant or at best marginal to these domains because they have few formal political and economic rights and make a limited contribution to formal domains.[81]

However, Nadia al-Ali maintains that women have organized themselves in the Middle East for a century to challenge oppressive structures and practices.[82]

Though several studies appearing in the 1990s demonstrated a growing awareness of the void in the study and/or misrepresentation of civil society in the Arab world, in-depth case study documentation and research on women's activities as a whole is still lacking. As noted before, this is partly due to the fact that scholarly work still largely follows the dichotomy between the public and the private. The private sphere is typically defined as the realm that comprises the family (though it is sometimes viewed as encompassing the neighborhood or even the community) as well as interpersonal relations between friends and acquaintances. As a result, women's roles are defined by and, to a large extent, limited to the private sphere and their activities deemed unimportant. As such, what is termed as unimportant will be eliminated as insignificant for the study of civil and political society. Orthodox political science democratization literature is characterized by "narrow definitions of democracy, politics, and citizenship, the concentration on the public sphere and the use of simplistic notions of civil society."[83]

In addressing the issue of bias against women in political science research, scholars might have thought that turning to feminist works would help fill this void, but feminist literature does not always do justice to women's struggles either. Instead, feminist literature continues to discriminate against Middle Eastern women by giving research on them an "orientalist" interpretation. The "Woman Question" has been pivotal to the Western critique of Islam.[84] Here, the privileging of dichotomies has restricted studies on Middle Eastern women to dress, segregation, polygamy, and female genital mutilation (FGM), relating these to the main cultural determinant—Islam.[85] Again essentializing, the result is that Middle Eastern women are depicted as passive actors in the public domain.

However, through growing efforts, which mostly involve studies on women in terms of economic effects during political change, crises, or installation of economic programs, the disregard for research on, and biases against, women and their participation has been partly remedied. Latin America and Eastern Europe remain the regions of concentration, but even so, the relationship between women and political liberalization in the Middle East has begun to be investigated by a growing number of authors.[86] There is a small body of literature for the Middle East that looks at resistance movements and women's movements in relation to nationalism,[87] and women's participation in development has also found growing interest.[88] Women's participation in Islamic pietist movements and organizations is small, especially in relation to the study of men in these forums.[89] Similarly, research on the role of women's participation in civil society in the Middle East has been taken up only by a small number of researchers,[90] while women's participation through networking in the Middle East is a newer area of study investigated by even fewer authors.[91] Research on women's participation in women's organizations, specifically in the Arab Gulf, also forms a newly opened up body of literature,[92] although, like most studies on women's organizations in the Middle East, the associations chosen and their leaders involve highly elitist sectors of society. Rather than passive beings, these women may well be "architects of political change and struggle."[93]

However, because very little research has been conducted on women in the Emirates, the present study has necessarily to rely heavily on field research. In her pioneering work, Linda Soffan examines the factors that have had an influence on the position of women in the UAE. But today some of these findings need revisiting, since the UAE has been undergoing a profoundly rapid transformation since the discovery of oil. Mohamad al-Zekri researched folk beliefs of Emirati women in Dubai prior to the discovery of oil (1966),[94] Razan Abdul Majeed looked into divorce in Dubai,[95] Nora al-Zaabi studied the results of the rising marriage age of UAE women,[96] while Hessah Abdullah researched UAE women's image in the media[97] and is currently part of a team of researchers at the UAE University exploring this area further. Hind Al-Qasimi looked at the role of culture in the lives of UAE women,[98] Mouza Ghubash researched development in the UAE, including its impact on women,[99] and Maytha al-Shamsi and Abdallah Coulon also studied Emirati women and development.[100] Suaad Al-Oraimi examined the factors that promote and hinder women's political and economic participation,[101] and a male researcher, Mohamed Mahmoud, looked at laws governing women in the UAE.[102] Rima Sabban diverged from studies on UAE women to research the position of foreign female domestic workers in the UAE.[103] This diverse assortment of studies, consisting mostly of works by local academics, explores various aspects of the UAE woman. Even so, the role played by women in civil society needs investigation.

By examining the agency of these women in their social context in the post-oil era, this book offers a critical study of the assumptions that obscure a better understanding of women's roles, specifically in civil society within the Arab Gulf. It investigates whether women are transcending the public/private divide through various actions that are not yet fully recognized in the broader body of literature. Carole Pateman argued in her pioneering work that, "The assumptions and practices which govern the everyday, personal lives of women and men, including their sexual lives, can no longer be treated as matters remote from political life."[104]

Activities that are not fully recognized in the literature are also those that are indigenous in nature. As professor of Anthropology, Suad Joseph emphasizes: "Neither women nor men are political or apolitical in the abstract. How their activities come to carry a political charge must be understood in the context of their particular histories and cultures."[105] An example would be the *jam'iayat* (informal co-op) within which women participate in order to advance their economic position, and which represents a model of association different from the liberal-individualist models of civil society that are based on contract and the market. This and other cases should not be dismissed as "primordial" because of religion. These activities of women may also be referred to as "networking," described by Diane Singerman as, "the political lifeline of the community, allowing individuals and groups to cooperate with other members of the community to achieve individual and collective goals."[106]

CIVIL SOCIETY EXPANSION IN A TRIBAL RENTIER STATE

It is claimed that oil-rich rentier states cannot witness civil society expansion. The argument is found in the literature that speaks of civil society in connection with liberalization. The Arab Gulf comes under greater scrutiny for a number of factors, one major reason being the prevalence of tribalism.

Philip Khoury and Joseph Kostiner define a tribe as "a localized group in which kinship is the dominant idiom of organization, and whose members consider themselves culturally distinct in terms of customs, dialect or language, and origins; tribes are usually politically unified."[107] Other definitions often view a tribe as a primordial grouping. The tribes of the UAE are based on patrilineal descent. Each of the seven emirates is headed by a ruling family belonging to a specific tribe.

Economist Hussein Mahdavy is widely acknowledged for having given the term *rentier state* its current definition of a state that receives substantial rents from "foreign individuals, concerns or governments."[108] Beblawi is also widely cited for refining the definition to refer to rents being paid by foreign actors and accrued directly to the state, and where "only a few are engaged in the generation of this rent (wealth), the majority being only involved in the distribution or utilization of it."[109] Such a state is concerned domestically with "distribution," "circulation," or "allocation."[110]

Rentier state scholarship forms two categories—one considers the political effect of rents, and the other concerns the economic effect of a state's dependence on natural resource exports. Subsequently, with the first category, the principal claims suggest oil wealth is an obstacle to civil society growth; with the second, its scholars suggest that oil wealth is an impediment to effective economic development. Both claims are conflated.[111]

The UAE has the characteristics of a rentier state, being oil-wealthy and with a low population. It can, therefore, be criticized on the basis that these characteristics are obstacles to civil society, and to political and economic development.[112] The UAE often provides resources to its citizens, from jobs or free housing to electricity and water. In the UAE, every citizen is supposedly "entitled" to three plots of land for housing, planting, and business activities.[113] It is said that in this way, an oil-rich rentier state effectively thwarts civil society and participation; hence, the slogan, "no representation without taxation."

Rentierism has produced what is called a "rentier society," in which citizens are enabled to have an income without doing any work. An example of this is the requirement that expatriates wishing to open a business must establish the business or company in the name of an Emirati citizen who automatically takes a percentage of the profit, typically 51 percent of the profits.[114] When there is no strict "work ethic," a kind of "rentier mentality" may be expected to prevail in such a society.[115]

However, scholars are increasingly raising objections to the predominant rentier state paradigm on the Arab Gulf. First, they claim that other variables have been excluded in favor of attesting to the role of oil wealth, and that the rentier state theory has been stretched too far. Political scientist Michael Herb reminds us that poverty is a part of all Gulf rentier states, as they have emerged from a background of poverty.[116] Okruhlik explains that almost all governments in the Middle East have a strong element of authoritarianism and patrimonialism in the way they have led their countries, especially out of poverty. Looney reasserts the claim that the variable of authoritarianism cannot be ignored,[117] while Bellin argues that it is necessary to consider the role of a coercive state apparatus, which may be supported by oil wealth, but that oil wealth should not be blamed for authoritarianism.[118] Gwenn Okruhlik observes, "The idea of the rentier state has come to imply so much that it has lost its content."[119]

Needless to say, rentier state theory "ignores" the possibility that oil revenues might have positive effects on civil society, which, as Clark argues is the case for political liberalization and even democratization.[120] Herb explains that it makes little sense to blame oil if oil wealth also has positive effects, but having studied variables that might specifically affect democracy, concludes that rent wealth has neither positive nor negative effects on democracy.[121] Thus, he maintains, "the more ambitious formulations of the theory 'no representation without taxation' can be retired."[122]

Second, there is evidence that civil society sectors are not subdued, as they have been perceived in the literature. Jill Crystal, an advocate of the rentier state theory, yet points out, "incipient pressures from Islamist, human rights, tribal, technocratic, and other groups have in fact appeared in the Gulf."[123] Herb suggests that countries under monarchic dynasties, such as the UAE, in fact present greater promise for true and peaceful democratic development.[124] Obviously, the rentier state paradigm cannot adequately explain why pressures are mounting within civil society. In fact, when regimes attempt to buy off dissent by distributing oil wealth among citizens, they may actually be causing more dissent.

The Study: Methods and Indices

Here I describe the sample of UAE women activists and describe the indicators used to identify the impact made by these women on civil society. I aimed to learn about the activities, motivations, needs, and goals of UAE women activists and their consequent effect primarily through interviews. Ghubash noted that at the turn of the century, 21 percent of existing registered NGOs were women's organizations,[125] a statistic that did not include charitable or Islamic organizations run by women. Nor did it encompass women's committees formed under male-headed organizations, or women's *halaqas*. Nonetheless, these are included in my case study sample.

The forms of collaboration included in this study comprise (1) the official UAE women's associations and clubs; (2) Islamic associations and *halaqas* (religious study circles); and (3) women's networks. The official UAE women's organizations are located in each emirate (except Fujairah, which has a sister club in Sharjah) and are headed by the Women's Union in Abu Dhabi under Sheikha Fatima bint Mubarak, widow of the former president of the UAE, Sheikh Zayed bin Sultan al-Nahayan. Women's Islamic-oriented associations are guided by Islamic principles, according to association leaders or association mission statements. *Halaqas* or learning circles are also places where women gather to advance their religious knowledge. Networks here refer to women who collaborate informally with one another to achieve shared goals. In the UAE, such goals often include human rights issues, *dawa* (propagation), and collaborative philanthropic work.

In order to assess the extent to which these women's actions contribute to civil society, as outlined here, three main indicators were developed: participation, civility, and empowerment. I analyze the level of *participation*, which I use to mean some active involvement on part of the volunteers. Participation is said to occur when people organize around specific interests, negotiate, and collaborate to reach particular ends. In a largely quantitative assessment, an inquiry is made in terms of volunteerism levels, growth in numbers of participants, activities/programs, and size of the structures that accommodate larger numbers of people. The analysis of the empirical evidence in this study is, however, necessarily heavily qualitative. As such, under participation, I also study the values, such as those ascribed to Islam as a belief system, which can be put into practice by the participants and influence society.

The *empowerment process* has traditionally been left out of the analysis of social movements and associational activism. In defining empowerment, feminists have emphasized the effects a woman has on her institutional environment as "circumventing, changing, or eliminating the society's values, practices, norms and laws in order to lessen the extent to which they constrain her activities and choices."[126] In this vein, Ann Bookman and Sandra Morgen assert, "For these women, empowerment begins when they change their ideas about the causes of their powerlessness, when they recognize the systemic forces that oppress them, and when they act to change the conditions of their lives."[127] This conceptualization of empowerment is, indeed, an important one, but such a rendering could miss important actions that equally serve an empowerment process. Jo Rowlands adds that it is also important in the developmental context when women assert their right to "control resources which will assist in challenging and eliminating their own subordination."[128] Greater focus must be on the agency of women in their own right. The onus on autonomy from men or the state derives from a Western *Weltanschauung* (worldview), and presupposes that the individual shares the same societal experiences in which these terms for empowerment have been developed, namely, a Western discursive tradition determined by liberalism and a specific language on freedoms.

Furthermore, as Barbara Einhorn and Charlotte Sever remind us, "women's movements are not part of a single linear trajectory towards equality, but are in fact time- and context-specific and are part of wider political and ideological currents."[129] While autonomy is stressed in the literature as a fundamental indicator for an assessment of empowerment, it is not a goal pursued by all women around the globe for happiness, fulfillment, and security. Arab women most often view the Western conception of empowerment as directly related to men, and translated into Arabic implies taking on unfeminine characteristics in order to challenge men. While self-reliance and independence might provide women with greater power over their own lives and destiny, most women in this study also reject the form of autonomy described by Western feminists.

Thus, unequal power relations that affect women should not be placed solely within a gender framework. Women identify various other sources of contention and competition that may include women of different classes and backgrounds, government, or globalization. As such, and in order to assess women's impact on civil society through the empowerment process, I explore, through their own narrations, any form of agency from which greater fulfillment, satisfaction, consciousness-raising, skills development, or piety may result. Understanding empowerment relies on an acceptance that the desires and goals of women will differ. As Adam Ferguson comments, "The happiness of individuals is the great end of civil society: For, in what sense can a public enjoy any good, if its members, considered apart, be unhappy?"[130]

Civility is the third variable utilized to assess the interviewees' impact on civil society. Middle Eastern countries are classically presented as deficient in civility. Islamists and Islamic movements are categorized as antithetical to civil principles as supposedly embodied within democracy and feminism. While "tolerance towards the other," most often defined as synonymous with civility, is an indicator,[131] a wider range of "civil acts," or "values" are considered within the term *civility*. While agreeing with Schwedler that "tolerance toward those with different views is paramount"[132] to the study of civil society, following Antoun, "the practices and ideas that generate cooperation and trust for the purpose of accomplishing social goals"[133] must necessarily be part and parcel of the concept. Singerman emphasizes the important factors of "cooperation, trust, and mutual dependence";[134] Adam Seligman, professor of Religion, notes, "To call for the establishment of civil society without taking into consideration the fundamental terms of trust in society is but an empty rhetorical exercise."[135] Civility is understood here as the conduct of a person whose individual self-consciousness is partly superseded by his or her collective self-consciousness, with the society as a whole and the institution of civil society being the referents of her collective self-consciousness.[136]

Underpinning the concept of civility in one's dealings and behavior are the values of trust, reciprocity, cooperation, and tolerance.

"[A] specific form of generalized trust,"[137] is particularly important because patterns of solidarity and interaction in the UAE are premised on specific ethnicities, class, and ideologies. Shils defines ideological politics as follows:

First and above all, [it is] the assumption that politics should be conducted from the standpoint of a coherent, comprehensive set of beliefs which must override every other consideration. These beliefs attribute supreme significance to one group or class—and they correspondingly view as the seat and source of all evil a foreign power, an ethnic group like the Jews, or the bourgeois class.[138]

One need not prove that forms of interaction are completely detached from primordial, class or ideological solidarities in order for some level of trust to be established. But interests motivated from such bases to the exclusion of others signify rather a lack of trust between other solidarities. As Seligman stresses, "The continuity of ethnic loyalties and solidarities (and so also the potential for ethnic exclusion) within groups undercuts the very definition of universal citizenship within the nation-state."[139]

The variable of reciprocity will be identified through exchanges observed between participants and between organizations, in which information, money, favors, material goods, donations in kind, or any form of help is given freely and reciprocated. Reciprocity involves sharing, giving, and helping. Thereby, an ethic of giving, receiving, and sacrifice are spread among those who participate. Reciprocity strengthens relations between members and organizations, and solidifies networks in which members can rely on one another to cooperate.

The variable of cooperation helps to reveal how participants deal with others. It is important to know how establishments place themselves among the various organizations and institutions with which they can interact. However, internal forms of collaboration among the participants are also important. As Norton rightly notes, it is "as relevant to look for civility within associations as it is to observe it between them."[140] Since nondiscriminatory forms of cooperation are a key to establishing norms that support plurality, the inclusivity of participants within the associations is noted.

In assessing tolerance, one must accept the condition of a coexistence with people of diverse beliefs, traditions, and practices, with the appreciation that others have the same right as oneself to personal beliefs and ways of behaving, given that legal parameters that will curtail behavior that harms society must be in place. When groups pursue interests and a version of the common good among competing positions, they contribute to the vibrancy of a civil society. However, if intolerance toward competing beliefs and practices is articulated and practiced, then civility suffers. Activities and expressions will indicate the levels of tolerance found among the actors under study.

Key Questions

The United Arab Emirates (UAE) case adds a piece to the puzzle of civil society in the Gulf and the wider Middle East, and more globally, the role of women. In the UAE, some assert that women are not very active or coordinated and that women's activism is completely co-opted by the state. Others maintain that women do play a significant role in their personal development and in the development of their country.

Within the literature scholars question whether civil society associations may not actually hinder the development of civil society. As professor of International Relations, Andy Knight maintains, there can be a fusion of state interests that stifles the abilities of civil society associations to pursue their own interests.[141] As such, the Lockian view that assumes that civil society fosters participatory behavior is challenged by another contemporary view, the rejectionist (Marxist) view, which sees associations possibly as "a handmaiden in the state's project of domination."[142]

A further issue in the literature is the centrality of civil society actors. In reexamining the concept of civil society in the Arab Gulf, the study's approach includes a broadened definition of its possibilities, to allow for more than mere "civil society sightings," and takes issue with the view that civil society equals organizations.

There has, furthermore, been a blurring of Islamic activity with Islamist terrorist activity, and as such, Islamic forms of collaboration have been framed as antithetical to ideals of progress, civility, and democracy, most acutely in the post-9/11 era. Hence, I examine the view that those actors who form groups that are guided by ideology must necessarily become obstacles to the formation of a civil society.

I ask whether we can discern that women are articulating competing interests and competing notions of the common good? That is, are women collaborating to achieve common goals—hence demonstrating their participation capabilities? Do UAE women develop and spread values that foster civility? Are these women empowering themselves through their struggles? In sum, the book centers on the question: *What role do UAE women play in civil society development?*

Structure and Discussion

The book contains six chapters. This first chapter briefly introduced the key issues, relevant debates, literature, methodological considerations, and key questions. Chapter 2 provides a background to the UAE and Trucial Coast, and will outline women's participation in the past and present in light of rentier strategies and the quest for civil society. Chapter 3 focuses on women's GONGO organizations and explains their work in light of the issues raised and literature introduced in this chapter. Chapter 4 presents a study on UAE Islamism mainly through the Islamic-oriented associations and *halaqas* of UAE women, while chapter 5 looks at civil society actions of UAE women through their networking capabilities. The concluding chapter, chapter 6, compares and elaborates on the differing activisms captured in this book, and ends with suggestions for further research. It also discusses the problems of the mainstream civil society concept and related state-society paradigms in light of the activisms. Furthermore, it suggests a conceptual rearticulation based on the actions and strategies analyzed in UAE women's activism.

Chapter 2

Civil Society and Rentierism?
Challenges to the UAE Woman

Introduction

The sociohistorical background information given here helps place the subsequent chapters in their appropriate political, economic, and historical context, since it is important that women's struggles are analyzed within this wider experience. Following a country profile on the UAE and a historical overview of the state's formation, governmental structure, and modes of participation, the participation of UAE women is examined through a discussion of laws and norms, while a historical account of women's roles in family, tribe, and society before and after the oil boom shows the changes and the forces behind their status and marginalization. From this information, the significance of UAE women's activism can be better contextualized.

Geographical Setting and Population Statistics

The UAE is located in the lower Arab Gulf sharing borders with Oman and Saudi Arabia and separated from Qatar by a strip of land belonging to Saudi Arabia. The area of the UAE covers around 82,880 square km,[1] and is separated into seven tribal sheikhdoms. The largest in size and population is the emirate of Abu Dhabi, then Dubai, Sharjah, Ajman, Ras al-Khaima, Fujairah, and Umm al-Quwain.

UAE citizenship is not granted automatically to any resident of the UAE. Generally, only those who lived for an extended period of time

within the UAE borders before the early 1960s and their descendants
have citizenship. Because one had to relinquish one's citizenship at
naturalization, many Arabs from elsewhere retained their own citizenship, and although they have three generations of descendants, citizenship can only be granted by sheikhly decree. Because citizenship is
a key security, social, and economic concern, tight, yet unclear laws
meant that hardly any people were granted citizenship after the discovery of oil. Except for Arab Gulf citizens, there are very few excep-
tions.[2]

Classes are clearly stratified, cutting along socioeconomic and ethnic lines. UAE[3] nationals rank first, but within the category of nationals they are also differentiated by further groupings, being divided
into what locals (*muwātiniīn*) refer to as Arabs, *'ajams,* and *baluch.*
The category of Arabs is further divided into two groups, those that
came from the Bedouin or *bedu* (e.g., the al-Nahayan family of the
al Bu Falah clan) and those from the settled people or *hadar* (e.g.,
the al-Qasimi royal family). The *'ajams* are also split into two groups:
those who came from the "Trucial Arabs" and those who originate
from the Iranians. Some of the original Arab Emiratis lived in what is
now the Persian coast and were made to leave as Iran expanded its
borders. Those of this category have a dialect among themselves that
contains a mixture of Arabic and Farsi. The *baluch* came originally
from Makran, in present-day Pakistan (referred to as Baluchistan).
Some *baluch* have Omani citizenship (or both UAE and Omani)
while they consider themselves Emirati. Their *baluchi* forefathers had
settled in Oman before their parents moved to the UAE while the region comprised the Trucial Coast.

In spite of these three broad categories, the issue of who makes an
Emirati citizen is complex. Especially in the northern emirates
(mostly Ajman and Ras al-Khaima), some men married young Indian
women in the early 1970s and, thus, their children are half Indian. In
other parts of the emirates, some locals have Yemini, Bahraini, or
Omani parents. In the following decade, a number of men (thousands,
according to Murr) established families with Moroccan or Egyptian
wives, among others.[4]

Class divisions across lineages become most evident in marriage
choices. According to "locals," the first two categories are considered
"local," and while the first category will prefer to marry within its
group, the first and second category will, nevertheless, intermarry
freely. On the whole, men from the first two categories marry members of the third less often. It is alleged that members of the third
group have simply lived in the UAE or, indeed, do perhaps have a rel-

ative who is a "pure" local and, therefore, the majority have UAE citizenship. Nonetheless, locals often claim the latter cause the majority of social problems in terms of drug use and crime. Regarding their status, it is difficult for a member of this group, particularly a male, to marry someone from the other two groups, especially the first.

There is a gross misperception about the wealth of people living in the UAE. While luxury is definitely part of the Emirati lifestyle, many citizens just about get by after the guaranteed provision of subsidized housing allotted by the state and interest-free bank loans.[5] There are no statistics as to how many people live in what can be thought of as poverty. However, some villages and areas within the cities can be very poor. In contrast to all the readily visible "glitter," one can find East Asians (mostly from Pakistan or Baluchistan), or Arabs (mostly from Iranian islands), who lack passports or identity cards and whose conditions are often desperate. These are referred to as *bedoon*, which means they have no passport and legal status, and some have lived in the country for up to 30 years.

The UAE has one of the lowest citizen populations but highest growth rates in the world. According to the U.S. Department of State, the population in 2005 was 4.5 million.[6] In 2005, the CIA *World Factbook* estimated that UAE citizens made up 19 percent of the population;[7] however, in 2004 Sheikh Zayed announced in a speech that the national population had fallen as low as 15 percent.[8] Foreigners account for approximately 90 percent of the 1.7 million labor force[9] and 98 percent of the private sector workforce.[10] The government does not publish its census reports to account for the population of nationals nor the population increase for nationals alone. However, calculating numbers from the Ministry of Planning, the number of citizens born in the UAE in the year 2000 was 22,451 and the total number of deceased was 2,158. Therefore, the increase in the population of citizens is the difference, amounting to 20,293. Given that the number of UAE citizens in the year 2000 was 559,440 (i.e., 18 percent of 3,108,000, which was the total population for the year 2000), the growth rate in that year was 3.6 percent. According to the government's mid-year estimates, there were 1,129,000 females and 2,359,000 males in the population.[11] The large numbers of male South Asian workers account for this imbalance.

Despite the majority of the population being non-Arab, the UAE government imparts a picture of the country as Arab and Muslim. As expressed in Article 7 of the Constitution, Islam is recognized as the official religion of the union. According to the country's first census in 2001, 76 percent of the population was Muslim, 9 percent Christian, and 15 percent other religions.[12] Those of other religions included mainly Hindus, Buddhists, Sikhs, and also a small percentage of Jews. Muslim residents consisted of Sunnis, Shi'is, and Ibadis.

WOMEN'S TRADITIONAL POSITION
AND CHANGING STATUS

The traditional roots, environment, and natural resources help in gaining an understanding of the contemporary position and role of women, as well as their challenges. Throughout various historical periods different Arab tribes, sedentary to nomadic, settled in the UAE region. During the eighteenth and nineteenth centuries, the two major and established tribal groups were the Bani Yas and the Al Qawasim, each of which had at least ten subtribes.[13] The effect of the British intervention was the freezing of the principal power relationships of tribal groupings, that is, the Al Qawasim. The Al Qawasim had ruled the area covering all five northern emirates and much of Dubai; they now rule over Sharjah and Ras al-Khaima only. In 1904, J. G. Lorimer set the number of tribes in the region of the UAE at 44, comprising 80,000 people.[14]

Most nationals can quote a tribal name or *nisbah* as rightfully his or hers.[15] Because some of these tribes or *qabilah* are huge, many local families derive their last names from one of the several possible subdivisions or *afkhadh* of the original tribe.[16] A person's existence is embedded in this group. Each member of this group also has a corporate responsibility to provide support and protection to its members.[17] It is particularly important to emphasize this aspect of UAE heritage to make sense of contemporary forms of patrimonialism and power of political authority.

In the era before oil, women played an active role in their societies, tribes, and families, whether they resided in the mountains or in the desert oases.[18] Bedouin women were entrusted with difficult and dangerous tasks, such as fetching water from the wells, which were usually a great distance away and where they might also meet strangers.

Some women also played a major role in the running of tribal affairs, though generally behind the scenes. This, for instance, was the case with the Al Rashid tribe, whose members sometimes also carried the name of their mothers.[19] Sheikha Salama bint Buti, Sheikh Zayed's mother, too, was also responsible for the way in which her four sons worked together from the late 1920s for more than 30 years to bring the emirate of Abu Dhabi through the adversity of economic depression and the Second World War.[20] Sheikha Salama was consulted by her sons on a daily basis, and she is known to have made them promise not to use violence toward each other if one were to be deposed by another as ruler.[21] This promise was instrumental in ending a long history of bloody succession struggles within the ruling family.[22] In Dubai, Sheikha Hussa bint al Murr, the grandmother of Sheikh Maktoum bin Rashid al Maktoum, (ruler of Dubai until 2004), was the most powerful personality in that sheikhdom and the Trucial States until al Maktoum's father, Sheikh Rashid bin Sa'id (her son and ruler from 1958 until his death in 1990), reached ruling age.[23] Aside from trading, she regularly held a public *majlis* of her own that was attended by men, and it is even said that hers was more crowded than her husband's, though he was the ruler.[24] When pearling and fishing were the primary sources of income (until the 1930s/1940s), it was not unusual to find women owning many of the ships used. As Soffan notes, "Some of the trading merchants were female, but they have always conducted their business through men acting on their behalf, and continue to do so."[25]

The raw materials of the UAE economy were fish and pearls. In this unforgiving environment both men and women fought heat, disease, and famine to make a living. Occupations ranged from slaves who dived for pearls and artisans who hammered coffee pots or stitched sandals, to wealthy pearl merchants and powerful sheikhs. Many of the pearl merchants were also landholders and moneylenders who gained political influence through their wealth and connections. In addition, there were cultivators of dates in oases, nomadic animal herders, and small-scale traders.[26]

These forms of subsistence activities shaped the role of women. For pearl diving activities men would leave their families, sometimes for three months or more. As a result women were in charge of maintaining the affairs of the entire household.[27] Not only did women care for all family members, look after the food, clothing, and even the building of houses but they also had occupations as spiritual and herbal healers. They would weave and color the palm leaves from which houses were mainly built.[28] Moreover, they were fully responsible for the care and/or milking of the animals, usually sheep and camels,[29] as well as for the making and maintenance of equipment for fishing, pearl diving, and food storage.[30] When the men went out fishing the women would sell the catch at the market, and would then purchase necessary household items with the earnings.[31] Women often sold items collected by their husbands,[32] which might even be empty tins and bottles, pieces of rope, scraps of metal, corks, or strips of cloth.[33]

Though family sizes are becoming smaller, until recently the family unit consisted of an extended household. The father or eldest male has always been viewed as the highest authority in the household that followed a gender-segregated order. As a result, again until recently, socialization was not only clearly divided within society, but also within the home. Although it was permissible to have more than one wife at a time, in practice few men could afford more than one.[34] However, because many women died in childbirth, it was not uncommon for a man to have several wives in succession.[35] There was no stigma attached to divorced women in the UAE, as has been the case for most Arab women,[36] nor was it uncommon for a woman to have married several men throughout her lifetime.[37]

Even though the social and developmental impact of oil was not felt by the citizens of the country until around the emergence of the UAE as a modern state,[38] the discovery and export of petroleum resulted in a major transformation of a barren country to a prosperous and rich welfare state.[39] The rapid development can be viewed from photos of the city of Dubai within a span of just 14 years where, for example, seven buildings lined Sheikh Zayed road in 1990 and merely 15 years later high rises tower along the road on both sides.

In 1980, the citizens of the UAE were rated as having the world's wealthiest per capita income, reaching US$ 100,000,[40] and the UAE still has one of the highest per capita GNPs in the world. In fact, with the oil boom the UAE attained the fastest rate of development and economic growth in the world, often attributed to Sheikh Zayed.

The UAE's proven oil reserves are the fourth largest in the world, after Saudi Arabia, Iraq, and Iran.[41] Oil revenues became significant in Abu Dhabi in 1963, in Dubai in 1970, in Sharjah in 1975, and in Ras al-Khaima in 1984.[42] In 1991, the governments of Abu Dhabi and Dubai together accounted for 99 percent of the UAE's production.[43] Abu Dhabi, by far the largest oil producer, exceeded Dubai's production almost twelve-fold, with 1,906,000 bd. per day for 1994.[44] Together, these two emirates spend significant portions of their oil revenues on infrastructure development, education, health, and social services. Abu Dhabi, in particular, distributes its oil wealth to the poorer emirates. At the current production rate of 2.2 million barrels per day, oil reserves are sufficient to last more than a hundred years.[45]

Before the discovery of oil the educational level of women was extremely low,[46] and in the 1950s, illiteracy in general was probably at 98 percent.[47] However, the first school was not opened until 1953 in the Sharjah emirate; Sharjah was also the first emirate to open a girls' school, in 1955. Except for Dubai, other emirates did not start opening schools until a decade later. In 1970, women accounted for only 4 percent of the literate population,[48] and as late as 1980, 51 percent of UAE men and 77.6 percent of women over the age of 45 were still illiterate. However, by 1990, the percentages had fallen to 40 and 65.4 percent respectively. By 1995, the overall illiteracy level had fallen to 22 percent.[49] From a 1995 estimate for the whole population, of those who were 15 years old and above, 79.2 percent were literate (with males at 78.9 percent and females 79.8 percent).[50] Although men were more literate than women, women have been moving ahead swiftly. Of those participating in the labor force in 1980, only 9.8 percent of the UAE women had university degrees. A decade later, however, the proportions had reversed, with 40.7 percent of UAE women in the labor force having had a university education.[51]

GOVERNMENT SYSTEM AND MODES OF PARTICIPATION: PAST AND PRESENT

The UAE has been in existence as a federation of the seven states only since 1971. It emerged on 2 December 1971 as a result of the uniting of six emirates, and Ras al-Khaima joined two months later in February 1972. Bahrain and Qatar were to join but pulled out of the process before the agreement was signed. What had bound these states together up to the point of signing the agreement of unity were the treaties signed in the early nineteenth century, according to which they had been referred to as the Trucial Coast or Trucial Oman.[52] Tangible benefits worked to the advantage of Abu Dhabi, since Abu Dhabi, under the direction of Sheikh Zayed ibn Sultan al-Nahayan, could provide the financial means. The extraordinary ability of Sheikh Zayed to sway the people, particularly the tribes, is also a factor.[53] However, as Jane Bristol-Rhys forcefully states, there are at least four narrations of UAE history, the dominant narratives ignoring the effects of over 200 years of British occupancy.[54]

After the creation of a modern nation-state in 1971, a provisional constitution was established that provided for the separation of powers into executive, legislative, and judicial branches, with the legislative and executive powers split into federal and emirate jurisdictions. The Supreme Council of the Union (sometimes referred to as the Supreme Council of Federation), the Federal National Council, and the Cabinet of Ministers were also formed. The Constitution was made permanent in 1996.

The executive branch consists of the Supreme Council of the Union (SCU), the Council of Ministers (the cabinet), and the presidency.

The SCU, which is made up of the rulers of the seven emirates, functions as the highest federal authority in executive and legislative capacities. Besides selecting the president of the UAE, it elects a chairman and a vice chairman from among its members, who serve for a term of five years. The SCU formulates general policy, legislation on all matters of state, ratification of federal laws and decrees, ratification of international treaties and agreements, and ascent to the appointment of the prime minister and Supreme Court of the Union judges. The rulers make decisions by a simple majority vote, except on substantive issues. Substantive issues require a two-thirds majority (five of seven rulers) that must include the votes of both Abu Dhabi and Dubai.[55]

The Council of Ministers administers federal affairs. In 1992, there were 25 ministers, including the prime minister and deputy prime minister. UAE citizenship is a requirement for appointment as a minister. All ministers are individually and collectively answerable to the president and the SCU. In addition to its executive duties, the Council of Ministers is responsible for drafting bills for formal enactment.[56] The Federal National Council (FNC) is the principal legislative authority, but in reality its function is limited to consultation. From early 2005, half of its 40 members were to be elected, whereas previously all 40 were appointed for two-year terms at the discretion of each emirate ruler, in accordance with a constitutionally fixed quota that allotted proportionately more members to the wealthiest and most populous emirates.[57]

The head of state is UAE's president Sheikh Khalifa bin Zayed al-Nahayan (since 3 November 2004) and ruler of Abu Dhabi (since 4 November 2004) after succeeding his father Sheikh Zayed al-Nahayan. The vice president is Sheikh Mohammed bin Rashid al-Maktoum, ruler of Dubai, who automatically took over the rulership after the death of his brother Sheikh Maktoum bin Rashid al-Maktoum (ruler from 8 October 1990 until 3 January 2006). The president serves as chairman of the SCU, head of state, and commander of the Union Defence Force (UDF). The president convenes the SCU and appoints the prime minister, the two deputy prime ministers, the cabinet ministers, and other senior civil and military officials. He has the power to proclaim martial law and to carry out a variety of functions usually associated with the chief executive.[58]

The social and political formation of the UAE does not reflect the "modern European state."[59] In fact, despite all the changes due to oil wealth, of the world's eight remaining absolute monarchies, the UAE is ranked second after Saudi Arabia by Freedom House.[60] Despite the formal branches of government, the *amirs* and their families, particularly those of Abu Dhabi and Dubai, are the most important political actors, holding the key political offices. Certain powers, including foreign policy, defense, security, immigration, and communications, are expressly reserved for the central government. The individual emirates exercise residual powers within the federal government and continue to have jurisdiction over their own individual territory. Formal participation in political society is severely constrained. Traditional consultation and *diwaniyya* meetings still occur to some extent, but apparently not to the level seen before the oil boom. Moreover, with its formalization of politics, the modern state has diminished the roles of women's participation in public life. Despite the pursuit of rapid economic liberalization, some tribes are becoming even more powerful.[61] Hence, notwithstanding talk about greater freedoms and democracy for the region, the tribal monarchy has not embarked upon any serious transition to greater political liberalization. The ruling elite has created mechanisms not only for the state's continued survival but also for greater powers over political society, civil society, and what has come to be known as the private realm.

CORPORATISM

The UAE state has salient features of the corporatist model as it intervenes in the market and civil society realms by organizing constituent parts. Tribal or familial interests are a crucial determinant for the UAE political system. One could speak of "community-based corporatism" in the UAE case, since the "tribal *Gemeinschaft*" attempts to channelize political and social interests from the top down.[62] Its policies and decisions may be motivated through external pressures or internal pressures. Globalization and the issue of migrants, for example, provide an impetus for action toward identity building. The following will highlight mechanisms to strengthen legitimacy authority, such as co-optation, the fashioning of tradition (*turath*), and state feminism.

Civil Society: Historical Development and Challenges

A mode of activism that has recently been subject to aggressive co-optation is volunteer-oriented activity. During the period before the nation-state was in place and, in fact, over many centuries, the concept of volunteering took a different shape from its contemporary definition. There were at least three main forms. First, it could be found through communal collaboration. Community "volunteerism" was known, mostly among town dwellers, as a system of *faz'ah* (literally, "panic situation"). Members of a household who faced an emergency would announce that they needed help, and the community was expected to show up at their house and offer the required assistance.[63] Communities were usually small and everyone knew each other. They supported each other whenever they were needed. For example, a mother who was unable to breastfeed her baby would have no difficulty finding a neighbor who could along with her own.[64] Second, there was philanthropy,[65] where a person would give money or, in most cases, food or other items to needy persons. This often took the form of "exchange," since members of a community depended on each other for survival. Third, volunteerism occurred within civil organizations taking on the role of what governments would normally have offered in terms of provision of help and services.[66] The third form of civil society activism began in the UAE in the 1960s. Here, women's groups were emerging (first in Ras-al Khaima) to take care of the needs of women and their families: The government would later take on this role through the Ministry of Labor and Social Affairs.

In 1974, Law No. 6 was issued on the governing of organizations. Article 33, in particular, was the foundation for the legislative hierarchy regarding civil society organizations. It states that the freedom of congregation and the establishment of organizations are accepted within the lawful limits.[67] Law No. 6 defines "organizations for public benefit" as every group that is organized and characterized by continuity for a certain period or unlimited time, and that is composed of a number of individuals or legal persons in order to achieve a social, religious, cultural, or educational goal, a needed technical activity, provision of humanitarian services, fulfillment of charitable needs, or other forms of care. Organizations should work for public welfare only and not financial benefit.[68]

Thereafter, the mushrooming of registrations with the government revealed the growing number of organizations. In 1974, 11 organizations were established, of which four were women's organizations, four were Arab and immigrant organizations, plus one religious, one folkloric, and one cultural.[69] By 1980, 42 organizations had established themselves under the law and by the end of the 1980s the number had increased to 80.[70]

Amendments to the law soon followed that granted the state greater powers of intervention and control. Law No. 6 of 1974 was amended in 1980 to prevent immigrants from establishing organizations (unless done through a local group), since these were increasing too quickly in number. By 1978, there were 17 and they had become the second largest category after folkloric organizations.[71] The establishment of organizations became limited to nationals, as also did full time membership in any existing organization. A further amendment in 1981 was issued to suspend the issuing of licences to community associations, on the grounds that their existence posed "a significant threat to internal security."[72] Significantly, the law will soon give the ministries full legal interventionist powers over the programs, projects, and finances of organizations.[73]

With the state's economic corporatism, the tribal leaders own the big oil corporations. Furthermore, the main corporations into which UAE business is organized are the Chambers of Commerce. The government supervises elections to the boards and appoints a large number of the board members. Membership is obligatory for all businesses in the chambers of commerce that, with their societal corporatism, attempt to form or co-opt NGOs. The state, in addition, attempts to bring under firm control the spaces in which the most potentially powerful opposition might germinate. It produces the outline of the Friday *khutba* (sermon) for each *khateeb* to follow in thousands of mosques. It funds the Human Rights Committee of the Jurists' Association, and under the police administration has established a human rights department. This has extended government control over an area that otherwise would be taken up by organizations dealing with human rights issues and that have so far been prevented from becoming involved. This is significant since any human rights case that might be levied against government actors or high-ranking individuals cannot be brought forward through a state organ. The state establishes what is determined to be a human rights issue and what is not.

As well as forbidding any independent human rights organization thus far to operate, no political parties, trade and labor unions, or Islamist organizations are allowed to function either. The only workers' associations that are permitted are professional associations (e.g., teachers, jurists, engineers, medical professionals, and social workers). Most members of these associations are locals and only citizens can vote or be on the boards. While strikes in the public sector are forbidden, strikes and collective bargaining committees for private sector employees are neither explicitly prohibited nor does the labor law explicitly permit them.

Several groups have submitted applications to the Ministry of Labor and Social Affairs to establish organizations and have been denied authorization.[74] An example is the faculty of the United Arab Emirates

University, whose application in 1991 remains unanswered. They therefore proclaimed themselves an organization without governmental approval and since function in clear view. During 2004, three separate groups applied to the Ministry of Labor and Social Affairs for registration as independent human rights NGOs. Although the ministry, by its own regulations, is required to act on all such applications within 30 days of receipt, it had not acted by the end of the year.[75] All organizations are required to register with the Ministry of Labor and Social Affairs and most are granted subsidies from the government.

The result of such monitoring and intervention is that organizations in the UAE are generally weakened, and those that would function to monitor human rights issues and policies are not allowed. Therefore, a lot of activities among individuals are not observed through their participation in formal organizations. Rather, they collaborate to pursue interests via informal methods.

Clients, Culture, and Religion as Political Projects

To varying extents, Middle Eastern states will also rely on and exploit patrimonial and patriarchal relationships.[76] The UAE state has put great effort into building up its legitimacy. As legitimacy and identities are fragile, considerable energy is put into their development and formation. This political project has two not unrelated objectives. First, as Christopher Davidson argues, there is a need to legitimize and reinforce the ruler's position at the head of a contemporary patriarchal and patrimonial society.[77] Second, in the face of globalizing forces, it is essential to restore and embellish the past in order to anchor and strengthen a local identity. Relying upon a balance of personal, patrimonial, cultural, and religious resources,[78] the UAE government utilizes a number of techniques of governmentality to achieve these two goals.

The project involves the application of various symbols and a "controlled-consociationalism."[79] Visual symbols are used to bring the past into a collective consciousness. In the middle of several cities one can find roundabouts decorated with sculptures of oysters with pearls, dedicated to the memory of pearl diving. The pearling industry's history is also captured through sculptures of vessels and the restored ships that line the harbors within cities. Along the waterfronts one will also find cafés shaped as traditional buildings, serving Emirati food and refreshments, and providing *shisha* (pipe-smoking), even though it was not a local tradition. Within the cities and along the coasts, traditional forts and towers are being restored.

Figure 2.1   Photograph taken by author at Dubai Heritage Village. Live portrayals of the past are presented, here with a woman in traditional dress making traditional foods.

Museums, especially in Sharjah, have been given a greater role in reviving an imagined past in the face of globalizing forces. Emirati tourism departments oversee the development of these reconstitutions of UAE identity. As Sulayman Khalaf argues, there is now a crucial need for the development of "living museums" and "imagined communities."[80] Examples of such constructs of the past may be found at the Dubai Heritage Village, the Pearling Village, and the Hatta Heritage Village (figure 2.1). Davidson notes that the production of "living memories" is of particular significance and that, in terms of tourism, the growing infrastructure of museums and heritage centers is performing a role in the country's economic diversification. The government's cultural production is integral to its technologies of legitimacy.[81]

Camel racing, a national sport unique to the region, is a further symbol that has an emotive quality and, thus, functions as a unifying force. To preserve part of the Bedouin heritage, the rulers have spent millions of dirhams on racing circuits, prizes, and racing camels.[82] As Sa'id Abu 'Athira noted, "Camel races used to be run [only] on special occasions such as weddings; now they are sponsored by governments to help people keep their camels and not lose their traditional way of life."[83]

In its consociationalist corporatism, the state's tactic involves widening the circle of allied groups in the interest of finding legitimacy. This organization comprises the ruling families at the top of the pyramid and tribal, commercial, and professional groups.[84] Oil has been instrumental in enabling the state to structure existing groups into a patron-client order as part of its strategy of inclusionary corporatism.[85] A rentier-based "ruling bargain" is forged between the elite state actors and the technocrats of the new middle class that are typical of Gulf countries. Relative autonomy is accorded to the technocrats. This is achieved by expanding their role toward the promotion of modernization. Importantly, however, this "pact" is meant to ensure a source of legitimacy for the state.[86]

The inclusion of Islamic groupings has also comprised part of the state's strategy to anchor its legitimacy. The state poses as the protector of Islam and Islamic identity. Yet Islamic groups and extremism are among the major political threats to the ruling elites of many of the countries and the greatest sources of internal security problems in the region. Hence, there is a crucial need to incorporate mainstream Islamic resources.[87] This, as already noted, includes funding the building of mosques and overseeing and controlling the lessons that take place. Importantly, funding is poured into lectures and speakers who highlight issues that are deemed apolitical in substance.

Inclusionary corporatism has been a strategy that has served to strengthen and legitimize state actors. However, because of growing challenges posed to the state, inclusionary corporatism has needed revision. The new middle class is "pushing hard for too much modernization too fast,"[88] and more dangerously, is becoming dissatisfied at being confined to the purely "technical" areas assigned by the state. Its members, with their demands, are beginning to encroach upon the political area that includes the privileges of the ruler, the basis of state legitimacy, and the religious and cultural underpinnings of both.[89] While it currently remains relatively stable, this slow encroachment on the political sphere shows how oil, though a cornerstone in the consociational bargain, also has its limitations.

The state's control over Islamic groupings through its inclusionary corporatism is also eroding. Noting that the UAE provided the pilot of the second aircraft in the 9/11 attacks in New York in 2001, Davidson comments that, "home-grown nationals [will be] disaffected with the weakening ruling bargain."[90] Shortly before 9/11, the state's strategy had shifted along the continuum toward the exclusionary direction. Its hard interventionist strategies (to balance its soft interventionist strategy of wealth distribution) included the dismantling of several bases of Islamic activity and created an atmosphere of fear about state wrath against any Islamic activity neither organized nor sanctioned from above.

Globalizing forces threaten the legitimacy of the ruling elite and an Emirati identity that has evolved only over the last three decades out of collectivities of various *bedu* tribes and *hadar* groupings. The state, most forcefully the emirate of Dubai, embraces capitalism and economic liberalization as an inevitable process and aims to take full advantage of globalization.[91] However, among those who have long opposed any form of liberalization that serves Western interests one can hear individuals beginning to question the benefit of the capitalist path upon which the UAE has embarked. As Davidson suggests, this path upsets the patrimonial, cultural, and religious resources that make up the "ruling bargain" between the state and its citizens.[92]

Women's Empowerment: A State Strategy

The UAE state reproduces itself by engaging in a discourse of unity and nation-building, conducted largely via media forums. As part of its initiative to take control over internal security, economic threats, and perceived attacks on local culture imposed by the high volume of expatriates, the state vigorously supports the education of its citizens. Importantly, however, and like most states in the Gulf, the UAE government makes a point of increasing education for women as indispensable for national development. Women's educational empowerment serves unity, identity building, and stability.

Part of the project has enabled literacy and education among women to occur at a staggering rate. Sheikh Zayed's wife, the first lady, Sheikha Fatima Bint Mubarak, president of the UAE Women's Federation, has also played a leading role, along with several other female members of the royal families. She has pushed for a national strategy with clearly defined goals.[93] Among Sheikha Fatima's numerous accomplishments is the initial plan drafted by her for the eradication of illiteracy, which has been an impressive success.[94] To some extent, women are entering fields traditionally allocated for men. Emirati women have joined the police force, armed forces, and other regular troops.[95] Women are also infiltrating into other fields of work, including engineering, computer science, the media, academia, and business.

Women are becoming more actively involved in formal politics. Sheikh Sultan bin Muhammad al-Qasimi appointed five of these women in 2001 and soon afterward two more, making them the first women to hold political posts in the UAE. In late 2004, the first female within the cabinet, Sheikha Lubna al-Qasimi, was appointed Minister of Economy, and in early 2006, Mariam Mohammed Khalfan al-Roumi was appointed Minister of Social Affairs.[96] After long debate, in June 2007 nine women were appointed (one voted in) to the all male Federal National Council, representing 22.5 percent of the parliament and instantly sweeping the UAE up to a ranking of having one of the highest female parliamentarians in the world.

Because of societal stratification and norms of segregation, supported by both society and the ruling elite, Emirati women are diverted into jobs deemed suitable for females. Sheikh Zayed defined the kind of work that was suitable for women's mission: "I encourage women's labor at work sites that is congruent with their nature and which preserves [their] dignity and honor as mothers and generation makers."[97] Many local women are allocated jobs within the ministries, banks, or schools where they will only interact with the female public. Civil Service Commission figures show that in 1996 44.3 percent of federal government employees were women;[98] in 1998 this figure rose to 47 percent.[99] These statistics are used to support the argument that women are well placed to have an effective impact upon the development of the country's political, economic, educational, and social goals.[100] However, as Davidson argues, the ministries are "bloated bureaucracies" that have come to function as a means for employment in place of state handouts.[101]

Notably, the speeches draw a clear link between a woman's natural propensities and her duty toward her nation, thus, directing both the aspirations for action and the kinds of employment women should take up. Sheikh Zayed established the view that women were indispensable to the development of the country and the preservation of its heritage and identity. His speeches emphasized that Emirati women had a major responsibility for shaping future generations and UAE society. For women to carry these responsibilities, he emphasized that they had to arm themselves with education: "Education is like a beacon lighting your way in the darkness. It teaches you many things, the most important of which is to know your duties towards your nation, homeland, families, and the realities relating to your present, future, and your past."[102] He confirmed that women were not only half the society in terms of numbers, but half in terms of their participation in shouldering the responsibility of the upbringing of generations: "Woman is one of the pillars of the UAE society, because she is the daughter, the sister and the mother who nurtures and raises the new generation."[103] Furthermore, "I am sure that women in our prospering country realize the importance of preserving our original customs which are derived from the true teachings of Islam. A woman is the foundation on which a family is built and the family is the force which propels the whole society."[104] The speeches of the elite systematically emphasize a woman's primary roles and duties to her family and nation.

Establishing women as "mothers of the nation" with responsibility for "maintaining the traditional family structure"[105] is one of the crucial means through which the UAE government pursues its project of identity building. The state fears not only the security implications and instability caused by the flood of expatriates, but also their impact on the culture, hearts, and minds of the local population. Armed with education, citizens are expected to Emiratize a country overflowing with migrants. But more importantly, women are directed to use the tools that the state has provided them to contribute to the project of identity building and internal stability. This project builds on the idea that the citizens are the ruler's children and the ruler is seen as their *baba*.[106] In line with the national family structure, women have a defined role to play in a general project of Gulf states.

Beyond education, the "stable family" has also been a project aimed at social development and identity building. Finding a suitable marriage partner for local women has been fraught with difficulties. The project for stable families has alleviated some of these difficulties by making marriage to local women financially easier.[107] At the beginning of 1994, Sheikh Zayed created a marriage fund to encourage national men to marry national women, to lessen the burden of expensive weddings, and help promote stable families (since no funding is provided for subsequent marriages). As anthropologist Paul Dresch has noted, "The Fund represents a massive attempt at social engineering. Nor is it just 'top-down.' . . . [I]t does a remarkable job not just of organizing talks and seminars but of intervening as a social service and mobilizing other services to solve family problems."[108] By organizing society's private sphere as the state sees fit, the state has made private interests into public matters, subject to control and containment. However, with the state's constricted definition of a citizen, it is in the interest of the common good of its citizens that such strategies aim to protect unity and build identity.

CHALLENGES WOMEN FACE IN THE UAE

Article 14 of the UAE Constitution suggests that the law does not distinguish between men and women, since it states that, "Equality and social justice, ensuring safety and security and equality of opportunity for all citizens shall be the pillars of the society." This article is quoted by women's GONGO associations and the government administration as proof that women as a category are not discriminated against. And it is true that UAE women have comparatively considerable power in the home. However, women continue to face several challenges, such as, laws, policies, societal norms, religious authorities or reigning religious interpretations, or lack of access to basic rights; many of these are interrelated.[109]

Since it is really only men who have (at least until very recently) been in positions of authority vis-à-vis policy-making authority, laws will inevitably be concerned primarily with the interests of men and will, thus, be disadvantageous to women. Until 2004, political positions within the federal government had been exclusively filled by men. Beginning 2008, women could be judges and public prosecutors according to the Federal Judicial Authority law. However, Emirati women, whose children are born to non-Emirati men, are forbidden to pass on citizenship to their children.[110] A woman may marry a man from the GCC countries without any legal repercussions.[111] On the other hand, a man can marry a foreigner and men have loudly asserted this right in the face of women's demands for it to be altered.[112] Drawing on religious orthodoxy, the state also criminalizes any Emirati woman who marries a non-Muslim.[113] Furthermore, the women who have reached positions of authority are mostly chosen from among elite families in a move that ensures shared goals with state leaders.

Women are left with fewer choices for marriage than men. Men face no legal repercussions marrying nonlocal women, irrespective of religion or country of origin. Furthermore, women are generally more educated than men. The more educated a woman becomes, the more difficult it is for her to find a partner with at least the same educational level; before the oil boom the opposite was mostly the case. In informal interviews with national men the view was expressed that education was important in marriage, but that they would not wish to marry someone more educated than themselves. Local men also maintained that a woman who gave up education to guard her morals and the honor of the family by taking all measures to segregate herself was much more highly valued in terms of marriage. The latter is an issue of norms in UAE society, and is particularly predominant in, but not exclusive to, rural areas. Because marriage is an integral part of UAE society, failure to find a partner and the related causes is of concern among local women. The state's restriction of their choice to males within the nation-state is a means of control continued across other Arab countries.[114] While there is no law within the Official Gazette that bans women from marrying foreigners, various orders were issued.[115]

Women are marginalized in the workforce because of the view that men and women should observe strict separation of sexes. The home is prescribed as the best place for women and the public sphere for men. In 1980, females constituted 3.4 percent of the labor force.[116] By 2000, this figure, including nonnationals, had risen to 15 percent,[117] despite the fact that the majority of university graduates from universities in the UAE are women.[118] UAE society continues to be highly segregated. As Mona al-Bahr remarked, "If all universities in the UAE all of a sudden became mixed, you would probably see 50 percent of the female students dropping out."[119]

Moreover, discrimination persists against women in the way they conduct public affairs.[120] Some of this is due to informal restrictions. For example, there are reports that women attempting to license businesses in the import-export sector encounter greater scrutiny than men.[121] As guaranteed in the law, women and men receive equal pay for equal work. However, women who work outside the home usually do not receive equal benefits, such as housing, and may face discrimination in promotion.[122] Husbands may prevent their wives and children from leaving the country and a married woman cannot accept employment without her husband's written consent.[123] Labor codes in both the public and private sectors often fail to honor the rights of women according to international labor standards.[124]

The marginalization of women also derives in part from prevailing religious understandings, however much these appear to be mixed with norms and/or state laws. An example is reflected in increasing divorce rates and the marriage of males to more than one female. From informal interviews, Dubai had the lowest incidences of polygamy as compared to the northern emirates, in particular Ras al-Khaima where a conservative estimate might be 70 percent. Abu Dhabi had the second lowest rate, again a conservative figure of 35 percent; some participants attributed this to education. With all the emirates put together and from all the estimates I gathered, it would seem that at least 50 percent of marriages are to more than one wife. Although Ras al-Khaima is the poorest emirate, nearly all the men questioned stated that a man marries another wife once he is able to afford to do so. Some women maintained that this issue was actually the greatest challenge facing Emirati women since a woman was "consumed with thinking of ways to keep her husband."

Previous court cases where national women[125] have sought divorces in the UAE demonstrate that women face numerous obstacles that hinder divorce procedures,[126] and that they are harshly ruled against for child custody. This is despite clear misconduct, such as physical abuse, on the part of the husband.[127] The state sanctions polygyny, and anyway many marriages are not registered. Like registered marriages, unregistered (or customary, *'urfi*) marriages can end with the man divorcing the woman on the spot without recourse to formal divorce procedures. Interviewees stated that marriage to a second wife, often 20 years younger than the first, was a major problem facing probably 50 percent of all married Emirati women.[128] A study on divorce stated reasons "on the men's part, marriage to another woman, inability to meet the financial demands of the family, and negligence. Sometimes the wife would file for divorce if the husband beat her frequently, was an alcoholic or had an affair."[129]

As these above examples illustrate, women face numerous challenges. Certainly, just as in any society, women in the UAE comprise a disadvantaged group, based on their gender. As such, studies looking into the motivations of women do need to begin with an overview of potential sites of contestation. In this quest, however, studies often miss other equally important sites of contention and activation when the historical context, such as tribe, and other crucial variables, such as globalization, are ignored. First, as the country has been transformed at an unprecedented rate, numerous tensions have resulted that should not be overshadowed by what Western researchers tend to place in a hierarchy as the more oppressive challenges. It will be argued in the following chapters that despite the discriminations and marginalization of women, matters such as the threat of globalizing forces and the legitimacy of state (or other) actors, form the more pressing issues and interests of women in the UAE. Second, women in the UAE do not form a cohesive group. Women will debate and contest meanings of equality and women's roles from different positions and viewpoints. Because women's identities are embedded in a particular class, lineage, tribe, or ethnicity, gender is not a determining factor for their actions and aspirations.

CHAPTER 3

RENTIER GOVERNMENTALITY:
ACTIVISM IN UAE WOMEN'S
ORGANIZATIONS AND CLUBS

INTRODUCTION

Chapters 3, 4, and 5 analyze the impact of women's activism on civil society development through case studies on three different forms of women's collaboration found in the UAE. This chapter looks at official UAE women's societies and clubs, and chapter 4 examines Islamic-oriented women's organizations and *halakas*. Chapter 5 studies women's networks. The major difference between the organizations described in this chapter and those covered in chapters 4 and 5 is their relationship to government. The organizations described in this chapter can be termed GONGOs, while those discussed in chapter 4 are not government-created although some are government-supported; furthermore, they are Islamic-oriented. The "networks" covered in chapter 5 are distinctive in that the women who participate in them interact with one or more persons to achieve specific aims and interests. The specific question asked was whether these organizations and networks served to contribute to civil society development in the UAE.

To better understanding of how differing forms of women's association affect a country's political landscape, this chapter analyzes the kinds of "selves" created by UAE women's societies and women's clubs and the consequent effect on civil society in the UAE. The self is a vital element to power and authenticity, since "governing society has come to require governing subjectivity [which] has taken shape through the proliferation of a complex and heterogeneous assemblage of technologies."[1] The governing of subjectivities refers to the kinds of strategies and apparatuses used, such as design of curricula in lessons or the connection of what is learned or motivated to embody larger assemblages, such as a self evident Islam, directed to inspire certain capacities, desires, or virtues within the self. Three indices—participation, "civility," and empowerment—were utilized here to explore the kinds of subjectivities shaped by the programs of these organizations. There are important achievements among government-run organizations; however, they are currently unable to effectively expand civil society. I argue that instead they function, in effect, as one of the most powerful mechanisms through which the state co-opts civil society.

I question assumptions about the clear boundaries between state and society, in which the state is a coherent entity and only site of politically relevant action. Such statist accounts of the state overlook the presence and power of representatives of the state.[2] They do not take account of, for example, traditional patterns of family obligations and tribal loyalty as crucial determinants of the Arab Gulf. Thus, the chapter attempts to understand how an Arab Gulf state is shaped and expanded through women's organizations.

Utilizing civil society literature for analyzing state-run associations could not provide a comprehensive picture of their participation. Drawing especially on Michel Foucault, Mitchell Dean, James Ferguson, and Akhil Gupta with regard to governmentality, I was able to scrutinize these organizations and their role in government conduct and production in detail. This chapter is concerned with the "programs, strategies, techniques for acting upon the action of others towards certain ends."[3] As discussed in chapter 2, the UAE state constructs itself through particular imaginary and symbolic devices, such as the (re)articulation of culture and tradition. This process is illustrated here through the agency of the state's official women's organizations. Employing the terms of verticality and encompassment,[4] the present chapter delineates how the state and official women's associations (re)configure the state and civil society sectors in terms of hierarchy and space.

Within the larger theoretical development in which GONGO associations have been viewed as part of the neoliberal process, and in which the nation-state cedes power to what are usually state-developed agencies and institutions, this study shows that GONGOs are, in most ways, empowered to fulfill functions of the welfare (specifically rentier) state. As sociologist Nikolas Rose explains, "Political forces seek to give effect to their strategies, not only through the utilization of laws, bureaucracies, funding regimes and authoritative state agencies and agents, but through utilizing and instrumentalizing forms of authority other than those of the 'State' in order to govern—spatially and constitutionally—'at a distance.' "[5]

Yet, in contrast with the theoretical underpinnings of neoliberal governmentality, a decentralization of power is not at stake in the case of the UAE. In fact, the state bolsters its powers through the vertical encompassment[6] of civil society sectors, made possible largely through rentierism and authoritarian technologies of governmentality. Authoritarian governmentality occurs when the state "does not rely on the choices, aspirations or capacities of the individual subject."[7] Inducements and coercion are techniques of power implemented by the UAE government alongside a "watered down" version of neoliberal ruling techniques and are used in the process of development plans to take better control over civil society. Hence, I refer to the rationalities of rule of the rentier state as "rentier governmentality," to describe a form of rule that aims to take greater control of civil society through the strategies of co-optation, facilitated predominantly through rentierism, and also through coercion and assisted by a limited and controlled form of "responsibilization" in the quest for development.

In referring to the rationalities of this form of rule of the rentier state, tribalism plays an important role. In fact, an accurate understanding of the state in the Arab Gulf cannot be reached without reference to patterns of tribal organization and hierarchy.[8] Until the 1960s, the governing system for centuries was largely tribal. Thus, as discussed earlier, a form of the nation-state is very recent. Sayyid Hurreiz maintains, the structure of government "merges into the clan, sub-tribe, tribe and tribal confederation,"[9] and asserts "that traditional UAE society is not a thing of the past, and that it has not been entirely superseded by modern political systems."[10] Although women played central roles in the family and society, a woman's role was also defined in respect to her gender. The norms of tribalism governed the conduct of each member of the household and each had inescapable obligations of mutual assistance.[11] With the concept of loyalty as a paramount value, the woman, as each member, conducted actions as expected to protect the honor of the family and tribe. The chief had also obligations to protect his group; consequently, loyal to his people, a leader was expected to provide, ensure peace, and guide through mechanisms of patrimony. Thus, as detailed in chapter 2, clearly understood value systems and civility formed a sort of civil society long before the advent of contemporary associations in the 1960s. These value systems, in which patrimony and patriarchy played central roles, are evident in the political system and, hence, the rationalities of the state, made up of tribal leaders, reflects these tribal institutions of behavior.

The first section of this chapter describes the UAE Federation of Women's associations and clubs and participants' profiles, the second section examines "participation," and the third looks at "empowerment." The fourth section considers "civility." In the fifth section, I discuss the ways in which the confederation of women's associations and clubs impact civil society and specifically how they seek to establish certain "natures" among the women and the consequences of this construction for UAE civil society.

OVERVIEW OF UAE FEDERATION OF WOMEN'S ASSOCIATIONS / CLUBS AND ACTIVITIES

The Jam'iat Nahdhat al-Mar'ah al-Dhabiyaniyya (Abu Dhabi Women's Development Society) was officially founded in early 1973 as the first women's association, and was headed by Sheikha Fatima bint Mubarak, wife of the country's former president, Sheikh Zayed bin Sultan al-Nahayan. The Jam'iat al-Nahda al-Nisa'iyya (Women's Development Society) followed in Dubai in 1974; the Jam'iat al-Ittihad al-Nisa'iah (Women's Union Society) in Sharjah in 1973; the Jam'iat Umm al-Mu'mineen al-Nisa'iyah (Umm al-Mu'mineen Women Association) in Ajman in 1974; and the Jam'iat Nahdhat al-Mar'ah (Women's Development Society) in Umm al-Quwain was formed also in 1973. A few associations had been set up informally much earlier. For example, the Ras al-Khaima Jam'iat Nahdhat al-Mar'ah (Women's Development Society) was organized as early as 1966 but only established itself officially in 1976.

These six organizations had already become modalities of governance by 1979, when they were subsumed under Sheikha Fatima's umbrella organization in Abu Dhabi, the al-Ittihad al-Nisa'i (Women's Union). This made a total of seven official women's organizations in the UAE. Each emirate organization is led by a sheikha (or sheikhas) of the emirate in which it is located; and each has branches located in other cities or villages of its respective emirate. The organizations are found in the emirate capitals, but their activities often extend to rural settings. This hierarchy has granted them not only an elitist character but also a mainly urban orientation.

They direct their activities to areas regarded as apolitical. Lessons, lectures, conferences, and seminars focus on four main areas: religion, health and beauty, family issues, and general skills development. Great emphasis is placed on Islamic education. Topics within the lessons include women's familial role, society, the environment, *da'wa*, prayer, mysticism, charity, fasting, and child-raising. All conference lectures are in Arabic but a few associations have lessons for non-Arabic speakers. Women are producers of the nation and pass down knowledge; hence, Islamic knowledge is emphasized.

Lectures and courses are given in the area of health and beauty to help raise women's awareness of illnesses, such as breast cancer. As women are the prime caregivers, there are also lessons dealing with children's nutrition and general well-being, drug administration or use, vaccination and breastfeeding. Beauty courses are offered on makeup, henna, or tips for hair. Conferences and lectures deal with women's roles, parenting, and how to be a good spouse (lectures have also included men). General skills development is achieved through literacy classes, although associations in urban areas have shifted attention to other activities. Specialized courses typically include computer skills, painting, drawing, cake decorating, baking, etiquette, fruit carving, cooking, or flower arranging. A further illustration of the gendered nature of women's roles is the initiative to revive "traditions," through learning to make handicrafts, dresses, and other sewing/stitching activities. Children's activities are also offered. All associations have summer programs for children as well as poetry, artwork, science, Qur'an recitation, and sports (see appendix table 1 for an overview). Activities are sometimes provided within children's orphanages.

While the associations share great similarities, they differ depending on the emirate, the leaders' goals, size, and funding. As each emirate is headed by a different ruler or sheikh, each association is headed by a different sheikha and management team. One interviewee explains their differences: "The goals of each association depend on its management and the vision of its leaders." Participants often defined their emirate and association through comparisons with the Dubai emirate and its association(s). A participant in Dubai's association compared its openness[12] to the Dubai government's diversification objective. The participants of one association pointed to the "downfall" of Dubai to explain why their activities focused on the preservation of local traditions, and resisted assimilation and moral degradation. However, all organizations geared their activities toward the protection of local customs.

Associations differed in size and the number of women who could be accommodated. In terms of the women using the services, a large association will have around 1,000 attendees. Associations will typically accommodate 150 to 350 women at their conferences. It was reported that those who benefited from services of all associations combined numbered up to 100,000.[13] Keeping in mind the small size of the country, the rather large number of women to whom these associations extend their services should give a picture of how potentially influential this medium of learning and information flow can be.

Associations differed vastly in how much funding they had at their disposal. While each emirate women's association received aid from the head of state and from Sheikha Fatima through the Ministry of Social Affairs, much of the funding was dependent upon the wealth of its home emirate. The rulers in Abu Dhabi were able to provide its women's associations much more funding than an emirate without oil resources, such as Ajman. In fact, Sheikha Fatima was said to provide extra funding to finance specific events, at least in Abu Dhabi. The Women's Union in Abu Dhabi was also granted a new building in 1998, worth DH22 million, and its main branch (Bateen) was also provided with a new building in 2003. Sheikh al-Maktoum, ruler of Dubai, provided the Dubai Women's association with DH20 million for its new building whose construction started in 2000. Interviewees reported that funding was a major challenge for poorer emirates. Making an analogy to explain the differences in wealth distribution among emirates, an interviewee stated, "Sheikh Zayed's children are different from his grandchildren. We are like his grandchildren, not his children. He feels more strongly about his children. They receive first." Electricity and water are free for all associations. The ruling elite in Sharjah speak frequently of developing a civil society (from the top down) and here, nonprofit organizations are additionally provided with a furnished workplace. In theory, all UAE nonprofit organizations could find funding through the Ministry of Social Affairs and sometimes directly through the *diwan al-hakim* (the ruler's office). Yet, most associations and clubs, even those in Abu Dhabi, needed to find funds from sponsors: other government charities; businesspersons; courses; income from galleries and parties; renting of wedding halls or, in one case, running a tailoring shop. Except for the case of clubs, membership fees made up a small portion of revenue.

Profile of Interviewees

The women who took part in the interviews are categorized in table 3 in the appendix. Two-thirds of the participants interviewed were local, a percentage that seems to accurately reflect actual local to nonlocal ratios within the organizations, except for clubs that had a significant proportion of nonnationals. Length of residency in the UAE among activists is generally longer than among nonactivists. Nonnationals within networks mostly had permanent residency, followed by those in Islamic organizations who mostly do not but often choose the UAE for an Islamic lifestyle, then these organizations. Their participation is a reflection of their concern for the community and society. Hence, they do have great potential to effect change in their pursuits. That said, however, locals and Islamic activists articulate the profound effect transient residents also have on shaping local behavior and even state policies!

Other characteristics noted were age, marital status, length of time at the organization, and level of activity outside the association. While the mean age of all women interviewed for government-run organizations was 30, ages ranged from 22 to 45. Just over half of the women were married. Only two interviewees reported divorcee status. The mean number of 1.6 children is distributed among all interviewees, including those without children. However, of the women who had children, the mean is three children to each woman. Of the sample of 28 women, 20 reported their length of time as participants in the association. The average was 2.6 years of participation. However, there was a split between those who participated one year or below (50 percent) and those who were with the association five years and above (30 percent). Those who were with the association at least five years were all nationals. This last group was in higher positions within the organizations illustrating a lack of inclusivity at decision-making levels.

Four women or 14 percent reported participating in other organizational or networking activities outside the association. Three of the women volunteered for the Red Crescent Society. None of the participants worked anywhere else outside the organization. The vast majority of women, 24 out of the 28, were paid on a full-time basis for the work they did in the associations. One of the four not paid was fulfilling the work experience required by her university in the last year of her B.A. degree, and chose a women's association in particular "to gain experience." Hence, volunteerism is lacking.

All women interviewed, except one, had some level of a postsecondary education. A degree from B.A./B.Sc. and above is counted here only if it has been completed. As can be seen from the table, a bachelor degree was attained by the overwhelming majority of women. Of those with a B.A., 54 percent had degrees in social sciences, which comprised 25 percent in family sciences, language, psychology, social work, media, and economics; 18 percent in management, business, commerce, and accounting; and 11 percent in Islamic theology. Forty-six percent had their degrees in computer related or technical studies. Seventy-nine percent received their education in the UAE and 21 percent (all non-Emirati) in other Arab or Western countries. One person was working on an M.A. A participant attested, "Anyone who works here must be educated."

PARTICIPATION

Quantitative Indicators

Associations have increased through the founding of new branches and programs offered. Dubai's women's association heads three branches; Abu Dhabi's Al-Bateen (located in the locality of Bateen, Abu Dhabi) heads 11 other associations in the emirate of Abu Dhabi. These are located within the main cities (Abu Dhabi and one in Al-Ain), in smaller cities (Shahama), and in more rural areas such as the island of Delma or in the south near the border of Qatar. Sharjah, Umm al-Quwain, and Ras al-Khaima did not have any further branches because of the smaller size of these emirates. Fujairah lacked an association of its own but had a small club. Informants in Fujairah explained that they could use the services and facilities of Dubai's Jam'iat al-Nahda al-Nisa'iyya. Otherwise, the associations will go into poorer areas to provide courses on various development goals, particularly literacy, and thereby can be considered to have further branches. While there were privately run gyms for women scattered around the country, clubs were found in Sharjah (with a small branch in Fujairah) and Abu Dhabi. A club opened in 2003 in Dubai. The ladies club in Ras al-Khaima closed down in 2002.

From the time of their establishment, all organizations under study had demonstrated an increase in activity level. Many facilities were still under construction. During the course of this study, I saw organizations move to much larger buildings in both Abu Dhabi and Dubai. In terms of horizontal growth of organizations, a notable and consistent growth occurred in numbers of workers. Certainly, the women's state-run associations have proved to have potential to affect a larger population through the increasing numbers of participants, programs offered, and organizational size.

Paid Work and the Concept of Volunteerism

Despite the growing organizational sizes and membership numbers, reference to volunteerism is problematic in describing the participation. Civil society organizations are the organs through which individuals are exposed to the spirit of volunteerism. This particular disciplinary technique of government is lacking among the organizations visited. As noted in appendix table 3, except for four interviewees (11 percent), women were paid for the work they did in these organizations.

Moreover, of the two broad goals guiding most women's participation—a salary and a segregated work opportunity, the salary comes first. An overwhelming majority of foreign participants spoke of their positions as a job they had landed. A nonlocal participant said, "First I was working a split shift in Dubai. I had no time to rest. . . . Here they said the salary would be very low, but I took it because of one shift. Also there's a nursery here, so my baby is here," or, "It was an accident! My company sent me here." Another expatriate explained how she landed the position: "I saw an advertisement in the newspaper and got an interview." Posts were advertised as a job, not as volunteer work, and the women who applied were motivated by the potential for work rather than by the desire to contribute to a greater good. A local participant told how she viewed nonlocals' participation: "A foreigner works for work!" Several women, especially locals, expressed the view that a women's association was the only suitable place to work as one worked with women and must not mingle with men. Another said, "The women choose this work because it is social work. They prefer it because when they get married maybe the husband will agree." Thus the position was taken up in the interest of continuing a job acceptable to some potential husband.

Hence, devices and techniques to involve women in associational public life consisted mainly of monetary incentives. Foreigners are lured to participate predominantly through monetary reward, since techniques of citizenship and its related forms of responsibilization are not viable for this category. The "political bargain" is not extended to this group. However, locals are also lured into "participating."

Nonetheless, both locals and nonlocals can be drawn to working in a segregated environment because this is part of their moral consciousness. The role played by these women's associations is one of entrenching this kind of moral subjectivity. Women who subscribe to the socially inscribed preference will find empowerment in having secured a job in a segregated environment. Most locals, as well most

Islamic activists, are not aiming to secure equality between men and women as society views men and women occupying different roles. Similarly, the associations support the kinds of subjectivities that uphold this system although increasingly some local women aspire to a gendered public space in which women can have the same choices and opportunities as men. Rather, these organizations enforce existing power relations in which men's place is in the public sphere and women's is in a feminized or private sphere, vertically situated below the public.

Participation occurs under three main circumstances. The first and most familiar form occurred under a system through which participants expected that, by demonstrating good working skills, they might be granted a position. This category of volunteers included new university graduates. Interviewees expressed their hopes of being able to land paid jobs in a process that would usually take a year.

This first type of participants has a number of consequences for civil society volunteerism. First, a larger proportion of these volunteers develop misconceptions about volunteer work. Understandably, focus can be lost when one volunteers under the goal of eventually landing a paid job. Second, government successfully shapes the desires, loyalties, and goals of the prospective worker through the organization.[14] She submits willingly because a salaried position in a socially honored place is her incentive. Third, as an interviewee remarked, "the volunteers shy away from feeling responsibilities. When you ask one to do something she replies, 'I am just a volunteer.'" Thus an ethos of volunteerism is not inculcated within the self, despite some associational leaders listing the opposite as part of their educational goals. Rather, these associations structure participation vertically, within the layers of state and society in which volunteerism is allotted a rank and from which participants ascend when they are taken into the association. In this ascent they find themselves in a position of stability—responsibility that is materially rewarded.

The second form of participation generally consists of older local women of higher status, who attend general association meetings and important events. This group also comprises those women who ensure that the activities of the associations are in line with the wishes of the sheikhas. The status of these women is above that of those who are rewarded materially. Besides the titles or certain family names that some may carry, their identity as volunteers denotes a specific rank in the hierarchy of state-society actors and, consequently, greater influence.

The third form of participation was that made up of women who participated for no material benefit or prestige. I interviewed one person from this third group who was indeed highly active. An interviewee noted, "[Such] volunteers are never in decision-making places." Containment of activism is thus achieved through a salary as a mechanism of participant regulation and monitoring. No one "off the street" can enter the association and exert influence to make a change in the direction she has envisioned. Rentier governmentality is the dominant mode of operation to ensure the production of citizens who are supportive of state goals. Volunteerism threatens authority and set modes of patrimonialism, which is, in fact, viewed by some state leaders as the ideal mode of community organization similar to the family structure that must be protected.

There were women who understood and practiced volunteerism until their arrival at the association. Two expatriate Arab participants told how active they had been in various forms of activity until coming to the UAE and the associations in which they now participated. The first exclaimed, "Here there are many costs. I don't rest here. Now all I think about is how to bring money." The other spoke of how active she had been in Islamic activism in her country of origin, but noted that in the UAE she only thought of her family and work. Several non-case study interviewees explained that when people came to the Emirates they did so to make money. Many had homes or apartments in their countries of origin that they need to save up for or to finance. Some expected to retire after their time in the Gulf. Some Islamists were not willing to risk their livelihood for activism given the threat of deportation (an issue that will be further examined in chapter 4). Thus, some, though not all, who had been active before and understood the concept of volunteerism curtailed their activism in these associations. In this way, mechanisms of incentives and coercion operate. In this way, rentier governmentality serves to contain civil society rather than to facilitate its expansion.

While participation in these state-run associations can lead to the encompassment and containment of civil society, one must note other processes that, at the same time, serve to contribute to a civil society. One participant who joined the association initially through volunteer work explained, "Of course I wanted to get the job. Even though I was volunteering I still needed money to pay for food, to live." The by-product of this form of *hiring* was that some of those who had to "get up early to take the bus to be here at 8 and work until 1 for free . . . [and] work sometimes until 9," developed an understanding of some aspects of volunteerism through this experience. Another participant asserted: "Before, I did not know what volunteerism meant. Before, I sat at home. After college I did not know what to do. But here I learned to give. I come from 8–1:30. But sometimes I am here until 9 or 10. . . . If you work you will know how to volunteer." And as one participant claimed, "It will take time for people to understand volunteerism. They don't understand Islam. They lost Islam. They go their own way. People are not educated. . . . It is only now that people are slowly beginning to understand Islam and understand people."

While some non-case study and one case study interviewees believed the associations were "using volunteers," some women were slowly becoming aware of what it meant to sacrifice time and effort. Lamenting the state of volunteerism, one participant explained that it was the association that taught her the concept:

I stayed home two years after graduation. I did not know what volunteering meant. At first I was not allowed to come here and work for free. My family did not like the idea of me working. And when I told them I want to spend my free time at the organization instead of at home they said that the organization was taking advantage of me. I was not allowed to even drive a car. I still am not. But I fought for them to let me volunteer. Now I am allowed.

An unintended outcome is a subjectivation in which participants acquire an understanding of sacrifice for a common good.

Sacrificing and giving selves are produced through other byproducts of a paid position in these associations. Displaying her hours of work on a monthly schedule, one participant pointed out how many days she worked extra hours without any extra pay, and how often she worked or participated in some activity on her days off at the expense of tending to her family. She did not hesitate to point to a CD writer and explain how, due to budgetary restrictions, she paid for items out of her own pocket. To her it was important to make a difference in the place through sacrifice. Hence, at the same time the state expands itself through "employing participants," subjectivities emerge that demonstrate capacities for sacrifice. These examples illustrate that a single form of subjectivation does not occur. Rather, there are various processes at work in shaping individuals' conduct and the way in which they interpret their actions. However, a rentier-based form of governmentality is generally not productive of the kinds of capacities that enable the sacrificial self.

EMPOWERMENT

Women's Associations: A State Organ?

There are a number of studies on women's organizations in the Middle East that have recognized the instrumental value of women's organizations to the state. Several authors discuss this issue within the volume by Dawn Chatty and Annika Rabo; Haya al-Mughni found that the Kuwaiti state has attempted throughout its existence to manipulate women's groups to maintain its stability and continuity;[15] while Suad Joseph described the politics of women's organizations in which the interests of the state were reproduced through them by the elite leaders.[16] Valentine Moghadam illustrated the close affiliations between the ruling parties and the major women's organizations in Palestine, Tunisia, Syria, and earlier in Iraq.[17] Indeed, "women's main role in the Middle Eastern political process has been as actors in the larger national politics,"[18] and the state's use of women's organizations as a device of governmentality is a phenomenon across the Middle East.[19] Corporatist politics of the state are also at work in the UAE women's GONGO associations.

State-run women's associations in the UAE function as one of the most powerful forms of organization through which the state pursues its agenda of legitimacy and identity building. No other organizations exist in the UAE that extend in the way the UAE women's societies and clubs do into virtually every corner of every emirate, and with their numerous branches subsumed under one umbrella. Neither, as mentioned previously, does any other organization receive as much state funding. Aside from ensuring "participants" execute roles to which they have been assigned through a salary, the state reproduces itself through further mechanisms of control. It selects and appoints leaders of the associations from the government ministries and formulates the agendas that participants are required to pursue, including the Emiratization plan (slowly replace workforce of expatriates with locals). Hence, participation through these state-run associations is contributing extensively to state priorities, not only through usual techniques of governmentality, but also through direct forms of corporatism. Participation in these organizations enables wider state powers over sectors of society.

A question asked concerning who formulates the programs received the reply that, "All clubs belong to Sheikha Fatima. She divides the activities." Another participant explained the relationship of the Women's Union and emirates' associations: "Sheikha Fatima is the leader. She gives us and the other emirates general goals to work on." According to participants, the associations' achievements are dependent upon Sheikha Fatima's endorsement of goals and her desire to implement them. The best strategy to attain goals from government is to rely on the power of Sheikha Fatima and the rulers. A participant confirmed this: "When you have the sheikh behind you, you have power in society," and another participant confirmed that, "with the women around her, Sheikha Fatima can achieve our rights. She is encouraging women. The government is trying to help a lot." A respondent explained,

Sheikha Fatima is the leader of the Women's Union and is the decision maker. She exerts pressure, if she believes in what she is asking for. We always try to work with ministries. We try to get everyone involved in our plans and strategies. We convince through research. We study the experiences of other countries in the Arab world. We choose what suits our society.

The idea many of the women hoped to convey was that they had power *because* they worked under the auspices of the ruling families. Participants were keenly aware of the authority that was carried through the name of their associations when they dealt with the public. The sheikhas' creation and endorsement of their activities positioned these actors in a way that enabled them forcefully to blur the boundaries between the state and civil society and to situate one over the other. Further, the idea formulated by the elite state actors and perpetuated through the associational actors is that it is the state's duty to initiate greater rights for women. This sense of *duty* did not appear out of a vacuum; rather, it is a remnant of the tribal ethos of the responsibility of the leader to guide. But it is also a purposefully continued ethos. In terms of vertical construction, not the tribal leader, but the state is now produced by actors embedded within the state and associations not only through referring to the value system of obligation and loyalty, but also through large monetary incentives. The notion of reliance on the state for one's rights is, consequently, a construct of rentier governmentality, which in effect produces dependency, not self-reliant selves.

 The most important link between the associations and government are the sheikhas. But contributing to this link are other women in high-level positions, such as those in managerial jobs, who have often been appointed to their posts by the ministries in which they worked, or directly through Sheikha Fatima's office. A participant, aspiring to contribute to her country's development, told how she received her post: "The chairwoman [a sheikha who runs the association] helped me get my position after I had volunteered here for two months. I don't care about the salary. I studied hard and got excellent marks. I want to see results of my studies by developing something new." Another participant said that, "Sheikha xxx called me to work here because of my skills." Some at the managerial level were sheikhas and received no pay. Although not all women were asked whether they had been appointed, 21 percent or seven interviewees reported that the government had appointed them, either through a ministry in which they had originally worked, or the appointment had been made by the sheikha. While most of the other interviewees were paid by the association, these participants continued to receive their salary from the ministry. Such a mechanism of encompassment has grave consequences for civil society.

Corporatist politics, such as government appointments, ensures that goals devised at the government level are implemented in the organizations. Having a person from the ministry present within the association at the managerial level enables her to take firmer control over activities on the ground. Through close scrutiny, she can oversee that participants conform to the objectives of the sheikhas. A participant from one of the smaller associations confirmed such a role: "One manager is employed by the Ministry of Education and follows up on the work in the association."[20] In practice, the ability of a state appointee forcefully to invade the participants' space for the purpose of monitoring the organization's programs defines the hegemonic positioning of state over society. Furthermore, participation is constrained from the top down in which participants are monitored through state appointees.

The state ensures the chosen person fulfills "her duties towards her nation" through several mechanisms. First, several of the women at the highest levels below the sheikhas' leadership are chosen on the basis of their family lineage. The family names of several (not all) managers and probably all directors reveal that they belong to elite tribal families related to the ruling families. As such, many of the appointed women have a vested interest in protecting family interests that are not distinct from the interests of the ruling elite. Second, being appointed through the ministry or handpicked by the sheikha entails a sense of responsibility to honor the distinction given by the royal family and which takes precedence over a woman's possible other goals. State actors invest the role of serving the sheikh/a with symbols of prestige and honor that already have long-standing meaning. The consequence is that a participant may have a sense of

compassion toward women as a group, but if there is a conflict between duties for women and those for the state, she is unlikely to
risk her government job, not to mention the trust of her leaders, for
the sake of women's solidarity.

Third, a woman's subjectivity is shaped by the discourse of her environment and dominant discourses on national women's duties toward their nation. However much the state may also fabricate an
enemy, the state leaders have reason to worry that their traditions and
Emirati identity (in its ongoing formulation) will evaporate with the
predominantly nonlocal population. Hence, a discourse has developed around the dangers of losing one's identity and religion. To
combat this onslaught of foreign ideas and lifestyles, the state's Emiratization plan is pursued through numerous techniques. The media
functions as an important avenue for the state to produce a discourse
around the dangers. However, the women's associations play a crucial
role in the implementation of the Emiratization plan.

Part of the plan implemented through the media and associations
is to produce subjectivities conducive to adopting feminine roles in
development, in line with the way in which family is valued and differing roles are thought to ensure its resilience. The goals for this development are carefully constructed through effectual techniques
of loyalty. The technologies of loyalty entail identity within a constructed family and the attendant responsibilities as members of this
family just as had long been important for the peaceful coexistence
among one's tribe. Several participants joined associations for the
purpose of serving their country. A participant said,

I joined because first this club is for Sheikha Fatima. It is also run by another
sheikha who is the chairwoman. I love this place. It is important that sheikhas
lead the place. It makes you more respectable in front of others. I love my
country, Sheikha Fatima and Sheikh Zayed and I really want to work under
their umbrella.

In line with the same rationalities, now nationalist sentiments play on
the subjectivity of participants to fulfill the roles laid down by the
country's leaders. Citizens understand that the associations belong to
the ruling families and, hence, that acts of patriotism and development of the country will be achieved through their participation in
these associations.

The *baba*, as head of state, leads his "children" to prosperity and
the good life within the national "family" that transcends the private
and public often espoused by governments in the Gulf. Through

these associations, a specific model is promoted as the ideal woman along with her ideal roles. The leaders of these associations construct the idea that a woman must sacrifice for the sake of her country and family. The family is thought of as the basic unit of the society. The woman is responsible for the functioning of this basic unit or "family" and then, by extension, the country. As with al-Mughni's case study on Kuwait, where political power is hereditary, "the assimilation of the concept of family with that of *watan* is crucial to the perpetuation of the regime."[21] As a participant emphasized, "I have to feel what my country needs and give back what it has given me." Another stated, "Through this association Sheikha Amina [of Dubai] gives us a chance to improve our country. We learn we must give to the country." Thus, participants express a desire that has been fashioned through their subjectivation within a discourse on *watan* and duty. "[I]ndividuals are to fulfil their obligations not through their relations of dependency and obligation to one another, but through seeking to *fulfil themselves.*"[22]

Leaders view women themselves as crucial to the protection of UAE security. At one association I was promised an interview once I had provided a certain required letter, but upon arrival I was denied the interview. The explanation given by the director was that she also represented the UAE and was "responsible for the security of the UAE." As such, a director's position is tied in with that of state security. Women's roles in security can also be understood through the Emiratization plan. It does not allow for women to sit at home in the long term. As a leader pointed out, "We have a lot of imbalances. The labor market, for example, creates a security problem. Women can reduce this security issue. We discuss how she can contribute to her home and here. . . . We also try to put nurseries next to their work places and in the future provide flexible working hours." For a market solution, as Dean has argued in relation to the notion of neoliberal governmentality, one would need to empower the marginalized.[23]

However, just as the state consists of persons who implement the goals of the ruling sheikhs while pursuing other agendas, women within these associations must also be recognized as individuals whose agency is a product not only of the dominant programs of the ruling families, but also of other influences and priorities. Just as some women give priority to ruling tribal clans in their activism within the associations, others base their participation on allegiance to less powerful tribes, economic circumstance, a sense of a common good that extends past a good formulated for nationals, or Islamist group embeddedness. As Suaad al-Oraimi points out, while the majority of elite women (most often not from the ruling class) do not feel they can effect change through these associations, some attempt to work through these organizations to promote their goals of "bringing about the new balance of political power." They do this by taking a nonconfrontational stance with government, and acting as "a hub for positive leadership."[24]

Two of the women interviewed belonged to Islamist groups. Others did not identify themselves as Islamists or as belonging to any Islamist group; yet, their statements and rhetoric confirmed Islamist positions and goals as pursued by specific Islamist groups. Others collaborated with Islamic activists on an individual basis. Some of these women derided the leaders of the associations and their practices. In fact, a notable number (also non-Islamists) vented their frustrations about the management, which, again, is usually made up of elite actors. Such a position demonstrates a "quiet" disavowal of the nationalist agenda pursued by the associations, a subjectivity that has been awaked by the fact that they are (though not all!) nonnational, and their identities as women or Muslims have not provided a cause for solidarity with their elite co-participants. One interviewee noted that Islamization is pursued through the associations. She revealed that Islamists can Islamize society "without needing to have the *halaqas* in secret or pay for many things." These associations function as a state organ that controls society through vertical encompassment, but they can also be used by women as a legitimate avenue to pursue various interests "behind the backs of or against the wills of even the most powerful actors."[25]

State Feminism as a Mode of Governmentality

An empowerment process takes place through some aspects of the programs offered by the state-run organizations and through the work of women in the organizations. But empowerment is curtailed in specific areas because these organizations function as the major means through which the government, in practical terms, pursues its state feminism. State feminism is used in much of the literature to refer to the process by which the state takes on women's interests.[26] However, the following demonstrates numerous contradictions in the commitment to women's issues.

The modality of state feminism as part of a mechanism of governmentality has enabled women to acquire some form of greater independence and self-development. Indeed, Sheikha Fatima has helped women to enjoy several achievements, including education and work possibilities. Certainly the organizations have also been the means through which women have been able to attain certain competencies and skills. Because they are crucial to the development of the country, the associations channel women's actions so that an empowerment process will occur in several areas. Women have acquired the sort of skills that are sometimes commensurate with challenging or high profile positions. Some of the (elite) women who have been part of these organizations have moved on to take up prominent positions of responsibility outside the organizations, as has been notably the case within the Dubai Festival City.

However, the associational leaders, being the sheikhas among the ruling elite, lead the associations toward the goals that are congruent with the political aspirations of the monarchy. They operate within a framework in which women's actions are directed to nationalist interests, to which only a fraction of the population may be steered through emotive technologies or from which they may benefit through the "ruling bargain." The constraints placed by a modality of governmentality on women's empowerment through state feminism may be understood through the strategies implemented within the associations. These include (1) building a consciousness that women have been given all they need, since women must otherwise rely on the sheikhs and sheikhas to initiate any cause on their behalf; (2) establishing that women's natures cannot permit them to function as full citizens; and (3) channeling talk and activity toward issues devoid of any controversial, legal or political content.

Despite all the means through which women in the UAE are marginalized, as detailed in chapter 2, women believe that they have been given all their rights. Elite leaders in government, together with leaders in the associations, maintain that the constitution has already protected women's rights, as if this entity were a living lawgiver, ensuring that women would have no legal worries. As a participant in a managerial position claimed: "Women have all their rights. Our constitution makes no difference between men or women. . . . The sheikh already made sure women are taken care of." This leader's statement was repeated in various ways by numerous interviewees at higher and lower levels within the associations. The assertion that women have everything they need is often followed by a statement about the sheikh providing for women or for the nation in general.

From the statements that followed or the views expressed by other women that there were only minor issues of contention that related to society rather than government, it could be discerned that, in fact, not everything was wonderful. A smaller number of women's statements indicated a perception that some things were far from perfect. However, because women kept repeating, "the sheikh provides," a complacent subjectivity seemed to have resulted. Women had learned not to place any demands or convey any message that they were ungrateful because, through the leaders' speeches, the government-controlled media, and their parents, they had developed an awareness that their material needs had been generously provided for. Thus, the subject was conceptualized as a means for securitization, in which rights to social welfare and economic advantages were provided "in return for duties of social obligation [. . . ,] social responsibility"[27] and, most importantly, loyalty.

As such, not only the state leaders but also the women themselves confirmed that there were no pressing issues on which to lobby government, but that if they wished to pursue anything the government had the ultimate authority to decide if it was worth considering. Women in leadership positions seemed to agree that to protest against government policies or to lobby was "not necessary in the UAE." As a participant remarked, "Here it is different from other countries. We like things done smoothly. We don't fight. Say what you want in a good and decent way and you will get it. Sheikh Zayed is in support of women. So we make up a proposal and they study it. The government never says no unless there are disadvantages." Not only do the speeches by ruling elites that are covered in the media reaffirm the notion that the citizenry must rely on the wise guidance of the leadership, but also those given within the associations convey the same explicit message.

Patrimonialism and patriarchy had been viewed quite differently to the Western conceptions, in the sense that the family cohesiveness, responsibility, and loyalty are integral, moral, and healthy in its larger manifestation comprising state and society. Currently, they are understood to secure a form of civility in a time of great change. However, curtailing action on the part of women does hinder civil society development, regardless. Concerns for society some local women had, they acknowledged, were in need of being addressed and were left so particularly because of a patrimonial structure. Significantly, other locals, although claiming they yet felt strongly part of a larger family, expressed they are beginning to view this configuration as oppressive and their own (extended) families are disadvantaged in this larger configuration. A few conceded the merit in patrimonialism and patriarchy was for some and not others! While patrimonialism may not have been viewed as oppressive features of tribal forms of organizing, rentier politics, particularly the accruement of oil money to the power holders, has changed the meanings attached to patrimonialism with its more obvious authoritarian character. As one interviewee outside this case study sample noted, "Women cannot make any changes through those associations. Any woman who wants to change the system would never try through these associations. She must use other avenues."[28]

Indeed, an institution directed by the ruling elite cannot criticize the ruling elite, and especially so in a country in which the laws criminalize a person who criticizes state actors. Disempowerment may result when women's agency is directed to acts of complacency because they learn that in order to achieve a goal they must rely on an authority whose primary interest is its own perpetuity and survival. Some elite women accommodate what may appear to be a passive stance, but have, in fact, consciously directed their agency not to take a confrontationalist approach in order to pursue their goals. They feel that working from inside rather than outside the politically powerful institutions will eventually prove more successful. Disempowerment, however, will not be uniform across all classes and groups, as some of the women who strive to protect state interests through the associations seek also to secure their positions of advantage within the social hierarchy.

The state exercises mechanisms to control the sexual and reproductive capacities of women by keeping marriage within the confines of the nation. One technique it utilizes is to categorize acceptable and unacceptable behavior by branding anyone who breaches rules governing women's sexuality as rebelling against the state. No women's association has sought to change this notion. On the contrary, a participant in a managerial position linked the way that Emirati women are marrying foreign men to religious and cultural rebelliousness: "They are becoming educated and open-minded, but are not following Islamic teachings. They do not respect those who pass rules. They are not wearing the *abaya* and *shayla*. They are wearing short dresses and marry from other nationalities." She approved that such women were stripped of their citizenship saying that this was the way it should be, in order to "protect society from foreign influences." The position expressed within the top ranks of an association was that the taking away of citizenship was done for the good of society. Thus, women's happiness and basic rights were being sidelined for the anticipated success of nationalist patriarchal policies, to which some of the most powerful women chose to subscribe.[29] They opted to adhere to patrimonialism because their position within the hierarchy of power relations would be secured by the structure.

Women's incapability is constructed when sexual differences are strongly emphasized. Women in managerial positions within the associations conveyed the message that women were not as competent as men to take on leadership roles in society. According to an organizational leader, "She has to be ready for political participation. . . . She is not ready. It is a new country. It is only 35 years old and small and unique." Participants explained that women did not have the experience that men had and so could not be entrusted with governmental political leadership positions. As an interviewee in a leadership position noted, "There are things just for men and just for women. It is not right that a woman takes up a man's job. . . . It is nice to see women in the police, but not in other places. She can't be a president. She can't be in *majlis al-shura* or *majlis al-watani*. It is too difficult for them. Besides, men will not accept that women are in these places." Another participant restricted women's roles to advising: "The UAE's leadership is men. Men are better at coordinating and planning because the way men think is more logical. Women follow their feelings. But women advise men."

Women in managerial positions within associations deny women other positions of power in their discourse of sexual difference. Another organizational leader said, "Women cannot be judges—women are led by passion and their hearts more than their minds. She should concentrate on cultural things and sports in which she can do her best. A woman should focus on religion, as well." Another participant in a leadership position agreed that, "Women should not be judges. They do not solve problems with their heads, but with their hearts. A woman is full of emotions, but a man is tough and works with his mind. This is from our Islam." Sexual difference is another technique employed by elite women to restrict women from aspiring to positions of political influence that would destabilize the current political order of the tribal monarchies in the most powerful government and economic positions. The discourse on women's sexuality is fixed by the Islamic discourses perpetuated through the ruling elite in state-run (and also in some private) study circles that draw on select interpretations. Such articulations are given legitimacy and sanctity.

What Yael Narravo-Yashin terms "faces of the state" are also found in society.[30] Numerous interviews with people outside this case study sample confirmed a belief in the division of labor. In particular, interviews with men revealed prevailing notions of women's (in)capabilities, and religious disapproval of women in various positions. However, instead of challenging views that serve to undermine women's roles and status, the associations function as an important means through which these patriarchal notions have been confirmed and reproduced. An Islamic-feminism in which scripts are reinterpreted from a gender perspective is absent among the women guiding the association programs. Leaders of associations, along with other participants, reduce women's ability to take on responsible positions by referring to women's "incapability" as fact. It is fact because, again "according to Islam," women by nature are not as adequate as men for public roles. Islam is not a fixed entity. Yet, the Islamic discursive tradition that has mostly evolved from *ahadith,* in which women were supposedly narrated to be less than men in mental capacities, is the tool used by these women to translate patriarchal notions into subjectivities that mark them as incapable of taking on responsibilities related to positions of power. Such tools are utilized in numerous religious study circles, both private and those held in state-funded organizations.

Rentier governmentality does, however, have its limits. Not all women in leadership positions advocate the exclusion of women from parliament, which further demonstrates that a state organ can exhibit contradictory agenda formulations. One participant argued for a gendering of parliament: "A woman in parliament will voice the concerns of women. She will point out things she finds shameful that men might not. She will critique society. A man's ideas in society are not enough. We need women's ideas." Moreover, Sheikha Fatima has affirmed that, "It is a woman's right to enter politics according to the constitution,"[31] and has publicly stated that women can theoretically fill the position of president.[32] When the presidential *diwan* decreed that women had to be stripped of their citizenship upon marriage to a nonnational, Sheikha Fatima discussed a survey of women married to nonnationals as if the decree had never been made.[33] These initiatives indicate that although she heads the women's associations through the Women's Union, her position on the role of women in development differs notably from the dominant discourse on women's roles within the associations. A participant who worked in Sheikha Fatima's office told me that the positions adopted by Sheikha Fatima in her public speeches are dependent on the close circle of women who advise her. However, if her advisers also hold such liberal positions, this perhaps indicates that women among the ruling elite do not necessarily form cohesive opinions about women's subordination to the development plans devised by the monarchies.

The activities of a sheikha in Ras al-Khaima support this proposition. Sheikha Fawqai, the wife of the former crown prince of Ras al-Khaima, supported women's rights along with her husband, Sheikh Khalid,[34] who advocated voting and women's full political participation. Some interviewees felt that Sheikha Fawqai's husband had been stripped of his title as crown prince precisely because the couple was too vocal about women's rights and political rights. While the powerful elite has a vested interest in protecting its power and wealth in the tribal strongholds, this elite also includes individuals who have risked their positions for a notion of the common good, in which power may be transferred to more elements in society. Such persons form a minority and are subject to censorship because their objective of changing power relations directly threatens the state's legitimacy.[35]

On the whole, I did not discern a strategic plan of action within the associations themselves for tackling patriarchy or unequal power relations, either on an intellectual or practical level.[36] Rather, women in managerial positions valued familial, societal, and state stability as most important. And they, thereby, applied a glass ceiling to other women by reminding them that they were not permitted to step outside some imagined "boundaries," and by referring to patriarchal-dominated religious discourses and discourses on biological gender differences. The idea is pursued through lectures and materials distributed among association attendees, and the discourse is continued partly because the women's subjectivities have led them to understand their status and position as being naturally subordinate to men's. Indeed, through the agency of these managerial women, the state often succeeds in keeping women's actions within what a participant reiterated were "clear boundaries that cannot be disputed." Although many of the women who take part or use the services embrace the different roles in society according to gender as they see as necessary for its healthy functioning, disempowerment takes place when women are immobilized from functioning as full citizens.

In addition to limiting women's involvement in rights activism, political issues, or political office by fashioning dependent subjectivities, the associations act to restrict women's legal concerns by channeling discussion and activities toward issues devoid of any confrontational, legal, or political content. In a lengthy book on the achievements and goals of one large association, the words "legal" or "political" are not mentioned, nor are significant legal issues or laws of concern to women dealt with openly. Thus, direct confrontation with sources that discriminate against and govern women's legal and political freedoms are not among the aims of this union of women's associations. Clearly, the need for this channeling is related to the prioritizing of challenges as seen by the state, notwithstanding shared by many of these women. With the heavy influx of foreigners with foreign lifestyles, the greatest priority is deemed survival. Stability and survival supersede other concerns, especially those that could further weaken stability.

As I argue in the next section, associational programs to teach women domestic skills have contributed to better productivity, some aspects of self-esteem, and a sense of purpose. At the same time, however, these courses, along with religious lessons and beauty classes, are used to "fill women's time." They are purposefully empty of any contentious, legal, or political ramifications. As one interviewee argued, "Women wanting to spend time with friends baking and learning Qur'an is important, but it is not enough. One has to apply ideas and because attention is paid to only one side of women's development, the activities are a waste of time. Part of the programs must include talking openly about social diseases where they can discuss and find solutions."

Because of the large amount of funding allotted to many of these organizations, the shaping of consumer subjectivities is a further consequence. Some non-case study interviewees pointed out that, in fact, the courses were a waste of money. One 6-hour course on makeup was offered at a cost of DH1,700 per person. Renting a conference room in a nice hotel where 37 women attended to learn flower arranging, or bringing in a group of Swedish experts to teach them table etiquette "because we felt the women needed it," is viewed by many as a waste of resources and money. This is especially the case when, as an interviewee from a poorer emirate explained, "funding and finding sponsors is a constant challenge."

Rights and issues concerning women, especially those in marginalized groups, may become sidelined for the sake of the state's pursuit of national development, identity-building, and stability. Because the associations are socially stratified and represent the concerns of locals, the problems faced, for example, by maidservants, are entirely disregarded. An activist explains,

In very exceptional situations, such as cases concerning Filipino maids that we have dealt with actively over the years, we may take up the cause of an individual who is in danger without that person having directly or indirectly requested our intervention. However, we would never extend this unilateral action to a program of advocacy and lobbying around legal reform. As there were no autonomous women's organizations within the UAE taking up these issues, the matter has sadly remained unaddressed.[37]

The importance of human rights issues is purposefully diminished. None of the state-run women's associations lobby the government about helping the thousands of maids who experience abuse, nor do they pursue any activities to heighten awareness of the situation of these women. As human rights reports indicate, those who are accused and punished of crimes such as fornication are almost always Filipino domestic workers. No women's organization investigates the circumstances of such accusations (such as whether the woman had actually been raped by her employer!). None question why the law on *zina* is applied mostly to certain nationalities or the lower classes, or disputes the fairness of these criminal punishments (*huddud*) either in a broad human rights framework or through Islamic reinterpretation, or investigate such notions that govern the lives of one gender so much more invasively. Nor do the associations present any mission statement or program geared toward lobbying for legal changes. *Shari'a* law interpretations that have been highly discriminatory to women have been left untouched.[38]

Domestic abuse is a problem, especially in recent years, and partly a product of the immense tensions and stress resulting from the large influx of expatriates. In pursuit of creating "stable families," the issue of physical or psychological abuse is secondary to keeping families intact. Some associations offer legal services to couples who have marital problems, are in abusive situations, or want a divorce. Rather than filing complaints about abuse in hospitals or police stations, local women often keep the situation as private as possible. If they allow the information to leave the family, the issue is disclosed to the department for legal services within an association. Usually the family intervenes in the disputes between the daughter and her husband, providing advice to both, and admonishing the husband. If all fails, normally they take their daughter into their home until the husband, mindful of his obligation to respect her parents as his own, resolves to show kindness. Once the dynamics of abuse are divulged or become obvious to the woman's family, the family plays a continued role.

One organization claimed that 98 percent of all their cases, many of which included abuse, were resolved. This *success rate* indicates that the aim is to keep couples from separating at all costs, although valued as indicative for the upkeep of a moral society, an important government objective to ensure social and political stability. In terms of cases of abuse, a participant explained how the association resolved the problem: "We talk with the couple and before they leave we make the man promise never to hit his wife again." The impersonal treatment of these cases shows also that the women dealing with issues of abuse have little understanding of how potentially dangerous spousal abuse can be. As a non-case study interviewee remarked, "the officer comes from a wealthy privileged family. How can she help the women if she does not know what abuse is?"

Starting in 2003, a group of women who also belonged to the associations formulated a proposal to draft some amendments to the personal status laws. Among the issues that the women wanted to alter were the following: changing the article that states that the responsibility of the household goes to the husband; raising the age of marriage from 15 to 18; lifting the limitation on the dowry; changing the stipulation that a working wife must pay for the housemaid; including within the support of a wife a monthly allowance in addition to payment for the food, clothing, and shelter already stipulated; setting a minimum amount of maintenance to be paid from a poor husband; reinstating the clause stipulating that a husband must furnish a house; in child custody cases, raising the age at which the child *must* return to the father; establishing the irrevocability of a divorce that the husband has stated is irrevocable; and applying the provision found in the Egyptian Personal Status law whereby a woman can request a divorce if she returns the dowry. To support their arguments the women referred to the "majority of clerics," or the *maliki madhab*.[39]

The proposed amendments show that women's concerns and demands are placed within a framework where women are dependent upon men and men should be made even more responsible financially for women's upkeep. Even so, this is an example where women are voicing their concerns and making demands, and represents a significant step toward pursuing and protecting interests that must be termed "civil society activism" even if the struggle is for changes within the home. The slogan "the personal is political," coined by Carole Pateman, finds resonance here where private everyday concerns in the home become significant to the relationship between the micro- and macro-level of politics. As Hurreiz has argued, marriage in the UAE "is considered a communal social affair rather than a private personal matter. It promotes group solidarity by reinforcing already existing ties, as well as through establishing new linkages between families and tribes."[40] Women do not view these issues as private matters. It has, furthermore, been argued that, different to the West, women in such localities will, in fact, work toward the kinds of changes in laws that give them more rights within the family.[41] Exercising power within the so-called private sphere in such example is often of crucially greater importance than in other defined spheres.

Empowerment of Beneficiaries

Potentially, empowerment of the women who use the services offered by the associations can occur. Empowered subjects emerge when government builds upon the capacities that also serve to enhance individual development and a sense of productivity. Empowerment, as such, occurs through the following: (1) learning basic skills and finding opportunities to mitigate structural constraints; (2) finding a forum for women to socialize; and (3) gaining religious knowledge and piety.

As discussed in chapter 2, the teaching of basic skills has, over recent decades, included a massive campaign to eradicate illiteracy. Even so, the associations graduate women each year who have dropped out of school, usually because the parents have not insisted that their children finish school (a greater incidence occurs among those with large families in the northern emirates), or have not had access to a nearby school (often the case among residents in rural mountain areas), or when the young person has been married at an early age. The rural branches, and to some extent the associations in the northern emirates, continue to emphasize the problem of illiteracy caused by continuing need. By 1995, as noted in chapter 2, 79.2 percent of the population was literate (78.9 of males and 79.8 of females over the age of 15).[42] This is a huge achievement given that in 1980, 51 percent of UAE men and 77.6 percent of women over the age of 45 were still illiterate.[43] Under the direction of Sheikha Fatima, the female literacy rate increased over the years, largely through the programs offered to women by these associations.

Furthermore, both associations and clubs functioned as the means through which women could learn new skills. The acquiring of such skills could enable subjectivities to emerge that in some respects were more self-reliant. Regarding programs for teenage girls, a participant described how,

We take the girls to parks, boating, or camping in the desert or on the lawn outside. This is to develop the personality and to teach them how to depend on themselves and how to cooperate with people. So, for example, when they go camping or on a picnic we only give them the address so that they have to organize themselves. . . . The girls develop their abilities when they have to depend on each other for finding their own transportation, and making calls to the place they are going to.

Sports classes found in clubs offered women the opportunity to practice leading healthier lifestyles, or to improve their skills and compete regionally. The policy of the clubs is to ensure that women can practice sports and swim at beaches segregated from men, which is in accordance with these women's sense of morals; hence, they have great functionality in a largely segregated society. The issue of women wasting time at home or shopping was raised in several interviews. Associations and clubs offer a partial solution to this concern as women are encouraged to use their time in a productive way by practicing sports and learning new hobbies. Furthermore, the organizations offer courses to enable women to gain the skills needed to enter the workforce. One beneficiary felt she had achieved empowerment through a computer course taken at one of the associations, since as the course provided her with expertise that she found useful for her non-job related goals. However, as al-Oraimi points out, most women who graduate from these programs still lack skills commensurate with the demands of the market.[44] Several local women exclaimed that, among other skills, they needed to improve their English and had found no way of reaching the level of their foreign competitors.

Some women who benefited from the services of the associations and clubs needed to support themselves, such as those who were widowed, divorced, abandoned, or who had an insufficient family income. In one association, widows received monthly payments. Women whose income was inadequate were given the opportunity to sell homemade items at fairs held and advertized by the organizations. Such items included *bukhur* (incense), ladies perfumes, creams and deodorants, makeup such as *kohl* (similar to a black eyeliner), perfumes for upholstery and furniture, sweets, spices, pickled foods, *abayas*, or scarves. To demonstrate what they could achieve, female prisoners too were taught the necessary skills to produce items for sale at these fairs, at which women could also advertize and establish regular customers. As one woman noted, some could, in fact, make a considerable amount of money. Economic empowerment involves changes in women's status in terms of the reordering of power relations throughout society and possibly within the family.[45]

Furthermore, these associations and clubs function as places where women can socialize with other women. Some interviewees were of the opinion that women should not leave their homes for aimless activity. The country's leaders encourage people to put their trust in these associations so that women are *allowed* to spend their time there. Some fathers with teenage daughters have met women participants to confirm that their girls will be supervised and their activities in the organizations are appropriate. Because it is against the norm for a woman to be seen jogging in a public place, or walking along a less populated road except out of necessity, a place where women can exercise is of tremendous value. As a beneficiary explained, "The association is the best place for women. My husband does not allow me to go anywhere. This is the only place outside the house where he allows me to go. This is where I talk to other women and socialize." Indeed, as a club member aged 22 commented:

Women are watched here. I cannot go out and come back a few hours later without being questioned. They will automatically suspect I have done something wrong. If I leave, I cannot come back. The other day I left with my car and returned with my brother's since mine was being fixed in the garage. XX questioned me immediately about the car I was driving and where I had been.

This is an environment that will allow some families to let their daughters venture into public spaces without a male guardian; hence, some women have achieved freedom through these clubs. Not all women shared the view that their attachment to a *mahrem* (male guardian) is disempowering; however, for others, freedom from a male guardian or, in particular, from having to stay at home is an empowerment that may not be found exceptional by a liberally minded individual disconnected from such a situation. Nonetheless, it is extremely important to the woman living in what the interviewees call traditional families. And, for example, since women will not find a swimming pool that is segregated regularly or on specific days, a Ladies Club is, in many cases, the only alternative. Moreover, as there are only a few such clubs in the UAE, women will even travel several hours by car to experience this *freedom*.

Again, the great value to these women of a forum in which they can meet other women is only understood through the fact that many of them are otherwise confined to the home for reasons that may extend beyond patriarchy. Being *allowed* to meet other women outside the home is something these women will look forward to, and seek out. The association is "a place where we can get out of the house and meet people and share our problems with other women," as a participant remarked. In such a place women can talk to other women about their challenges at home. Many of these problems were raised during (mostly informal) interviews, from experiencing physical abuse or the psychological pain of a husband's subsequent marriage, to disputing traditions used to limit women's freedoms. It is often psychologically empowering to be given an opportunity to discuss the similar challenges faced by other women.

At times, participants are even able to help attendees to achieve greater freedoms within the home. One participant described how she succeeded in changing what she referred to as the "traditional" views of some parents about the impossibility of women or teenage girls sleeping outside the home. She recounted how, on a four-day camp with a group of teenage girls, she was able to convince parents to let their girls stay out in the desert on the fourth night after three shorter day trips. She was viewed by the community as an example of a good *muslimah* since she was a regular speaker on religious programs. Thus, placing her argument squarely within the discursive tradition from which all the parents understood and attached meaning to proper conduct, she was able to argue that there was no such ban in Islam. Changing restrictive ideas among parents was a notable achievement on her part. Women listed other techniques to change "traditional" behaviors restricting women to the home, such as paying home visits personally or inviting men to a lecture at the association to discuss such familial issues.

Furthermore, the associations function as a means through which women can achieve moral and well-informed subjectivities, as defined by the associational educators and members. The dominant activity among the organizations (clubs concentrate primarily on sports) is the traditionally presented religious lessons and lectures, the primary focus of which is *ibadat* (rituals). Women find empowerment through practicing rituals and self-monitoring that will produce "better individuals." They aim to be closer to their Creator through acts of worship and the building of a more conscious self. For these women, being a good Muslim has a particularly liberating meaning that brings empowerment. These terms are embodied in the Islamic discourse in which the women situate themselves. They find peace, a sense of purpose and satisfaction through such a "subjectivation."

Thus, the federation of associations has produced a number of achievements for UAE women and society. These include raising literacy rates; graduating previous school dropouts; the recent increase in the period of maternity leave to three months with full pay and six additional months entitlement with half pay; providing regular charitable assistance for families and widowed women (the number of families helped increases each year); distributing aid packages to poor local families; developing (through the clubs) women's sporting abilities and enabling them to partake in regional competitions; through campaigns, raising overall numbers of women entering different fields of education and work; and generally contributing to aspects of empowerment through self-development projects.

CIVILITY

Civility through Cooperation

The increased strategies of co-optation pose challenges to civility. The level of civility was determined through the indices of cooperation, tolerance, trust, and reciprocity. Cooperation was evaluated by determining external and internal inclusivity. This was achieved by establishing whether an ethos of inclusivity was developed. Tolerance was ascertained in terms of the acceptance displayed toward the participation of women of differing backgrounds, ethnicities, and religious beliefs. Trust was evaluated in terms of the extent to which the participants could rely on one another to achieve their goals. Reciprocity was analyzed in terms of the kinds of subjectivities that are shaped by the acts of sharing, giving, and receiving.

Associations that practiced democratic acts produce the kinds of selves conducive to the development of a civil society. When women act on themselves in a way that causes a cooperative self to emerge, they can affect society at large because they disseminate these experiences. Thus, to learn whether leadership skills could be ascertained quantitatively, I tried to establish the extent to which management was inclusive of women in decision making by looking at women's suggestions, visions for development, experiences, and knowledge, and at whether rotation of leadership positions enhanced opportunities to improve these skills.

When asked whether the management of each emirate association requested opinions from the participants, or if suggestions were made to the management and were, in fact, implemented, participants frequently confirmed that they always brought up new ideas and suggestions. However, when I probed for examples, few proved to have contributed to any decision-making process, such as developing a new program. One local participant proudly spoke of a major project she had conceptualized that she claimed the manager of her organization would begin to implement in a year (which when last checked two years on never materialized). Even so, participants seemed in general to be free to suggest ideas related to their job duties. Suggestions were taken more seriously in an organization in one of the smaller emirates. Participants in this particular association all reported that their director encouraged input, and indeed often sent participants to other countries in the region to learn new ideas. Hence, in this emirate organization investment was made in human capital through "responsibilization," even though experiences were confined to what would be calculable within reasonably close environments. Nonetheless, the kind of power exercised among the associations was usually vertically inscribed through instruction on the main points and concerns for organizational leaders.

Rotation of leadership positions at the level of director or management is not part of the policy of these organizations. As Munira Fakhro observes, the composition of the boards has not changed since the organizations were first established.[46] Yet it could be established that participants did gain some leadership skills through the activities in which they participated, such as running camps for teenage girls, or leading educational classes or presentations. Women at managerial levels sometimes needed to take on additional responsibilities irrespective of their portfolios. One participant in a leadership position at a rapidly growing association described how she had started as manager of a single department but now managed four. As such, only a limited number of women are entrusted with leadership duties and a vertical construct of power relations is reified.

No association implemented any voting scheme for the election of a leader or for settling matters that were not agreed on unanimously. The absence of any such method of decision making is reflected throughout the country's political practices. However, collective decisions were made through consultation. Women explained that they would consult each other or particular women whose opinions and judgment they respected. However, descriptions by interviewees of the decision-making process confirmed that for larger matters, it was consistently top down. According to a nonlocal participant, "Each department brainstorms. But the top people choose. I don't choose." The decision-making process continues to be largely dependent upon the tribal consensus building in which the leader decides and is loyally followed. However, as women in managerial positions made clear their objectives were to attend to what they felt were the needs of the local women, decision making was purposefully top down to focus on identity-building and solidarity among local women.

Cooperative selves were also circumscribed by the dominant modes of decision making. One interviewee insisted that management did not want to see new projects suggested. She spoke of a conference she had attended in which Sheikha Fatima asked the women, mostly from higher positions, to suggest new projects for implementation. The whole room was silent, even after further prompting from Sheikha Fatima. When asked why management would not want to expand their projects, she stated, "simply laziness." As the interviewee points out, while laziness may be one reason for apathy on the part of some of the organizational leaders, the numerous mechanisms that have been put in place to forestall any change from the bottom up indicates a broader reason for a perceived apathy.

As discussed above in the section on volunteerism, cooperation becomes problematic when individuals aspire to effect changes in areas that management does not regard as a priority. Cooperation can also suffer when conflicting aspirations are resolved through utilization of the technique of containment. A participant described the challenges she experienced in her efforts to raise money for charity:

> They did not want my charity work. . . . I always want to bring in sponsors and the money to charity and she [the participant's supervisor] was not happy with that. . . . I was just stunned by that. The more money that came in the more successful she would seem to be. . . . I wanted to do things and I wanted to give the money to charity—kids' charity. She said, "There are enough people doing charity."

In fact, most women's associations contributed to charity and distributed some *zakat,* taking meticulous care to document this for public observation. However, from the participant's narration it seems that leaders did not involve the participants in charity collection and distribution, but rather obstructed such involvement. Sheikhas would enter the associations and announce the donation of a specific sum of money for a particular cause. Or donations would, for example, include bags of camel meat or other foodstuffs for poor local families. Typically, the bags would be dropped off by drivers, accompanied by workers who were sent to distribute the charity. The participants were rarely involved directly in the actual distribution of charity. As such, the form of cooperation normally involved in charity work within NGOs in the Arab world or Middle East was limited in these associations, due to the nature of participation.

Civility through Tolerance

As Amy Gutmann has observed, "the more economically, ethnically, and religiously heterogeneous the membership of an association, the greater is its capacity to cultivate the kind of public discourse and deliberation that is conducive to democratic citizenship."[47] In the analysis of tolerance, what these organizations make possible for many of the women who were previously confined to the home or extended families is the mixing with various elements of the society. Their mixing entails gaining firsthand experience with and knowledge about others of different ethnicities that should make possible greater tolerance. However, verticality was constructed within these associations on a number of levels. Interview participants were made up of locals, Arabs from other countries, and in one case a non-Arab. However, not one member from this case study sample identified herself as *'ajami*,[48] although the UAE heritage is built upon Arabs and *'ajam*. Instead of aiming to become more heterogeneous, associations were in the process of actively implementing the government-devised Emiratization plan. Otherwise, local Arab to foreign Arab participants were already two to one, in a country where locals are merely 15 to 18 percent of the population.

Some nonlocal women raised the issue of inequality within the associations. Their most common concerns were inequality in pay, job position, decision-making ability, and representation of ideas. Pay was according to ethnicity, so, for example, pay scales differed depending on whether the participant was local, Arab or non-Arab/non-Western. Referring to the pay of participants in managerial positions in a particular association, one interviewee described how the named locals received almost twice that of an Arab woman and three times that of a non-Western foreigner, all of them at the same level. I learned from the local participants that they were actually not paid by the association itself, but by the ministries that had appointed them to their positions in the association. Such difference in pay scales is not exclusive to women's organizations, being the rule in most firms throughout the UAE.[49] The only difference between firms and the women's federal associations is that some company employers sought ways of circumventing the system that stipulates the preference for locals over nonlocals and having, through various means, to pay more to locals. This economic interest is not found in these women's associations and thus no effort is made to reduce disparity in pay. On the contrary, rentierism and the doling out of salaries is another mechanism through which verticality is enforced, and these organizations can function as a "techne of government."

Other interviewees expressed contention over job positions. One participant explained that she would normally have a prestigious position in her country of origin, but that during the last two years (from the interview date) that was no longer possible in the women's associations. She, and others like her, had to take lower end positions and could not aspire to move beyond their levels into any management position since these were now reserved for locals. An Emirati participant in a managerial position confirmed that nonlocal women were gradually being replaced by local women. She explicitly commented that it was necessary for women in decision-making and planning positions to be Emirati, because nonlocals had a very different culture and could not possibly comprehend the challenges and needs of local women.

Further differentiations are commonplace among participants and attendees. Some nonlocals pointed out that representation of the association could only occur through nationals. Nonlocals cannot represent the organization or their own ideas to anyone outside the organization. Differentiation in types of membership was also made, depending on whether one was local or not. As one association stated, "The services are free of all charge only to locals." Another association confirmed that, "We have three types of membership. One is for locals, one for non-locals and one for the sheikhas. The one for sheikhas is free because they give money to the association."

However, cooperation is not only problematic between locals and nonlocals. Stratification is also noticeable between women in higher and in lower positions of responsibility and prestige. This was evident from details of family names and the family ties that some of the women divulged. Al-Oraimi notes that these organizations lack cooperation because the tribal elite ensures their interests are advanced:

[W]omen's unity in the UAE will not emerge from the efforts of the tribal elite because it is not in the interest of the larger group to support change that will challenge the current status quo. The advancement of women's unification or economic and political issues will not come from these organizations, as they are dependent on the state and headed primarily by the tribal elites. Therefore, it is necessary for women to organize their efforts, raise awareness about leadership skills, and establish their own independent institutions.[50]

Civility through Trust

The level of trust between participants of the associations was examined with regard to their capacity to rely on one another and have confidence in each other's abilities, intentions, and integrity. A sufficient level of trust existed in terms of sharing responsibilities in order to accomplish a stated task or project. In this sense, civility can be deducted from the successful completion of the participants' lists of agreed goals for which they needed to coordinate efforts. However, trust was constrained between groups of greater and those of lesser power.

On numerous occasions it was stated that locals were afraid that integration might undermine racial solidarity. Several non-case study interviewees, mostly local, noted that locals were confused and perhaps frightened about what course of action to take to protect their heritage from being assimilated with such an unprecedented influx of foreigners. Thus, the reaction was to strengthen their ties at various levels, including internally within the associations. However, in the case of the UAE, this occurs at the exclusion of the Other. As Rose argues:

Social insurance is an inclusive technology of government. It incarnates social solidarity in collectivizing the management of the individual and collective dangers posed. . . . And it enjoins solidarity in that the security of the individual across the vicissitudes of a life history is guaranteed by a mechanism that operates on the basis of what individuals and their families are thought to share by virtue of their common sociality.[51]

Hence, internal stratification is also purposefully deepened by associational leaders. If cooperation is inhibited between locals of higher status and nonlocals, trust will also be highly problematic. The women's associations are mostly concerned with the shaping of local women's subjectivities and, therefore, tailor their programs to deal with issues related to local women. As mentioned earlier, managers expressed the contention that nonlocal participants, in particular, did not understand the needs of the country or of Emirati families. Behind this stated contention lies the more profound fear that a cultural invasion might creep into society through the educational programs that the leaders seek to control in order to construct and reify a particular truth to the knowledge and authenticity of practices categorized as indigenous to the UAE. As such, the rationalities associated with identifying the Other as a threat to authenticity and legitimacy endanger civility.

Trust between the tribal elite and various groups, notably nonlocals, is circumscribed by the "racial discourse within a bio-politics of the population and its linkage with themes of sovereign identity, autonomy and political community"[52] and by " 'development' enabled by the rentier state . . . also tend[ing] to create a distinctive set of socio-spatial hierarchies, enclaves and zones."[53] Michel Foucault's discussion on National Socialism, as a particular articulation of certain elements of biopolitics,[54] is applicable to the UAE case, since the Emiratization plan is put in place to produce a similar "knowledge of populations" and races.[55] In fact, as Dean argues,

A political discourse that divides populations on the basis of race has certain fairly obvious political dangers. However, one that makes the welfare and life

of a racialized population the basis for national sovereignty and political community could be viewed as more clearly "demonic."[56]

The issues of genocide discussed by Foucault and Dean are, of course,
other matters; however, a discourse that is supported through policies
to separate constituent parts of the population does become a serious
matter, since there will be repercussions on the welfare of individuals
according to which side of the divide they fall.

Civility through Reciprocity

Participants identified "jealousy" as an obstacle to productivity within
the associations. Although I was surprised to learn that jealousy could
be viewed as an obstacle to women's development, the fact that so
many women mentioned this issue made me realize its significance to
civility. Though the issue of jealousy was also brought up in numerous
discussions and interviews outside the case study, its prevalence among
all forms of collaboration under study was most notable within the
government-run women's associations. As an interviewee stated,
"The problem facing women first of all is jealousy. Women are jealous
of women at the highest level." Jealousy of locals was evident among
nonlocals. Jealousy was "here in the association; if I have a lot of
skills, she is jealous." Jealousy was expressed toward volunteers who
joined with a mission to sacrifice time for goals within the association.
An interviewee said, "There is jealousy of some active members.
Some [volunteers] have the drive, but management does not so they
cripple their efforts." She explained, "They are afraid of volunteers.
Volunteers have different ideas and worries."

The problem of jealousy has two main consequences. First, it impacts on collaboration and trust between associational participants
and associations. Collaboration is impeded if competition for recognition supersedes peaceful cooperation. While there are a number of examples, one suffices here. A participant in a managerial position told
of how she and others worked overtime to prepare for an event that
would be attended by royalty. One of her colleagues, also at the managerial level, hardly showed up in her office but came on the day of
the event "covered in all her gold and literally elbowed her way
through the crowd of women to the front to take all the credit for our
work!"[57] As mentioned above, the goal of appearances for the sheikhs
takes priority over women's solidarity. When asked if the associations
collaborated with their sister organizations in the other emirates, the
usual reply was, "no," and that it only occurred through representa-

tives of the umbrella organization and Sheikha Fatima. In fact, three participants from two organizations stated that when they were implementing a new program they hid what they were doing from the other emirate organizations so that their organization would come out with the project first. One of these participants lamented such a situation, pointing out that secrecy was motivated by a spirit of jealousy. Such jealousy obstructed women's sharing of skills, knowledge, and experience at some level, and hence, contributed to enmity and rivalry.

Second, jealousy is another description among the participants for what is invariably control over civil society actors. The issue goes back to the problem of volunteerism in these associations. A person who demonstrates a desire to pursue goals for the common good through these associations, and who has not been appointed or undergone an interview process, hits a glass ceiling before she is in any position to effect control over program agendas or to implement ideas outside the scope of the sheikhas' Emiratization plans and legitimacy goals. "Jealousy" occurs when the individual proves she is capable of having an impact within the organization or when she shows zeal in pursuing interests. Her stated intention to volunteer is the first indicator that she does not play by the rules of a state-run association.

While jealousy was a notable obstacle, several of the interviewees also affirmed that women did share their experiences and skills with others. This took place, for example, in the form of teaching others how to perform certain tasks, providing others with experiences that would help in an education process, or using one's time to help another participant accomplish a project. Not only did women confirm that reciprocity was a practice; I also observed giving and sharing amongst participants in numerous settings. The issue is that when individuals collaborate for goals not primarily for the common good, in which sacrifice becomes a mode of action, the "self" is at risk of taking priority over "doing good" to help others.

THE ROLE OF THE WOMEN'S ASSOCIATIONS AND CLUBS

Women do play a significant role in how they impact on civil society through these state-run women's organizations and clubs. Certainly, the organizations have achieved empowerment of women and enabled the agency of women in contributing in numerous ways to the self and societal development. But are the official women's societies expanding a civil society in the UAE?

Arguably, if the goals of the associations represent the goals and needs of society in general, and can support an empowerment process, then it should not matter if the state or an autonomous source is behind the formation of the resultant subjectivity. The fact is the state often has interests that are congruent with the hopes and expectations of societal actors. Whenever a sheikh or sheikha visits an association to give a speech that is always permeated with the message of the importance of women to development and the leadership's commitment to the nation's prosperity, the attendees and participants infuse all subsequent discussion with expressions of their praise, admiration, love, gratefulness, and deep respect for the sheikh or sheikha. An interviewee explained to me that one had to see today's politics from a historical perspective, pointing out that women as young as 50 vividly remember the hardships they endured when they lived in tents and were exposed to the desert elements with little to eat. With this understanding, people can only be extremely grateful to the leadership. However, state actors invest this consciousness with symbols that serve to legitimize state power, since "[p]ublic veneration for the state re-erects mechanisms of state power."[58]

In addition, "[t]he way a sense of public is built into social interactions varies considerably with social context and notions of personality, responsibility, and justice inherited from older traditions."[59] The values and institutional practice coming from a strong tribal heritage must be calculated within current political practice and shaping of identities. In the non-state tribal structure, individuals paid allegiance to smaller tribal groups, tribal leaders viewed their positions as being ones of responsibility, and members did not see their identity as autonomous from their specific tribal groups. Their solidarity was with their tribal leader. Given a climate that is more unstable than is perhaps obvious, the state vigorously attempts to broaden the framework of reference—the family and tribe—to a single nation, through the revival of traditions and the rhetoric of national unity. Many (though not all) citizens now view their attachment to their leader through notions of family, as given.

An analysis cannot ignore the larger context of political and personal aspirations attached, more significantly, to the local group's survival. Women see their time and effort in these initiatives as beneficial or even crucial to a common good. As such, certainly, these programs have a positive impact on women. Through the programs bolstering religious identity, beneficiaries feel they are profiting spiritually and educationally. Additionally, most of the courses are geared toward helping women deal with family difficulties and contribute to their children's development. Attendees gain useful information for improving their health or the health of their families. As many individuals view globalizing forces as destructive to the self, their interests converge with those of the state. Women generally see themselves as operating within a framework that makes sense to them.

When a woman, especially after learning to read, becomes aware of a wealth of information, she has also learned how to unlock a fundamental door to her society. I met several women whose comments indicated that they felt their lives had been renewed through literacy skills, even if these were unrelated to obtaining a job. When women work at achieving goals that are meaningful to them and they get what they have been discursively directed to want or feel, they have benefited from the programs and lectures and an empowerment process has taken place. When they use their skills and knowledge to better their lives in the ways they have been conditioned to understand are worthy of those around them, they have effected social capital formation.

In assessing empowerment among the women beneficiaries, it is important that a Western conception is not forced into a context in which women have different perspectives about what is a good thing. So, for example, if women choose not to work, it does not mean they feel they are missing out on an opportunity for empowerment. My own preconceived notions of what all women around the globe should aspire to were shaken when one interviewee asked, "Did you ever see the movie *Mona Lisa Smile* with Julia Roberts? You have to understand, women here do not want to work! They simply want to stay at home and go shopping." Nonetheless, several interviewees in leadership positions argued that as the country is so new and because a balance must be stuck between traditions and modernity, women need to be guided. I would argue that this state feminism could be credited for the increasing numbers of women entering public arenas to contribute to their nation. The associations have encouraged women to pursue postsecondary education, and though it has never been a major campaign, have also encouraged women to pursue careers. Part of the Emiratization plan is to lessen the reliance of the UAE on foreign workers through women's increased participation in the workforce.

However, there are a number of obstacles to the effectiveness of these associations in contributing to the expansion of a civil society sphere. The assertion that women, as a group, need guidance may well be in accordance with societal ideals of the feminine role of women, but as it serves the reproduction of the patriarchal order, it undermines women's roles and position in various significant ways, and especially women among nonelite groupings. But more significantly, participants are operating within a system in which programs and aims have overarching goals of state legitimization and political stability. Because the nation-state subsumes various other collectivities and identities and since the organizations serve the interests of the state, they ignore the larger issues of women's well-being. Women's well-being will be subordinated to the stability of the family because the family is the basic unit of the nation.

Similarly, al-Mughni found that there was a strong resistance to any changes in women's status on the part of the Kuwaiti state and the elite women.[60] There are also parallels with Joseph's findings in her case study on Lebanese women's organizations. In Lebanon, leaders of women's organizations, belonging to the privileged class, reproduced male processes of political action and domination. Because they did not offer structural alternatives to men's patron-client based organizations, they did not offer a basis for an autonomous women's movement.[61] Authoritarian governmentality in the UAE leads to the same dynamics. In the UAE, the women's organizations serve the vertical encompassment of civil society when they reproduce the patrimonial hierarchy of royalty, tribes, ruling elite and men over the rest of the citizenry. Moreover, as with Joseph's study, UAE women's organizations do not transcend class lines. In fact, the associations serve to widen the gap between classes and ethnicities within a distinct hierarchy as a product of the Emiratization plan. Most problematic, such practices result in straining civility between groups and classes.

Grassroots initiatives are not encouraged in terms of ideas proposed or volunteerism. A significant number of the associations' participants are employed by ministries at leadership levels. The wives of state leaders dictate the parameters of programs. Participants emphasized that their legitimacy was because they functioned under the auspices of Sheikha Fatima. As an interviewee noted, "The name gives us trust. It gives us strength. People put trust in our organization because of the name." Because the associations are effectively co-opted by the state, the associations serve to co-opt civil society.

State leaders and the organizational leaders have emphasized how crucial women are to development and national goals. A few elite women have been admitted to parliament, perhaps to concede to the demand for women in parliament. After all, the UAE was the last among the Gulf states to appoint a female to a ministerial post. However, the main avenue through which women can influence other women is an official women's organization. An elite woman argued that a position in a woman's association had the same impact as a position in parliament: "Just because they are not in parliament, does not mean that women are not playing a political role. Through my position I am participating in organizations and represent the organization when I go out . . . The idea is to have a voice that is heard for the nation." However, the interviewee spoke for national interests and not for women across classes and ethnicities. She maintained that her voice was heard just as loudly as if she were a member of parliament and, thus, saw her position as one that allowed her to have similar powers to someone in a government post. In this way, the agency of women is crucial to the achievement of state goals but the women help to produce the gendered hierarchy of a "masculinized [. . .] vertically encompassing state"[62] and the feminization of their organizations. As Andrea Brown comments, "The masculinism of the state refers to those features of the state that signify, enact, sustain, and represent masculine power as a form of dominance."[63] Similarly, the women are reproducing the patriarchal notions of power in which the masculine and dominant sphere (the state) vertically encompasses a feminized dependent sphere at some lower level.

Even if Western feminist epistemology places greater importance on rights and personal achievements in the public sphere than do women and men in other localities and, hence, skews meanings attached to oppression, limits placed on women's mobility and access cannot be justified. It is, furthermore, not justified according to women—and men—themselves whose worldviews are simultaneously shaped by tribal modes of behavior and Islamic values. After all, tribal modes of behavior differ according to tribe, and members alter meanings attached to proper conduct through time based on changing circumstances. Thus, definitely not all UAE women view the exercise of power in the home as most important or the only means for their well-being. If power is not redistributed throughout society in a way that enables autonomous collectivities to pursue interests and achieve goals for the common good, that is, not narrowly for elite men and women, then these groups cannot effectively expand a civil society. Deniz Kandiyoti explains the result of such practice, as observed in the associations:

On the one hand, nationalist movements invite women to participate more fully in collective life by interpellating them as "national" actors: mothers, educators, workers and even fighters. On the other hand, they reaffirm the boundaries of culturally acceptable feminine conduct and exert pressure on women to articulate their gender interests within the terms set by nationalist discourse.[64]

In sum, UAE government-run women's associations and clubs are contributing to civil society in a limited sense through the fashioning of selves produced through many of the activities. Their challenges have reached a critical point with the almost sudden and overwhelming influx of ideas and people. However, in their quest to reconstruct identity to combat this onslaught and the state's objective of bolstering its legitimacy and power, the technologies at work within these organizations are contributing to the suffocation and manipulation of civil society. As such, the UAE women's GONGO associations, as with other states in the Middle East, demonstrate that state feminism has emerged as a key modality of governmentality. Through rentier governmentality, the official women's organizations have been effectively co-opted through direct corporatist politics, such as salaries, large provisions of state funding, operating under the auspices of an emirate sheikha, all lead by Sheikha Fatima, and controlled through the appointment of ministerial employees into sensitive and powerful positions. While women are empowered in many ways, a client mentality is fashioned. Subjects are guided to direct their acts to those of dependency on state leaders. The women's GONGO organizations function superbly as the UAE state's "techne of government" because their composition and "assemblage of techniques of power" instrumentalize "governing at a distance."

CHAPTER 4

WOMEN AND ISLAMIST POLITICS: ACTIVISM IN ISLAMIC-ORIENTED ASSOCIATIONS

INTRODUCTION

Civil society development in the Arab world has prompted much debate among academics and intellectuals. One critical viewpoint has been that civil society cannot flourish in the Middle East, not only because of authoritarianism, but also notably because of Islamism. After all, according to its scholars, Islam is a comprehensive mode of living that encompasses the public and the private, the political and the personal. This anomaly, posed to civil society theorists, results from the historical development of civil society. First, because the idea is historically and contextually situated within secular liberal thought, the civil society concept is unable to capture processes among peoples whose modalities of action are premised on a public arena where religious symbols, norms, and practices matter. Second, by designating a public and private divide and allocating actions that, for example, serve to transform individuals with respect to morality, ethics, and piety, privately oriented actions are deemed insignificant to a constructed public sphere.

With the example of the women's Islamic organizations and *halaqas,* this chapter interrogates the assumptions that the practices and ideas of the women participants are either inimical or inconsequential to civil society expansion. Women's activism in Islamic-oriented associations is one major source of struggle over the interpretation of their position and role. These women pose as major contenders because government has not been completely successful, in its rentier-based technologies of encompassment, in developing the kind of selves that necessarily support and legitimize state polices and interests. In their strategies these organizations also implement the use of symbols and metaphors to persuade and influence. As with the state or other institutions, the associations "represent locales of power, control, and ideology which work together in the social construction of reality."[1]

The women in Islamic-oriented organizations and *halaqas* did play a part in providing the building blocks for a civil society in the UAE. To interpret the capacities in which these women contributed to civil society, I asked about the nature of the subjectivities being produced. The organizations' technologies of governing their subjects can be seen in the way they enable participants to be " 'free to choose,' [. . . as their] lives become worthwhile to the extent that they are imbued with subjective feelings of meaningful pleasure."[2] Surely, organizational leaders implement technologies of governmentality purposefully. But as Nikolas Rose argues, one should not deny or diminish the genuineness of the concerns for individual well-being or social justice that their projects involve.[3] For this study, one should not view the subject "as an isolated automaton to be dominated and controlled. On the contrary, the subject is a free citizen, endowed with personal desires and enmeshed in a network of dynamic relations with others."[4]

Hence, I study the techniques that are utilized and how self-organizing capacities are fostered among Islamic activists. Importantly, I also ask what the consequences are of producing the kinds of subjectivities that these organizations and *halaqas* aspire to or fashion? I argue that these organizations are producing subjects that are conducive to: (1) contributing to participation levels of civil society activism; (2) being active in articulating their own needs and goals, engaging and contesting opposing views, and developing modes of being that furnish their empowerment and the transformation of society in many ways similar to Islamists; and (3) contributing to civility through the norms and practices they seek to produce and reproduce.

As such, I discuss how the organizations of this study fashion subjects that aspire to individual productivity, self and societal empowerment, and civility. Michel Foucault draws attention to the myriad ways in which the conduct of society is governed, that is, not only by the state, but also by institutions and agencies.[5] In fact, James Ferguson and Akhil Gupta suggest that it is necessary to treat state and non-state governmentality within the same frame, and to make no assumptions about the greater spatial reach, vertical height, or relation to the locale of one over the other.[6] Foucault notes that the techniques for governmentality include the discourses, norms, practices, and identities that are constructed, as well as those of self-discipline and care.[7]

By describing the goals and practices of Islamist groups in the UAE, the chapter elucidates congruency with women's associations and *halaqas*. Due to the nature of the authoritarian governance, the strategies of Islamist groups are nearly always directed toward reform on the individual and societal levels, rather than on the state level. Women in Islamic organizations place their goals for reform on the societal level and their strategic goals on the individual level. It is irrelevant if one asserts its intention for political reform and the other does not. Both Islamists and Islamic activists have a significant effect on public life in the UAE.

Of the seven sections of this chapter, the first details these indices and discusses the tradition of discourses in which the participants ground their articulations. The second provides a description of Islamist groups in the UAE and Islamic activity among the organizations examined in the study. A broad overview of Islamic activity in the UAE will also be provided to contextualize the case study. The third section discusses the profiles of women interviewed. The fourth, fifth and sixth sections examine the indices of participation, empowerment, and civility respectively, and the seventh discusses the impact of these associations on civil society, and thus, the implications of the practices of these organizations for the concept of civil society.

PARTICIPATION, EMPOWERMENT, AND CIVILITY WITHIN A TRADITION OF DISCOURSE

The three main indices used for the assessment of UAE women's role in the expansion of civil society are participation, empowerment, and civility. In a quantitative assessment of *participation,* an inquiry is made in terms of volunteerism levels, growth in participant numbers, activities/programs, and size of the structures. In a qualitative assessment, an inquiry is made in terms of the techniques implemented by organizational leaders and the modes of self-regulation adopted by organizational participants to achieve a subjectivity that is motivated to Islamic activism. The values ascribed to Islam that motivate subjects actively to seek specific ends are part of the investigation.

Applying an approach to empowerment that embraces "positive actions" that aim to gain access to, or to acquire spiritual or material benefits, power is no longer in finite form as "power over," as opposed to the "negative actions" embodied within mainstream feminism. Rather, the "power to," "power with," and "power from within" is studied. *Power over* is defined as controlling power that prompts a response of compliance or resistance. *Power to* is a generative or productive power that creates new possibilities and actions without domination. *Power with* "involves a sense of the whole being greater than the sum of the individuals, especially when a group tackles problems together." *Power from within* is "the spiritual strength and uniqueness that resides in each one of us and makes us truly human. Its basis is self-acceptance and self-respect which extend, in turn, to respect for and acceptance of others as equals."[8]

This rendering broadens the scope of possibilities for empowerment. Shirene Hafez provides a definition of empowerment especially useful for the case in hand. Hafez defines empowerment of Muslim women,

as the bolstering of women's self-esteem, solidarity, and confidence, which comes from an inner satisfaction brought by the improvements they implement in the community. It is an empowerment that is predicated upon relinquishing the forms of power deriving from overt resistance and relies instead on notions of perseverance, submission and higher levels of religious attainment.[9]

Rather than categorizing the women's modes of action as necessarily fitting either resistance initiatives or compliance, I seek to place their modalities of agency in a broader framework of power relations in order to uncover various other meanings that will inform an empowerment process.

Foucault has pointed out the failing of meta-narratives and argues discourse, which he sees as a historically, socially, and institutionally specific structure of statements, terms, categories, and beliefs, is the space where meanings are contested and power relations established.[10] Correspondingly, depending on the discourse that surrounds her, a woman might not feel disempowered in a situation a woman situated in the West might view as oppressive. The subject experiences and understands life within a discursive context constituted through complex historical circumstances. Hafez argues Islamic activists "force a re-examination of the issue of empowerment and agency, as these women who are clearly involved in processes of self-development and reinvention do not comply with feminist liberal paradigms that have traditionally been employed in interpreting women's agency in the Middle East."[11]

In this respect, I find Talal Asad's notion of a "discursive tradition" useful for situating the participants' discourses. Building on Foucault, Asad defines a discursive tradition as a discourse that seeks to instruct practitioners about the correct form and purpose of a given practice.[12] He argues that Islam is a discursive tradition that "includes and relates itself to the founding texts of the Qur'an and the hadith."[13] This interaction results in the production of an ongoing and long-standing discourse.

Asad's formulation of discursive tradition has been expanded. Adding to his notion of a larger tradition that includes the Qu'ran and *hadith,* John Bowen suggests that other texts or oral traditions and systems of cosmological speculation are part of the discourse.[14] Mark Woodward includes rituals, such as *hajj,* prayer, the Eids, and Ramadan alongside the core texts, and explains the portion of "universalist Islam" that becomes part of a specific local context is a "received Islam." "Local islams" are those rituals and texts, both oral and written that are not known outside a specific local context that arose from the interaction of a local culture and received Islam.[15] Scholars have also extended the locus for this discourse to include Islamic pedagogy within Islamic schools,[16] Friday *khutbas* (sermons),[17] and women's mosque *halaqas* (study circles).[18] In these three examples emphasis has been on the interaction between the textual or core traditions and the local and practical concerns of the practitioners in the discourse.

The periods of intense discussion about the nature of Islam and society have occurred particularly at times of political upheaval and change.[19] Thus, discourse may also include concerns about globalization, equality, justice, freedom, feminism, and development and absorbed within Islamic terms; principles underlying such subjects may also be articulated as antithetical to an Islamic core. Recognizing women's modes of action as falling within a tradition of discourses helps to capture the relevant meanings and significance of these actions with regard to the fostering of values of civility and empowerment. As Aihwa Ong argues, it is essential to "recognize other forms of gender- and culture-based subjectivities, and accept that others often choose to conduct their lives separate from our particular vision of the future."[20]

With Middle Eastern countries classically presented as deficient in civility, and terrorism singled out in support of this view, "civility" is studied. The literature blurs the differences between nonviolent and violent groups. Lumped together as one unchanging entity antithetical to civility, the different groups are stripped of their transformative power and ability to contribute to a common good. Hence, this study examines whether the kinds of subjectivities shaped through women's activisms in Islamic-oriented associations cannot contribute to civility.

ISLAMIST GROUPS AND ISLAMIC ACTIVITY IN THE UAE

The UAE, like most Arab Gulf countries, was a major center for the funding of Islamic projects outside the country. Fund-raisers flocked to this oil-rich country to visit wealthy merchants and tribal sheikhs in hopes of receiving funding from what the wealthy donors would usually set aside as a pool for *zakat* (obligatory annual charity) payment. Often lacking the time to manage the block of money set aside for use in the various project categories they had stipulated, such donors hired managers to deal with the *zakat* distribution when the expectant fund-raisers came knocking. This funding bonanza of monies leaving the UAE for Islamic projects almost ground to a halt around 11 September 2001.

Fund-raising remains a feature of Islamic activity but operates at a considerably lower level than was the case before the events of 9/11. The number of official fund-raisers making their annual trips has dwindled sharply, and others have left the country empty-handed. Shortly before 9/11, the government had banned the collecting of funds through organizations for Islamic projects, especially abroad, apart from a limited number of charities such as the Red Crescent and a few others directly under the auspices of emirate sheikhs, such as Sharjah Charity International. These cooperate with international organizations and provide charity to countries and communities in need, regardless of religion. Otherwise, most charity establishments have been, and continue to be, closed down, especially those that directed money and charitable goods specifically to Muslim communities. Comparatively, Dubai, Abu Dhabi, and then Ajman maintained a little more freedom in handling the closures, while Sharjah had the least. Most people who worked in charities lost their jobs (in the case of locals) or were "sent out of the country" (in the case of nonlocals). Those who were volunteers were removed and those who were active in the collection of funding remain under surveillance. As one interviewee put it, "the taps have been turned off."

Given the prevailing nervousness about state scrutiny, the government's sweeping measures to restrict the collection of charity as a way of curtailing the funding of violent Islamist activities abroad have affected civil society growth in several ways. Intensified intervention has clearly thwarted and discouraged much Islamic-oriented and Islamist activity. People participating in Islamic-oriented activities express fear that their efforts may be sabotaged, or that participants may be accused of Islamist political activity. As one participant said, "People are watched. I know some people who are watched as soon as they leave their houses. They are suspected of doing too much Islamic work." According to interviewees, monitoring methods are much more sophisticated and widespread; so such intrusion, thus, scares activists away from overt civil society activism, such as openly fund-raising, openly holding *halaqas,* and recruiting among moderate Islamists. However, civil society dynamism and political activity that fall outside the scope of civil society cannot be said to have dissipated as a result. The modes of action employed by activists have had to adapt and change accordingly. Thus, civil society will take on different shapes from those that are easily recognized in Western normative categorizations. These different forms are a product of the differing environments.

Islamist Groups

As an interviewee remarked, "Everybody is in the UAE, from the Ikhwan to Al-Qaeda." But because the state has always been suspicious of Islamist activity, moderate Islamists generally do not engage in extensive activity with Islamist groups to begin with. This is to avoid calling attention to their identity as Islamists in case they jeopardize their employment contracts and residency in the UAE. They come to the UAE for three reasons. The first is to seek a better standard of living; the second is to raise children in an "Islamic" environment. As a rule, these practical concerns override their most popular strategy of active recruitment, at least among the moderates. The third goal, as noted above, is for funding. Because of tightened laws governing the collection of funds, Islamists must collect on a more personal basis. A typology of Islamist activity will be provided as a backdrop to a broader understanding of civil society processes in which actors use Islamic discourses in their activism.

The Ikhwan al-Muslimin (Muslim Brotherhood), which originated in Egypt in the first half of the twentieth century, is the largest Islamist group in the Arab world, having spread to all Arab countries, Europe, and North America. While most of the current Islamist groups, violent and nonviolent, are formed by members who have split from this major group, the Ikhwan today is regarded as a moderate Islamist group. Ikhwan members exist in nearly all emirates of the

UAE. The UAE group is mostly made up of expatriates, who form subgroups with separate hierarchies for each nationality, except at the highest level where activities are loosely coordinated. Reportedly they have been told that if any member contacts members of other nationalities to coordinate activities he or she will be deported. A few cases occur each year. Especially the Emirati Ikhwan members are confined to their own nationality by the state, so as not to become too powerful, and are further restricted to participating in relief organizations. Between the Ikhwan of all nationalities, especially in Oman, Saudi Arabia and Kuwait, there are only loose haphazard networks, often based on friendship, running through the Gulf countries.

Besides dividing themselves into groups according to nationality, the Ikhwan have a strict organizational structure. A group is further broken down according to emirate with a further hierarchy of sections and subsections, typically classified according to emirate cities and rank of members, each with different *halaqas* having different curricula. Each subsection becomes relatively small and in order to avoid government scrutiny there is no coordination among the level of subsections.

The Ikhwan's activism is guided by internal and external interests. A group sends money to its group in its home country and sponsors projects, such as student scholarships and relief, especially in Palestine. Its members pay much more for membership than do the Ikhwan in most other countries, with fees that may reach up to ten percent of salaries. Internal activities include those related to Ramadan fasts, such as sponsoring and holding *iftars* (dinners to break the fast), as well as courses in members' houses for their *halaqas*.

The women hold *halaqas* in masjids (mosques) as well as in their homes. As with the men, they carry out activities through Islamic-oriented organizations, organizations that are independent, and also those that are affiliated to government-run women's associations. Their ability to infiltrate various forums for learning was evident, in that such women were among my case study sample for government-run women's associations, Islamic-oriented associations, and networks. If they are able to "penetrate" an organization they use its resources and its name as a "security cover." However, in terms of duties, their activities in the associations in which they participate are no different from those of nonmembers. It is thus impossible to differentiate between Islamist and Islamic women's activities.

The discourse of the expatriate Ikhwan is generally not of politics or government in the UAE. The talk concerns politics related to their home countries. Their modes of action in the Gulf are to diffuse their ideas at the societal level. As is the case across most Gulf countries, the Emirati Ikhwan members are less concerned with the state. As a Saudi Ikhwan noted, "The Ikhwan in other countries have problems with their governments because of economic problems. Here, what do we need democracy for? We're fine." In one of the emirates, however, the Emirati Ikhwan approached their sheikh declaring that while the group held the utmost respect for the ruling sheikh, its members did not seek any power, and that they requested cooperation with him. Thus, despite their marginal position in the power hierarchy, and perhaps their grudging willingness to work within the status quo, they envisioned a possibility for an incremental step toward power-sharing. The ruler responded by allowing the group to do charitable work, teaching of Qur'an, and organizing youth camps, and banning them from practicing politics of any nature or talking as a group in public.

The Ikhwan's discursive spaces take root in concrete settings, such as in the organizations in which they participate, the *halaqas* they control, the lectures they hold, or their places of work. Their agenda is pursued by speaking through their jobs and positions of influence. Teachers attempt to sway the youth through advice, giving their opinions, or less subtly, infusing programs with political ideas.[21] Local and other Arab professors in local and Western universities, some Ikhwan, some Salafi, some from other strains, have access to literally thousands of young minds. Their mode of action is to play the father figure, give advice, and teach the implications of globalization in classes. The theme of the inescapability of globalization, and how locals, Arabs, and Muslims must shape their own identities, is popular among university classes, lectures, speeches, and conferences, not to mention the media. Ikhwan members hold various media positions, such as in the Gulfian satellite stations or local newspapers. Along with Islamists from other groups and leanings, they try to mobilize UAE public opinion for the Palestinian cause. While the curriculum and agendas will be planned for the *halaqas* and lectures among Islamists, their modes of action within spaces of employment is largely dependent upon individual initiatives.

The Tablighi Jamat, which began in India in the late 1920s, is also active in the Southeast Asian community in the UAE, and includes members from Southeast Asia, Europe, and North America. The Tablighi Jamat follow their traditional method of gathering in a specific mosque for a speech, after which they call for recruits to go out and invite people (men only) to the mosque. Their mission is *dawa* or the propagation (*tabligh*) of Islam. They invite people to stay overnight in the mosque for up to ten days and if the recruit wishes they will send him on a *dawa* trip for up to 40 days in any other country. They are concentrated in the more populated emirates, especially Dubai and Abu Dhabi, and their targets for *dawa* are mostly Muslims who have apparently gone astray. The large number of discos and clubs are seen to be the means through which the West is corrupting Islamic society and values, and their activities are directed toward combating this assault on Islamic identity, culture, and belief. The motto of the Tablighi Jamat is no debates about Islamic groups, no debates about differences in opinion in law, and no involvement in politics.

Women associated with Tablighi members do not enter places such as clubs to bring "sinners" to the mosque. Rather, they hold *halaqas* in their homes that other women may be invited to attend. Like female Ikhwan members, they are active in Islamic-oriented associations but on a larger scale. They concentrate on *dawa* activities within these associations. Similar to Tablighi men, they invite attendees to a meal after lectures, in which a sense of sisterhood is strengthened and women are encouraged to be active. Unlike the female Ikhwan members, women associated with the Tablighis are open to a wider public (of women) for the sake of *dawa*.

Irrespective of their claim that they do not partake in politics, the Tablighis are shaping public opinion about the nature of Islamic identity and what is antithetical to it. Their thinking converges with Salafi and Sufi thought, since they concentrate on rituals and emphasize spiritual practices. They use discursive spaces such as *halaqas* and lectures to produce and reproduce their ideas, which include not confining themselves to the four schools of thought but practicing as the *salaf* did. By harking back to the practices of the Prophet and the *sahaba,* the Tablighi and Salafis shape those meanings in their interpretations and choices as to the practices and rituals to which they will adhere.

The Murabitun, a global movement, has also played a significant role in Islamist politics of the UAE. The Murabitun was founded by its spiritual leader, Abdalqadir as-Sufi al-Murabit (previously, Ian Dallas), a Scottish convert to Islam, in the 1970s in Britain (London's Soho area). Abdelqadir as-Sufi, a playwright and actor by profession, learned the Darqawi *tariqa* (a Sufi order) through his religious sheikh, Muhammed ibn-Habib, in Morocco in the 1960s, whose vision was that Islamic revival would take place in the West. Converts, mostly in Britain at the time, played an important role in its initial development, of which included Abdel Latif Whiteman, Peter Sanders, Hamza Yusuf, Anas Coburn, Abdel Sammer, Tabil Fehlhaber, and allegedly Yusuf Islam (Cat Stevens). All were directed to live extremely poor simple lives. The above mentioned and many of the earlier members completely severed their ties to the movement largely by the mid-1980s.

Abdalqadir and members went to Dubai and from a villa in Jumeira promoted their ideas. Their ideas include, foremost, waging an ideological war against Western capitalism and ushering in an "Islamic" form of trade in which the currency is gold and silver. The political leader of the Murabitun, 'Umar Ibrahim Vadillo, a Spanish convert, spearheaded this vision, outlining how the Islamic world could then both break with the West and break the West. They mint their own *dinars* and *dirhams* out of gold, and hold them in safes in Dubai, available through Thomas Cook, UAE and the Dubai Islamic Bank. In furthering their ideals of greater economic equality and the undermining of monopolies, banks and usury are to be abolished, individual and caravan trade is to be instituted, and Maliki "Islamic" commercial law is to be established. Importantly, these moves, when successful, are expected to bring back the Islamic Caliphate.

One strategy is to reestablish Islam in the West through Spain. Dubai's ruling family fund their villa in Jumeira from where they continue to promote the movement and receive further financial support for particular projects. They were welcomed, among other things, due to the shared Maliki school of thought. The return they speak of, in particular, is the return of Andalusia—including its return to the Maliki school. Abdalqadir approached Sheikh al-Qasimi, amir of Sharjah, who with others contributed to the building of a 4 million dollar mosque in Granada in 2003, one of two mosques in Granada to be funded by UAE leaders. It received much media attention as the first to have an official opening in Spain after 500 years. Sheikh Zayed had previously turned an old house into a mosque and commissioned two Mauritanian imams, unrelated to the Murabitun movement, to head this mosque, which still runs today. However, Abdalqadir soon sold their mosque, embittering those who lived off very little to contribute to such endeavors.

It is estimated that the movement today has three to four thousand members globally. Ex-members report that Abdalqadir played the modern depiction of the Pied Piper, the leading role he actually did play during his career as an actor, by leading members to live destitute lives in slums. While he now leads a following in South Africa, members continue their propagation of the Murabitun, although politically from Malaysia, from the villa in Jumeira. Although the economic system and theory of the Murabitun movement remains pronounced, their ideas are simultaneously growing wider in scope and in tolerance to the West. The general idea of their economic theory, although crit-icized for inconsistencies and its oversight that gold is not infinite, has been advocated by many other groups, including seculars, in a quest for greater human equality and justice. From this point of view, they are contesting structures and related ideas deemed oppressive in order to reach an economic "common good."

Another group operates transnationally between West and East. A movement associated with the Deen Intensive Program (DIP) in North America, and began by Hamza Yusuf after his learning with a sheikh in Morocco and others from London, also has few members dispersed throughout the larger emirates. The DIP is linked impor-tantly to a network of North American university student groups since the mid-1990s. It aims to host a one week "Deen Intensive Pro-gram" annually in a North American city to "learn intensively," but regularly holds a *rihla* (literally "travel") for four weeks during the summer, designed to develop individuals spiritually to work as a "bul-wark against global malaise." The *rihla*, attended by hundreds, has taken place in Granada, Spain.

Young men and women from North America additionally go to such Arab countries as Mauritania, Morocco, Syria, and Yemen, to learn, usually through small institutions. Men may also learn through the traditional *madrassa* method with a particular religious sheikh, ideally a few years. Their sheikhs are linked through a chain of scholars. The pupils are kept within the boundaries of one school of thought; in the UAE this is the Maliki school. Besides one-on-one learning with a religious sheikh in the UAE, members gather for *halaqas* in the home. They regularly cooperate in fund-raising for the needy abroad.

Sheikh Zayed had brought a number of Maliki scholars from Mau-ritania and North American scholars educated in the above Arabic countries. His vision was to promote a moderate form of Islam, espe-cially through the Western pupils. He funded their activities, such as publications and media work. They also formed a team to meet with politicians in Denmark during the Danish cartoon crisis, illustrating a marked difference to the above Western group in their approach to Western governments.

In the struggle to reproduce their thought within the Islamic dis-cursive tradition, the group claims authenticity through the chain of scholars that leads back to the Prophet's time. This chain has been uncorrupted since the sheikhs have, until recently, generally lived away from modernization. Superiority in knowledge is further se-cured through the practice of their sheikhs having passed down their knowledge orally from sheikh to sheikh/student. Much knowledge cannot be found in books. Thus, this specific form of knowledge transmission carries a special form of blessing as occurred between the archangel Gabriel and Prophet Mohammed.

As with the above mentioned groups, this very contestation over ownership of the most pristine Islam is a mode of action in discourse formation. Thus, through such techniques of contestation, actors can form a powerful resource for civil society activism. This is due to the virtue of contesting ideas in the mélange of competing opinions for what the actors regard as being for the good of society. Furthermore, this strong group solidarity, developed through rigorous personal training of the self, and the spiritual development that is so central to their objectives can contribute to the empowerment of group members.

Abdulkhaleq Abdullah states in his 1995 book that Islamic groups and organizations distance themselves from extremism and radical activism that do not suit the internal structure of Emirati society.[22] However, there are indications that modes of action among moderates and the political field for extremism in the UAE has shifted with changes in the region and the UAE itself. Many interviewees lament that the constricting of fund-raising had damaged their projects that were meant to help Muslim communities outside the country. As one participant said, "for the wrongdoings of a few, hundreds of thousands of people in Muslim countries are now starving because we cannot get any help to them anymore." Another participant expressed what many other interviewees believed: "I think America is just doing this as a plan to kill off the Muslim countries." Indeed, U.S. foreign policy in the region and what many interviewees referred to as the pressures placed on the sheikhs to accommodate these policies has had a significant effect on not only the charitable and humanitarian efforts of Islamic activists, but also the Islamists' typical modes of action observed previously.

A sense among many that, with the latest invasion of Iraq, the Middle East has fallen to American rule has led to the rise of a very small, though growing number of Islamists who have formed new solidarities or have perhaps split from existing nonviolent groups. As such, it is the tightening of control through extensive crackdowns on Islamists and Islamist activity since 9/11, the jailings and deportations of *jihadi* figures called al-Qaeda members by the government, and the government's seemingly full support for American military interests that have sparked a resurgence of extremist groupings. According to the Jamestown Foundation and the Site Institute, al-Qaeda's presence is growing. They point to letters that have been sent to the UAE government by groupings sometimes claiming al-Qaeda identity. In one letter dated 18 March 2005, the group demanded, after providing evidence, that the government cease to support America and warned Muslims to stay away from the port of Jebal Ali, Dubai International Airport, Abu Dhabi International Airport, and the Dubai Investment Collective Center.[23]

Finally, most Islamists and Islamic activists in the UAE do not operate within structured groups, but as individuals connected through networks based on a Muslim identity.[24] Consequently, it is a mistake among theorists searching for political change to focus on Islamists according to adherence to groups. Several interviewees said that they either did not join group activities as they would do in their own countries, or that they did not believe in belonging to any group. Those who were part of Islamist groups collaborated with others outside their confined circles to achieve similar agendas. Participation in Islamist groups is risky. Existing Islamist groups are not necessarily growing in number because they risk state interference by seeking recruits to join the group. Thus, while a lot of activity is, indeed, halted in the UAE under great pressure, much simply goes further underground and so is much harder to observe and detect. In effect, networking is becoming the dominant mode of action among those wanting to effect change and make a difference.

Islamic Activity in the UAE

The activities of Islamic-oriented associations are strikingly similar to those of Islamist groups. They work on two levels: one, collecting and distributing funds, and two, benefiting, developing, and shaping individuals and society through lessons, lectures, *halaqas,* and through the distribution of materials. The associations in the case study comprised four main types: *halaqas* (study circles); women's committees in a larger organization; information and learning centers; and Islamic student clubs. As can be seen in the appendix table 2, all but one of the organizations give prime importance to Qur'an memorization in their agenda. Individual spirituality and knowledge is sought through recitation. Individual knowledge is further enhanced through the learning of *tafseer* (interpretation of the Qur'anic text), *tajwid* (correct pronunciation of the Qur'an), and *hadith* (sayings of Prophet Mohamed). *Dawa* is a goal among Islamic-oriented associations, not only to non-Muslims, but also Muslims.

Organization number one refers to a *halaqa* that is part of a large number of *halakas* held in all public mosques in one of the emirates, under the auspices of its ruling sheikh. A *halaqa* leader estimated that over 600 *halaqas* (including men's) exist within this body of religious circles in the one emirate alone. In each mosque that subscribes to this body, two study groups are held daily, each for men and women. The first set is for beginners and the second for advanced students. These *halaqas* actually enable the ruler to place circles of religious study in places of potential gatherings that would otherwise be independently run; thus, they operate as massive apparatuses of control. Organisation number two refers to a *halaqa* that was held without official sanction in a mosque in the same emirate. The patriarchal order was similar to the first—the leader was female, and her supervisor was the mosque's imam.

Associations number three and four are both information and community centers. Anyone wanting to know more about Islam can ask for help or resources at these centers. They hold regular lessons and lectures to educate the public about Islam, and at least one such independent information center exists in most emirate capital cities. Association three also has a men's wing and has a few men on its board. The board of this association is headed by an *amir,* who must be male and who was voted in by the nine-member board. The association began in the home of a woman until it moved to a larger establishment about 20 years later in late 2002.

The founder of this association established the first women's shelter in the UAE in 2003, now called "the City of Hope," though the women who play leadership roles in the association had a few decades long hosted several women in need in their own homes. The shelter looks after women in various situations of oppression—abuse, threats by their families that they would be killed, or divorce from or death of a husband that has left a woman without any resources, etcetera. It is a place where, irrespective of religious affiliation, women can find security, open hearts, and an ear to listen to their problems. The shelter is always filled to capacity, and participants scrape together resources to keep the place running. The significance of the shelter is that it gives women a place to turn to when they are unable to utilize the traditional method of security in the Middle East, the family. As the director of the shelter modestly remarked, "The shelter is a first little step, it is not the solution, but a step." Many local men view the shelter as opposing the authority of the family institution, but recently a few police officers have referred women to it although it remains unregistered. The Red Crescent opened the second shelter in Abu Dhabi early 2008, particularly in efforts to combat trafficking of women.

Associations five, six, and seven focus on lessons for those who would like to develop themselves further, rather than on those contemplating conversion to Islam. Association five was the first Qur'an learning institute in the UAE established for women, and therefore attracted women from all over the emirates. It received a one-time government grant of DH10,000, and has no paid staff; however, participants receive a small honorarium. Association six has mostly paid staff, and association seven has some paid staff. Association six has been linked to one of the women's GONGO associations, and now is completely answerable to that association. Association seven is a women's committee in a larger organization. Similar to association six, association seven receives funding from its emirate government.

Associations eight and nine are university student associations. Association eight includes women and men; however, all but one of the board members were women, and as its president noted, "it is the sisters who are active, not the brothers." Association nine is the women's wing of the student Islamic club, which only rarely coordinates activities with the men's wing of the same university. Both associations eight and nine have similar activities, which include *dawa*, usually to nonpracticing Muslims, and the hosting of lectures. Both engage in collecting charitable donations for local causes. They also function as community centers where students find solidarity in practicing a conservative centrist interpretation of the Islamic faith.

PROFILES OF INTERVIEWEES

The women who took part in the interviews for Islamic-oriented organizations are categorized in table 4 in the appendix. As can be seen from table 4, the proportion of locals to nonlocals at 17 to 83 percent respectively is significant. Among nonlocals in the UAE, there were two Gulfians. If we categorize the two non-Emirati Gulfians with the locals the total percentage of Gulfians is 23 percent. In addition to nationality, further characteristics noted were age, marital status, level of activity outside the association, and education. The mean age of all women interviewed at 28 (ranging from 18 to 45) is slightly lower than interviewees in the government-run women's associations and clubs. Credit needed to be earned through a postgraduate certificate in order for one to participate in government-run women's associations, whereas a certificate was not a requirement for participation in Islamic-oriented associations and, thus, the Islamic-oriented associations are able to include younger participants. Thirty-seven percent of the participants were married (versus 54 percent of participants in the government-run associations). The lower number can be explained by the observation that students comprised a large number of participants and students rarely marry until after graduation. If the student factor is left out (students are not included), the percent married is almost the same as that of the government-run women's association (55 percent to 54 percent). The perception in the Gulf about foreign women in Islamic activity is that they are generally married and are accompanying their husbands in the emirates, whereas the sample here illustrates that almost half of those (excluding the sample of students who were all with their parents in the emirates) women in Islamic-oriented associations were not accompanying a spouse. Rather, these are women active in civil society work who are independently residing in the UAE. This is significant because despite the emphasis on women's proper role in the home among most Islamic-oriented associations, practically speaking, participants are not subscribing to the idea. The mean number of one child is distributed among all intervie wees, including those not married. However, of the women who had children, the mean was the same as for women in government-run associations, at three children to each woman.

Of the participants, 63 percent held jobs or invested much of their time in academic studies not related to their participation in Islamic-oriented organizations. This is significant compared to zero percent holding jobs among participants in the government-run associations (excluding the few participating as part of an academic requirement). This ratio exemplifies that state-run associations are really places of employment. Despite two-thirds employed or studying elsewhere, 73 percent of women reported participating in other organizational or networking activities outside the association. Not only do the overwhelming majority of women in Islamic-oriented associations stretch their time to participate in their respective associations, hold jobs or enroll for full-time study, but also volunteer their time elsewhere. This signifies a significant increase in activism level from those (at 14 percent) within the government-run women's associations and clubs outside respective associations. Moreover, the majority of women, 73 percent, were not paid for the work they did in the associations. A few women refused any honorarium or payment. This percentage is a significant difference to the participants interviewed for the federation of women's associations (at 14 percent).

All women interviewed, except one, had some level of a postsecondary education or were pursuing a postsecondary degree. As can be seen from the table, a B.A. degree was attained by 50 percent of women. Those pursuing a B.A. bring the number up to 83 percent.

Two women had two-year diplomas, one an M.A., and one a Ph.D. Three with degrees were pursuing further degrees (two in Islamic theology). Of those with at least a diploma, 50 percent had degrees in social sciences (family sciences, language, psychology, social work, media, and economics, six percent in management, business, commerce, accounting, or math, 22 percent dentistry or medicine, and 22 percent Islamic theology—55 percent included Islamic theology as a minor or additional degree pursued). Six of the 18 or 33 percent received their education in the UAE, 11 women or 55 percent received their educations from other mostly Arab countries, and one woman from the West. The area of study of nine of the ten students still pursuing a B.A. fell under the category including management, business, commerce, accounting, engineering, or math. The younger generation of women Islamic activists is acquiring skills and education that should enable the women to secure more leadership positions or enter employment traditionally not occupied by women. Very little variation can be noted for the social sciences when comparing area of study of or degrees held by women participating in the government-run associations. There is a notable emphasis on Islamic studies among participants in Islamic-oriented associations, indicating a desire among the women to understand their religion at a deeper level and further their activism through teaching Islamic knowledge. Also women educated in medicine and dentistry were absent in the case study sample for government-run associations.

PARTICIPATION

The first of the indices used, *participation,* draws on some of the data on the profile of participants to illustrate the nature and level of activism. Quantitative indicators show that women in Islamic-oriented associations are providing building blocks for a civil society in the UAE. Increase in participation was observed through vertical and horizontal growth within associations, often accomplished through grassroots mobilization, norms of segregation, and furnishing of value systems. As Salwa Ismail shows, "The investment of religious signs in domains of social practices, and the redefinition of norms in reference to a constructed orthodoxy, constitute strategies of action and mobilization."[25] As such, Islamic-oriented associations are able to contribute to civil society more effectively, not only because of growing membership, organizational expansion, and effective mobilization strategies, but also because they incorporate techniques that enable them to link to and have an impact on society at large.

The organizations and *halaqas* exhibited an ability to contribute to social capital through structural growth indicators. All associations studied started out as small enterprises with just a few members or students, located in basements, old buildings or homes. With time, all associations included more activities and membership increased over time. Gatherings proved their capacity to grow by moving on to locations that could accommodate the larger memberships. An organizational leader's account illustrates this typical process:

This association began six years ago. We began with 10 children, all girls. In the first three years we had no place for our activities. We held our classes in schools, going from school to school for each lesson. We did this for three years until we found this place. My father helped me establish the association. My father paid for the buses, phone, and electricity. He bought the buses. We asked the girls who came to pay for lessons, which we used to get the place running. At the time it was the only organization in the UAE where women could come and learn Qur'an, except for small gatherings, so we had women coming all the way from Abu Dhabi. Now we have 400 to 500 ladies coming to this association.

There was no decrease in the number of programs or membership in any Islamic association or *halaqa* in the case study, which represents 100 percent growth. Those organizations that can be said to have decreased faced forced dismantlement by the authorities. Hence, lack of interest among beneficiaries or even difficulties with funding did not contribute to an association ceasing to function. Associations grew with the interest in the programs offered, and the growing population size of the emirates.

Islamic-oriented associations incorporate a variety of techniques to increase participation levels and achieve spatialization of their goals and interests. The technique of language in participant recruitment, for example, motivates altruistic feelings. Participants are guided by religious injunctions to "do good" for the sake of Allah. Satisfaction that one is doing *khair* or good deeds is a motivator because it means accomplishing the goal of pleasing God. As a participant said, "When you love God and feel bad about what is going on around you and you taste the sweetness of what Islam has to offer you, you want everyone to taste it too. I am happy with my state and want others to also be content. It is about the Afterlife and the Day of Judgment." The obligation of *dawa* is also a major motivating factor. One participant expressed the idea of sharing, "I want to share the peace of Islam with others. It is a duty upon every Muslim to spread the message of God to humanity." Hence, desires developed within the context of Islamic directives for existential reward are important in successfully mobilizing for civil society participation.

Civic recruitment occurs most effectively when participants are drawn into the institutions of Islamically based participation through the technique of networking. Consequently, individuals find themselves connected to networks of good-doers. Participants involve members of their networks and members of their communities. As described in appendix table 4, despite two-thirds being employed or studying elsewhere, 73 percent of women reported participating in other organizational or networking activities outside the association. This is significantly higher than, for example, women in the women's government-run societies at 14 percent. Because women in Islamic-oriented associations participate through various other avenues, they are able to bridge their social capital capacities through these other avenues. As one woman said, "We all eventually take our neighbors and our sisters."

The strategy of segregation also enables higher levels of participation. Several studies on women in the Middle East have shown that at times women's solidarities formed out of norms of segregation have emancipatory functions.[26] Women felt freer to work closely alongside other women. In a sense, because social inhibitions that might curtail female participation in public life are eliminated, women were freer in terms of permissibility of leaving the home to partake in activities in places that ensured socially/Islamically prescribed conduct.

Some participants noted how the power of wearing of *hijab* enabled them to carve out spaces of movement for themselves outside the home. As an organizational leader attests, "People think that a woman with the *shayla* cannot be effective in society. You get this message through the media. The designers contribute to this message. I am always against this. I give the women the message that women can be very active with the *shayla*." Women are able to go out and take part in society or work because the *hijab* signifies a barrier or respected space between the woman and men.

Associations sought to include as many individuals as possible in unofficial activities that would not jeopardize the association, the project, or individuals. For example, after a lecture or during a meal following a *halaqa*, a leader or participant often announced an issue that some of the participants were dealing with, or that involved individuals outside the respective association. A plea would be made, such as for physical help, monetary contributions, or material contributions—the purchase of a fridge, air-conditioning system, or chairs for a poor school, medical assistance for an individual, a pledge to send some children to school, volunteers for a bake sale, to form a group for regular visits to the sick in a nearby hospital, and so on. In this way, the associations provide an important link between the participants and members and the wider society, in which individuals are motivated and encouraged to contribute.

This link between individuals and society is especially crucial in societies that experience a continuous stream of expatriates entering and leaving the country, such as in the UAE. A view states that persons who are not rooted in the community in which they live because of short-term residence are disinterested in contributing to the community as "good-doers" or pursuing interests for the common good. I argue, however, that certain mechanisms function not to just remedy, but also to take advantage of, such a situation. For example, Robert Putnam has recognized that religious organizations can play an important role in contributing to social capital formation by connecting new immigrants to society.[27] The Islamic-oriented associations similarly functioned as a base where women new to the country could meet other women who share their same faith-based interests. Social capital formation is enabled within a disaggregated society.

In the endeavor to impact on society, spatialization of a particular truth is achieved through the utilization of learning materials. Participants within the majority of associations distribute cassettes and CDs. This is an effective strategy. First, the cassettes and CDs include the sermons and speeches of well-known religious sheikhs. As such, unquestioned legitimacy is often established. Second, people do not need to attend a lecture within an organization. They can listen to a cassette or CD in their own homes or cars; therefore, the tapes can reach a wide audience with relative ease, including those who might be shy about appearing in a religious environment. They are distributed free or at a minimal cost. *Nashids* (Islamic songs) form a large part of the audio material distributed. Other cassettes and CDs include religious speakers, such as Harun Yahya, who synthesizes science with Islam, Bilal Phillips, who talks about purification of the soul and Islamic law, Amr Khalid, whose recent themes include taking the companions of the Prophet as role models and how to develop Muslim societies through Islamic values, Hamad al-Rifai, who talks about women's proper dress and appropriate behavior, Nabil al-Awadi, whose recent theme is personal and spiritual development before undertaking *jihad* against the Other, Muhamed Hassaan, who talks about politics, especially issues related to U.S. foreign policy, such as in Iraq and Afghanistan, and Mukhtar Mai, an academic who focuses on social problems specific to the Southeast Asian community.

Greater reach and encompassment is also achieved through information dissemination technologies due to the addressing of topics relating to new challenges and concerns. These speakers approach Islam from different angles—spirituality, science, the *halal* and *haram*, social problems, dress and behavior, politics and civil society. This indicates that, within the themes guiding the messages of these sources—proper practice, the Other, dress, morality, and revival of the *ummah*—listeners are incrementally introduced to a wider range of discourses. For example, discourse within the fields of science and civil society is rarely stressed among *halaqas*. Speaking about politics in lectures and study circles involves taking great risks; whereas distributing audio material containing political directives conveys the same message in a discreet manner. A reconfiguration of the line drawn around usual themes is indicative that a change in Islamic discourse is being effected locally. Several interviewees confirmed that tapes and CDs played an influential role in the way they sought knowledge and made changes in their lives. Islamic-oriented associations are thus able to circumvent restrictions placed on their discourses and activity within the associations.

Greater autonomy gives these associations greater ability to implement agendas. As Mai Yamani has argued, where the state seeks to coopt society, "it is often only religious organizations that retain enough autonomy or cohesion to shelter the vestiges of civil society."[28] Islamic-oriented associations have greater abilities to pursue their own agendas when compared to other associations. They enjoy greater autonomy from state control because of higher volunteerism levels (versus paid positions) and less government funding. In no association were women reported to have been appointed by government or a sheikha. While some funding is supposedly guaranteed, only two associations were completely supported through emirate funding, and some associational leaders attested they never received government funding. Even so, independent *halaqas* receive no government support, while government-controlled *halaqas* use the facilities of the mosques and their leaders are not paid.

EMPOWERMENT

The problems facing women in a developmental context are many and varied, as are their goals and desires. Confining all interpretation of women's struggles to contention, especially between men and the state, limits an understanding of these women's transformative capabilities. Rather, the examination must give importance to the redistribution of power women may influence. Activism in this vein could be manifested into two general, but not disconnected forms, as "governing society has come to require governing subjectivity."[29] The first is activism that involves technologies of the self. The second involves the shaping of public selves and methods of confronting the Other.

Power Over: Threat of the Other

According to Tobias Theiler,

> Humans inhabit a world in which there are few clear lines of division. . . . But this threatens to overwhelm our cognitive apparatus. . . . To counteract this [people use representations of "us" and "them" to order, systematize and simplify [their] field of perception.[30]

In other words, "frames," defined as "a cognitive order that relates events to one another,"[31] and which tells people how to think about things are strategically and conveniently used to place the dramatic changes in the UAE in intelligible terms. Establishing a source for erosive influences that threaten one's interests also produces a target and, hence, allows action to be more systematic. Such a technology of "assembling" good and bad feeds nearly into rhetoric that can mobilize to action. Thus, it is easier to guide a larger reach of people how to achieve or preserve the good life when a clear threat is established. Francis Fukuyama has noted among various sources of social capital the two most major sources: religion and globalization in developing countries. As he attests, "globalization injures indigenous cultures and threatens longstanding traditions. But it also leaves new ideas, habits, and practices in its wake."[32] These new habits and practices, thus, must be rooted out through classifications that are familiar and can, moreover, evoke emotive qualities. The cognitization of the Other among the Islamic based associations in the UAE is rooted in the discursive tradition of *dar al harb* and *dar al Islam,* in which the enemy embodied *dar al harb* and the "Islamic world" *dar al Islam.*

The genealogy of this discursive tradition shows it has been modified to fit modern dilemmas and ensure its continued relevance. This politically motivated division within traditional *fiqh* has been reformulated into the "occupier" and the Muslims. These terms are gaining more ground as the Other has become pervasive and intrusive within the "land of Islam," militarily and culturally. It is articulated through the narrations that young men and women are losing the strict segregation laid down by the religion, promiscuity is mounting, and women's dress is becoming more unIslamic. The roots of these problems they point to are the influences coming from the West through Western media, the flux of Westerners into the country, and the modernization projects pursued by the state. Muslims are falling prey to the influences because they do not know their religion. To heighten the seriousness of the threat within interviewees' narrative, among those in various positions are truly missionaries. In respect to the encroachment of this threat, an interviewee describes, "Everything is becoming Western. The companies here are Western. Sheikh Zayed Road is turning into a New York. We abandon our own skin and take on others." The symbolism articulated through reference to New York is that America is shaping the UAE into its likeness. Another interviewee confirms the source of threat and tells how she will choose to counter it: "I do not want to work. Instead I want to bring up my kids to be like Salah al-Din. Children do not know their Arabic history. They are only on the internet and in front of the TV. We are getting shaped by the US's perceptions. We are being shaped by the media and by the professors. They shape us the way they want."

The invasion, aside from the Westerner, includes the live-in maids from mostly the Philippines and India. Most are non-Muslim and pose a threat to the children they take care of. Stories abound on how they not only corrupt the children's language, but also distort their faith by introducing other religions—Christianity and Hinduism. The theme of maids is even more strongly communicated among state-run women's associations and among the various forms of literature. Thus, the narrations of Islamic-oriented and state-funded operatives converge, making the problem a major contention for all sectors. The narration continues on how women are neglecting their duties as mothers and wives. Narratives abound, furthermore, on how dutiful maids can be to their homes and so the husbands may be inclined to taking a maid as a wife. Such a major issue threatening society requires action. The appeal is targeted specifically at mothers. The emotion of fear is set within the narrative to encourage women to quickly resume their roles within the home. Shaping such selves is important for the Islamist goal and also for the state's interest of stability.

The Other is also found locally within the emirates among the liberals, thought by Islamists to teach secularism. In the mid-1980s, a small group of liberals was second to Islamic activists in the vocalization of its interests. A group of liberals began publishing their magazine in the 80s, but were soon banned from its publication because through it the liberals tried to push political change. Its journal, *Al-Azmina,* can now be found online and its contributors are currently London based. They pushed for change through acts, such as the demonstrations initiated at Al-Ain University, an event for which the military was called in. Today those in the UAE comprise an even smaller group, many of which are Western educated local academics, often professors, and businessmen. Some are in government positions; one became a minister. A few others are pushing for the establishment of one of the human rights organizations referred to earlier. Suaad Al-Oraimi argues that these liberals are a force within the UAE pushing for change, to eventually establish a modern state, while Islamists are struggling to establish an Islamic state. Accordingly, they do not collaborate.[33] She acknowledges, however, that the liberals have lost much influence in the UAE.

To counter the threat of the Other locally and "reawaken" a "lost" Islamic consciousness, the associations pursue a variety of projects in the form of lectures, *halaqas,* lessons, and dissemination of materials. In the following sections, I will delineate techniques through which their objectives are realized. Resistance to the effects of Western influences will be outlined in terms of *power to, power with* and *power from within.*

Power To: Well-Being, Education, and Skills

As *power to* involves the simple act of doing or the ability to act, it embraces capacities, skills, creativity and, at times, resistance.[34] Delineating how women claim the *power to* helps place their practices and aspirations in context of empowerment that is otherwise missed through analyses that place all action within the framework of subversion. I ask in what ways are participants claiming greater educational levels, skills, and well-being? As Connie Christiansen notes, Islamic activism enhances skills, knowledge, competencies, and the kind of self that is integral to a modern lifestyle.[35]

Fundamental to the attainment of well-being, education, and skills is, first, the *power to* organize. Collaboration then opens a wealth of opportunities or *power to* further one's education, broaden one's experiences, and attain a number of valuable skills essential to self-empowerment. The participants understand these opportunities to contribute to the betterment of the individual within their own traditionally grounded construction of what produces a better individual.

The sheer ability to establish a forum in which interests may be pursued is, in itself, an important step that can be richly empowering.

Reaching the goal of having a place where women can successfully meet at times derives great efforts on part of the women, which can include resistance. In one example, the *halaqa* leader's right to organize her study group could not be granted through any mosque authority. In the emirate in which she wanted to begin the *halaqa*, *halaqas* were already organized by the state. She was well aware that her agenda differed substantially from that of these organized *halaqas*. She was, however, granted access to a room in a mosque by the person she made her official *amir* of her *halaqa*. If her *halaqa* were to be discovered by authorities, she would need to face the consequences of it being terminated, she being perhaps interrogated by the authorities, her work contract terminated, and consequently her residency cancelled—a risk she was determined to take even though she was the sole breadwinner of her family of six. Despite the difficulty and threat of repercussions, she found the *power to* begin the *halaqa* through her belief that she carried the burden of bringing the truth to people and, hence, Allah would protect those who struggle in His way, as she affirmed.

In another example, the *amir* posed as the obstacle. The women had just moved their meeting from one of the participants' home to an official building as a registered association because the participants became too many to host in the home. As an Islamic center, however, the leaders decided they required a male *'alim* (religious scholar) to refer to, as they had received threats by men storming into the association that they would make sure the association is closed down since the women did not have a scholar to refer to. Subsequently, they found a scholar and made him the official *amir* of the association. No sooner, the *amir*[36] proclaimed that women are forbidden from entering public spaces unaccompanied by a male relative. Furthermore, as men could enter the association (a men's wing was being formed and men could certainly enter the association to find Islamic guidance), the women, including the director, were banned from entering the premises and attending their lectures. The *amir* simply locked himself inside the building the women had barely finished renovating. All classes were cancelled and the women protested by sitting daily outside the association on the steps. The director ardently fought to have the *amir* removed by asking prominent persons in the community to intervene and appealed to the Ministry of Islamic Affairs. However, having placed his name on legally binding documents, she and her cofounders met obstacles in this endeavor. After deliberation, the women opened a new association under a different name and cut their financial losses. In this example the women struggled against a patriarchal interpretation of rigid segregation that grants men access to public spaces and denies women entry into public spaces. Yet the women were still able to derive the *power to* continue their objectives by starting anew.

Power to establish a forum for learning and self-advancement from an Islamic angle, as seen in these two examples, often includes working within a patriarchal system in which legitimacy as knowledge bearers of Islam must be won under the guidance of a male scholar. One might argue that women are not pursuing their interests autonomously, and are rather submitting to male authority over women's issues and, thereby, question if empowerment is really occurring. Women, in such examples, might very well be securing subordination through some of their actions. However, one must bear in mind that empowerment does not occur inside a vacuum. In order to secure women's voices in the public realm, strategies for this goal must be resorted to that simultaneously build on patriarchy. If the only way to gain legitimacy is to place a male scholar within a decision-making position that allows the organization to function, then the women must work from within such social stipulations. To work outside what is acceptable within a powerful discursive tradition would be ineffectual.

Women developed skills through their participation. Participants were asked which skills they felt they had attained through their participation in their respective associations and *halaqas*. The most frequently quoted was communication and organizational skills. Interviewees learned means to articulate their views or get their ideas across in an influential manner. They expressed a better understanding of people different to them and an ability to deal with them. Participants also gained experience in managing and coordinating their programs, often "through trial and error," as one interviewee put it. These skills or competencies have been attained on the individual level and result in individual empowerment. Christiansen explains the link to society:

One result of successful education is a complying body. Paradoxically, it could be argued that the other side of this compliance is a process of empowerment: the acquisition of tools and skills with which to confront and influence the world. Competencies such as assertiveness, the construction of a coherent argument, and experiences with practical organization are outcomes of Islamic activism which, although not unwelcome, are not necessarily directly intended. Nonetheless, they are indispensable aspects of the skills and attitudes demanded of an influential group of people, an avant-garde, pushing other groups towards changing social practices and promoting new visions of society; in other words, a reform movement.[37]

Power to is achieved when women feel they are directing and developing their own programs and agendas. Empowerment is gained when a woman is able to influence change through suggesting, debating, or voting on a program. She gains a sense of control over her needs and interests by articulating what she as a woman wants to develop, learn, or see implemented for the benefit of other women or to accomplish the goal of reforming society. The second most frequently acquired skill identified for self-development was their decision-making skills in the areas they were responsible for. In these ways, these women acquired the skill and *power to* initiate steps toward fulfilling goals they planned themselves. This skill developed out of the typical Islamic association that included the input of its members, as there was often no plan of action for several activities along with their usual goals. In such a process she need not take power from anyone to see her agenda implemented. Power, as such, is infinite.

When the women opened the first shelter in the UAE for women, the empowerment gained for the participants was in the ability to or the "we can" effect a major change, by finding funding from donors, charity, or hosting weekly garage sales to support the project, and importantly, sheltering women from harm. The women who require use of the shelter find empowerment from various desperate situations, which include fear, hunger, poverty, in a number of cases sexual, physical, mental, or emotional abuse, or even threat of death, as was the concern of two women who ran away from their families at the time of interview. Thus, the power to give women a place in which they can find solace, counseling, and a place to rest without fear is a form of empowerment that is found and spread through society without the domination versus resistance/compliance dichotomy. This does not mean that resistance is not a function of these participants' actions. Simultaneously, the women are resisting notions, such as: The family has the right to take the law into their own hands and punish a daughter; abuse and disputes are a family matter; or that women must endure an abusive situation if family members fail to intervene successfully.

Knowledgeable subjectivities also emerged from women's participation. Women who attended the associations were also questioned as to what they gained from attending lectures and courses. A literacy class illustrates the profound effect an Islamic organization can have on women. Several literacy classes were offered at an organization in which the women learned to read by reciting the Qur'an while learning to recognize the letters and words within the text of the Qur'an. The women were demonstrably proud to read out what they had learned. One attendee expressed she could now read newspapers, though slowly. One attendee expressed she was pleased she could follow-up on her children's homework as a result of learning how to read through reciting Qur'an in the lessons. Self-reliance or the capacity to help one's children educationally is empowering for a woman who once felt helpless because she lacked the necessarily skills to contribute to her older children's educational development when they were younger. In front of her children she, and other women like her, feels a sense of competency and productivity. These women felt a sense of empowerment because they could seek knowledge from the source of their faith. This is especially empowering because the Qur'an is their most valuable source of knowledge, truth and, guidance and, hence, an immense source of motivation for learning.

Power With: The Ummah

In simply attending a gathering in which women could spend time with other Muslim women, participants found new sources of empowerment. As a participant elucidates, "There is a strong sisterhood here. Each woman wants for others what she wants for herself. I love to come here. There is sunshine here. We act as a family." In one example, a woman said she only stayed in her home and had never spoken a word to another Muslim woman for the two years she lived in the UAE until that day. She was so overjoyed she found the Islamic center, she busily asked ladies to exchange phone numbers with her. Her situation might sound absurd, but it is also not uncommon that many expatriate women in the UAE find it very difficult to connect with other women. Many women feel alienated and lonely, especially when their husbands are working the typically long hours required by most jobs for expatriates in the UAE. An experience where women connect at Islamic centers is, thus, especially empowering and therapeutic.[38]

Power with one another is exercised, furthermore, through the establishment of a conception of nationhood that offers the women a sense of identity and belonging and which forms the basis of the women's actions or *power to* achieve common goals, as with countering the Other. The notion of *ummah* is employed in a volatile situation of confusion in which identities are questioned and reordered. In this upheaval of identities, a sense of solidarity in pursuance of the good traditional life that is threatened by an identified Other is developed. In other words, associations are invoking subscription to an idea that provides a role in forming solidarity in reinscribing practices and rituals as understood to have been practiced by Islamic role models, whereas it is also a tool through which control is gained or a *power to* is acquired to combat forces of domination. Ira Lapidus explains the historical roots of the idea:

The growth of religious loyalty to *hadith* and the long struggle over doctrine and authority had crystallized a conception of the *umma* of Muslims as a community founded upon loyalty to religious principles. . . . Henceforth, the Caliphate was no longer the sole identifying symbol or the sole organizing institution, even for those Muslims who had been most closely identified with it.[39]

The concept of *ummah* was formulated when the Hanbali opposition mobilized the idea to delegitimize the Caliph who insisted all Muslims adhere to the Mu'tazali theological movement.[40] The context in which the idea of the *ummah* is emphasized in the UAE is much the same. The concept is reestablished in the UAE context of rapid modernization as a force to contest the power of the Other, identified as Westernization or globalization from the West. Calling for its reinstatement is a misnomer, as its formulation comprises articulations embedded in a local and modern context, in which an enemy has been identified and its usage should assuage an apparent threat produced by this enemy.

Because of rapid transformation of a social order, the state also seeks to promote unity of a nation based on its own narration of a local heritage. As Mehran Kamrava points out, the majority of Middle Eastern states have been highly effective in placating opposition by co-opting popular norms and values, often being religion.[41] In the UAE, the activation of an *ummah* as a force to contend with Westernization conveniently coincides with the state's agenda to build a narration of a common heritage and culture, which the state promotes through media, associations, policies, and programs. As Abdullah explains:

Executive leaderships of these Islamic associations and groups view the current political situation as the best possible alternative especially with the repeated official confirmation of the necessity of sticking to Islamic customs, culture, values, and belief. This compromising view is totally coherent with the specific patriarchal political culture that is prevailing in the UAE and this has added to the popularity of the religious stream in the UAE.[42]

As civil society theory is preoccupied with the function of civil society as a bulwark against the state, nationalist projects are expected to stir modes of resistance on part of the actors within society. Here, however, neither resistance, nor submission to state objectives takes place. Rather, the Islamic activists utilize the same techniques of identity formation and rhetoric as that of the state's to gain a stronger platform to challenge power relations with the hegemonic Other.

The consequence of this technique of power is its wide reach for mobilization. The concept of *ummah* encompasses a much wider circle, which in the UAE includes the locals and all believers of Islam, thereby, crossing boundaries of ethnicity and class. This gives the concept greater permanence, legitimacy, and applicability. Because a wider circle of participants is called upon to play a role, the idea provides for greater levels of participation than would the idea of nationalism, for example.

The activation of the concept of *ummah* is, furthermore, shared among men and women Islamic activists; activation is not confined to one gender. Feminist theory is preoccupied with women's struggles that are aimed at destabilizing men's domination. Here women are not identifying the source of their disempowerment within a category of gender but rather a category of power relations based on hegemonic ideas that threaten a lifestyle constituted through Islamic codes of being. Their objectives for the preservation of moral and social codes are shared with their male counterparts. Hence, when women promote the idea of a solidarity based on the needs of the *ummah*, they are tapping into resources for mobilization not only among women but also among men.

In its modern formulation, the concept of *ummah* presents the same patriarchal structure as the concept of nationhood utilized by state actors. Just as the state assigns women a defined role as protectors of the family unit, through use of media and women's GONGO associations, so do Islamic activists through the media and women's Islamic associations. The family unit, as viewed by state actors, forms the basis for the nation. The family unit according to Islamic activists is also seen as the critical unit upon which the *ummah* is built. Just as state actors view women as bearers and nurturers of this nation, Islamic activists situate women as pivotal in bringing up generations that will contribute to and develop a transnational *ummah*. Without their attentiveness to the husband and children the *ummah* will be weak. Thus, as within government-run women's associations, the rhetoric in Islamic women's associations places great value on the differing roles of men and women.

However, subordination to a patriarchal order is not the only process at work. As Saba Mahmood has argued, all forms of desire are discursively organized,[43] and as such, one needs to understand that the desires emerge out of practical and conceptual conditions in order to place the meaning of their activisms in their appropriate context. The conceptualization of *ummah* among the associations produces a focus on the reproductive role of mother and nurturer. Those women who are subscribing to the idea of an *ummah* are embracing the feminine roles and commitment it has come to outline within a historical context. Simultaneously, women are enriching their lives with a sense of *power to* engage a movement in which they have placed hopes and expectation of securing dignity.

While the acts of supporting and nurturing might be satisfying and rewarding, as can be deciphered from the discourse that imbues these acts with positive evaluations, what one is supporting must be analyzed to evaluate empowerment comprehensively. In a study circle three women vented their frustrations of feelings of oppression to each other and their *halaqa* leader over a number of weeks. In a way, they were seeking emotional support and advice about physically and emotionally abusive husbands. One day, the *halaqa* leader ended their grievances by instructing them to refrain from their "complaints" and be patient with their husbands because "if you divorce him you are neglecting your responsibility to your *ummah*. He is part of the same *ummah* you are part of. You have to mend him and take care of him. Whether you divorce him or stay with him he has a problem that needs to be mended, and who else is going to mend him if you divorce him?" Similar advice to women having trouble with husbands was typical among associations, using patience, Qur'anic verses, or *ahadith* as support. In fact, associations provided lessons specifically on this topic. In this example, a *halaqa* leader is able to suppress potential action that might disrupt the unit upon which the *ummah* stands.

Disempowerment occurs when one is emotionally or physically harmed. Thus, women whose activism guides them or their dependents to unsafe circumstances, in the above example emotional and physical abuse, empowerment cannot be part of the process. Here, the idea of an *ummah* is conceptualized within the Islamist discourse in which these women partake to supersede any consideration for safety. This particular discourse, among others, is made possible because the assertions are based on a shared logic that sacrifice is part and parcel of one's activism for the greater good of Muslims.

Piety and Power from Within

Women find within themselves abilities, strengths, and virtues that are developed either through intentional training to achieve greater piety or closeness to God, or through an unintentional consequence of their participation. Women felt that their participation brought virtues out from within themselves because of repeated practice of virtuous acts in face of ongoing challenges. The subjection to such circumstances is then embraced as the fulfillment of an Islamic objective.

The embodiment of such virtues is, moreover, crucial to effect change on the societal level. Having problematized the issue—a moral decline in society, brought on through the Other and Muslims lacking the Islamic education required for a pious and moral self, Islamic activists direct their activities to the reform of society. Thus, not only piety, but also the biological and psychological uniqueness that resides in each woman is evoked within the "epistemology of assemblage"[44] as the means to achieve a moral society. One can observe an emphasis among the participants on building a "pure" society through the developing of devout Muslims. Organizational leaders and participants produce these devout and sacrificing subjectivities by setting standards of behavior and goals for piety.

In producing the pious self, the notion of *jihad* is a central technique. Reference made to a commitment to *jihad* is a powerful means of mobilization as the word denotes an action essential to the formation of Muslim individuals true to the *ummah*. In one of its meanings *jihad* takes the form of struggle with the *nafs* (literally soul, meaning personal desires). In its characterization as struggle against one's earthly desires, participants seek *power over* these base desires and worldly inclinations. In her study on Moroccan women, Christiansen uses Foucault's notion of technologies of self to refer to the process in which women in Islamic lectures build the self in which these technologies permit "individuals to effect by their own means or with the help of others a certain number of operations on their own bodies and souls, thoughts, conduct, and way of being, so as to transform themselves in order to attain a certain state of happiness, purity, wisdom, perfection, or immortality."[45] As Christiansen argues, like any other type of technology (i.e. technology of production) these technologies result in the shaping of the individual and the acquisition of skills.[46] Hence, in submitting oneself to a notion, in our case *jihad*, that carries great weight in the collective psyche of what produces a virtuous self as a means to struggle in the way of Allah, the individual is engaging an empowerment process.

Such "technologies of self," in which the women develop themselves spiritually and educationally, are carried out highly systematically and purposefully. Subjectivity and its capacities enter the calculation of organizational leaders. The typical topics they cover in the lectures and *halaqas* included backbiting, wasting time, such as with watching too much TV or movies, talking too much on the phone, talking with friends about unimportant events, listening to music, etcetera. To mobilize attendees to change these habits and channel their activities, they will give advice to start praying, to switch from unimportant programs on TV to Islamic channels, instead of listening to music, to listen to Islamic tapes, etcetera. One popular technique of controlling the *nafs* was having participants resolve not to listen to music for five days, then ten days, etcetera until one is no longer "addicted" to the music. The method was also suggested for smoking. One is also advised to make a list of all the problems one has with oneself, and start eliminating the easiest first. By working on eliminating negative or sinful actions and replacing them with ones that nurture the soul, the goal is to improve one's relationship with God. In the process of personal enhancement, individuals attain greater piety through the cultivation of virtues that bring oneself to greater awareness of her Creator. In this endeavor, participants, individually and collectively, are constantly pursuing a goal of the embodiment of virtues.

Other strategies were utilized to develop productive and pious subjectivities. A typical technique found especially among *halaqas* was competing with one another to better the self. As a participant describes, "We have competitions to see who can learn the most *surahs*. We discuss issues together and try to correct each other. It is a learning atmosphere for all of us. We try to be the best we can. We try to be an example for each other." During and after lectures, talk sometimes revolved around how to be an example for others to follow. Such was a powerful motivating strategy as visual cues were sometimes provided, as with dress and what was defined as Islamic manners and virtues. Other times success stories were involved. One organization, for example, held a session in which converts were invited to give testimonies to how they transformed their selves from sinners to what was the example of sincere and struggling *Muslimeen*.

"Technologies of self" as a major part of Islamic associational activism is, however, not the only means through which pious selves is achieved. While piety is a goal in itself, it is also an outcome of various other processes that are sustained through the women's efforts. When asked what the participants had gained from their activism, in terms of virtues that cultivate piety, the most frequent reply was "patience."

In other words, they had found and developed *power from within* themselves to deal with everyday challenges and practical realities. This includes facing obstacles, such as funding, or convincing people who refuse to accept their views, goals, or strategies. Agreeing with other participants on how to accomplish a task was a learning experience that developed patience and communicative skills. As a participant tells, "Dealing with different people has its challenges. No one here is a professional. They participate from their hearts and because of enthusiasm. So, personal preferences and differences always get in the way. I learned to observe more and develop a lot of patience. These experiences have affected the way I behave." Patience that results from painful experiences is viewed by the participants in the same vein. As an interviewee exclaimed after telling she had endured some mishaps, "I think Allah is trying to make me a stronger Muslim." The women learn that they must embrace their tests that are part of God's divine plan to make someone a better individual. In this sense, women are acquiring and exercising the *power to* endure.

As is "given" within the Islamist project, a conscious link exists between the development of individuals and development of society. However, in several lectures a debate took place whether one should wait to practice *dawa* until one has achieved piety and a certain level of knowledge, or one should begin *dawa* while studying Islam. The latter was informed through a much cited *hadith*, "One must seek knowledge from the cradle to the grave." However, what most *da'iyas* agreed upon was that, as one put it, "You cannot change society unless you change yourself first," or another, "You cannot give what you do not have." A certain level of piety and religious knowledge had to be the foundation upon which an individual could then struggle to transform society. As Christiansen similarly concludes, "The ability of the body to become a means of social transformation is recognized and utilized among Islamists. Thus they have strongly objectified their own bodies and the working out of a program for one's own activities seem to be part of this objectification."[47] Transforming society is an interest like many other interests, and the women take significant steps in its enactment. The first step of such an "assemblage" is producing the kinds of subjectivities conducive to this endeavor.

The impact these associations and *halaqas* have on society was argued previously in quantitative terms; however, the very process of producing moral and pious selves accounts for the impact these forums for learning has on its attendees. Several women who attended to benefit from the associations asserted they derived several spiritual and educational benefits from attending the lessons and simply being part of the Islamic learning environment. As one attendee attests, "I love that my mind is changing. My mind is being developed in the right way. My thoughts are changing. My character is becoming better." Another participant emphasizes the spiritual satisfaction, "The *halaqa* is full of electric charge. When I enter the room I feel intense spiritual charges. Whenever I find people learning it charges me with energy." Guiding the attendees to learn how to cultivate piety and seeing the effects on the attendees gives the participants a sense of productivity and self-satisfaction. As a participant elucidates, "When I go to bed at night I feel I have accomplished something, for example that I convinced someone to put on the scarf, taught someone a *hadith,* gave someone charity. I see my deed in their eyes and in their expressions when I have made them happy." Experiencing success or the *power to* effect change, or importantly, produce happy individuals, as evinced through such markers, is empowering for the participants. Next, I will attempt to clarify the connection forged between individual practice and societal change in a discussion on the objective of morality.

The Production of a Moral Society in Face of Moral Decline

Not only is the major theme the corrupting effects through interaction with the Other, women are slowly taking up roles not traditionally accepted and are increasingly entering the work force. Thus, a tension between the ideal of a woman's role in the home and growing economic pressures along with the ideal for Western progression of women taking up other roles outside the home exists. In face of competing notions of women's position and roles, Islamic activists gear their activities toward a production of a notion of the moral society. I will focus on the discourses that assist women to view uniqueness within their gender as moral, caring, and sacrificial for personal and societal happiness and equilibrium.

Islamic activists launch their arguments for women's roles in the home and for social reform around the woman's biological, emotional, and psychological makeup. An interviewee gave her views within the popular discourse of women's role in the home:

I believe my mom as a Muslim woman has to stay at home. Her priorities should be us, her home, her husband, and then herself. She tries to give to us but she ends up giving most of herself to her career. She cannot do everything. So, she has ended up practically losing her husband. She is now older, and my dad is busy too, so he does not really notice anymore. In any case, she has ended up losing herself, her health. . . . I am only able to contact her when she has her break or lunch. I would love to be able to just come home and find my mom at home. . . . A typical Middle Eastern man would love to come home and find his wife at home with food prepared, etcetera. . . . We are used to moms at home. It is what we got used to. It is how society sees it. Even if the income is not great, everything is peaceful if the mom is at home. I have friends whose moms are at home. You can see the peace in their faces. I do not want to repeat this. My dad took a lot. I have to be home to help out with the house while she is out sometimes for 24 hours. Half of her friends are divorced or single. There is a verse in the Qur'an which reads, "The woman's best place is in the home."[48] This verse is always repeated in the lectures because women are beginning to go out of their homes. Lectures revolve around this issue because when women go out of their homes they have illegal relationships, incidences of rape increases, there are all sorts of illegal marriages, illegal children, HIV. The majority of this is happening because women are out of their homes with make up and dressed immorally.

Articulations around dress codes are another major technique in producing the notion of a moral society. Ills of society, as the narrator above asserts, are the result of women's mobility into society. This assertion is related to the discourse of women as temptresses. When women leave their homes or are in the presence of male unrelated kin, proper dress must be adhered to. Of the symbols found within the discourses of Islamic activists in the UAE for proper practice are the *hijab* or *shayla* and *abaya*. The *abaya* or long black thin coat, symbolizes adherence to Gulfian tradition and commitment to the principle of Islamic dress. Often women point to the Kuwaiti and Bahraini women who have led the way to corrupted moral behavior in the Gulf as signified through the shedding of their *abayas*. While the thin *shayla* pulled over the face as a face veil is acknowledged as a traditional dress that also signifies shyness, the *hijab* (covering at least the hair and neck) more significantly is understood to reflect inner chastity and submission to Allah's commands. However, as part of the *hijab*, a *niqab* is often viewed as mandatory.

Indeed, the *hijab* connotes something so powerful that it can surpass any other "obligation." In two associations participants exclaimed how shocked they were to see women dressed unchaste in the UAE and had made it a mission to educate women about how to dress appropriately. As one participant in another organization tells, "The last two years the biggest issue here has been women not covering. . . . We have had great success though. We have had several women put on the *hijab*, women who were not praying now do." As a participant laments, "People do not think about what is *halal* and *haram* anymore. The family lets its girls show their hair and other body parts." The wearing or not wearing of the *hijab* issue is elevated and framed in the discourse to something that should be accorded the category of *halal* versus *haram*. Elevating the seriousness of wearing *hijab* through the strategies of framing and categorizing is one of the most effective acts on part of the participants and leaders in the construction of moral subjectivities.

The subjectifying aspect of dress moves to a deeper level among participants. Such practical ways of formulating, understanding, and responding have become, as Rose argues, thoroughly "pychologized."[49] The way one dresses reflects the state of one's inner self. Through the wearing of *hijab*, women's consciousness of the way they deal with others and practice their religion is heightened. There is a direct relationship between the wearing of the *hijab* and bodily reform. Mahmood observes, "outward behavioral forms were not only expressions of their interiorized religiosity but also a necessary means of acquiring it."[50] She refers to this process in the Aristotelian sense of the word, "habitus" as "a conscious effort at reorienting desires concordance of inward motives, outward actions, inclinations, and emotional states through the repeated practice of virtuous deeds."[51] To instill in women the practice of *hijab*, techniques of praise, admonishing, but importantly responsibilization, were commonplace.

Motherhood is manifested as a woman's most important role and goal among both women's Islamic associations and state-run women's associations. Empowerment in the above narration is not dropping the shackles of traditional familial obligations and pursuing a career for fulfillment. For this Islamic activist, and many like her, a woman is, in fact, disempowered by the very act of "leaving the home" to take up a career. Women's entrance into the workforce is articulated as a new concept that has disrupted the way of life among Islamic societies and culture. Most importantly, a career or work outside the home undermines a woman's most valuable role in society. Thus, to define the Islamic position in regards to women's work outside the home, the dominant discourse places motherhood as a woman's most desirous and rewarding role that conflicts with other practices.

The manifestation of the responsible and caring subject entails that she makes prudent decisions in her capacity as the social and emotional support of a family. To ensure the needs of the children and the husband are attended to, a woman must put her personal desires last. If the woman puts herself first, as the narrator above stresses, the family and society will crumble. A woman's unique attributes as a wife are cultivated to protect the family unit and safeguard public morality. In this endeavor, women's success is measured, not only in terms of how well they can perform the duties that define a good mother, but also a good Muslim wife. If one fails by letting her ego get in the way, the consequence, as this activist pointed out, is that one loses her husband through divorce or building resentment.

Even though polygamy was uncommon 30 to 40 years ago, it has become a notable feature of Emirati and UAE society and even a part of the discourse on how to ensure a moral society. Religious male speakers point to the rising number of spinsters in UAE society and warn that such a situation is the worst in which a woman could find herself. The success of producing, sacrificing, and giving selves is evident as female interviewees supported such arguments. In a lecture on marriage, the *amir*[52] of the organization spoke about a man's right to marry more than one woman after an attendee asked if a man needed to ask the first wife if he can marry a second. The reply was, "no". And to bolster his argument on the importance of polygamy in solving moral ills in society, the speaker warned attendees of a *hadith* that states, "You must want for your brother/sister as you would want for yourself." The speaker then admonished, "You want to convert a sister and when she says, 'I want to marry your husband,' you tell her to get out the back door!?" And he explained, further, that women outnumbered men so it was unfair to other women that the married women should try to stop their husbands from being fair. He further exclaimed women must, in fact, enable their husbands to marry other women "or else all morality in society will collapse. You will see." The message this speaker is preaching has been echoed in *khutbas* (Friday sermons) that have been held in local mosques and regional TV programs. The imam[53] that one of the *halaqa* leaders of this case study placed as the *halaqa's* ultimate guide had also stated in a *khutba* that "it is recommended that a man marry two women together [in one marriage ceremony]," and supported this claim that it was the *sunnah* (Prophetic tradition) referring to one of the companions of the Prophet who had done exactly that (early eighth century C.E.).

Reference to *sahabah, hadith,* and religious sheikhs' opinions is a strategy through which the discursive tradition on polygamy is grounded. However, just as meaningful is action by example. Observably, many of these speakers have had several wives, and most often not in succession. Several male interviewees have explained that when a man takes more than one woman in marriage he is signaling he is a "man." He is respected by his friends and other men because he

proves to have enough wealth to afford more than one wife, and
wealth is one signifier of one's status. What the discourse, however,
signifies is that it is of vital interest for these men to use such discursive spaces to anchor such practice in a particular discursive tradition
in which the widespread practice of polygyny is an unquestioned
norm.

The messages that support polygamy preached through the associations, lectures, and *khutbas* do produce sacrificing and giving selves.
An interviewee explains,

I was once a co-wife. . . . He married a friend of mine who I felt needed a lot of
support. . . . I don't know how I did it, but it was my own personal *jihad* I had
to wage. . . . I just couldn't bear being in the house we all lived in together.

This interviewee's interpretation of struggle to become nearer to her
Lord was to endure something that would be nearly unbearable. She
found the *power from within* to sacrifice her own "selfish" needs. By
finding the power to conquer her selfishness she gained in one way a
strong sense of accomplishment. She triumphed over her bodily desires with hope to receive existential reward and with anguished satisfaction that she was able to help others. As Mahmood argues, not
only does the regulation of the body take place by male religious authority, but also the very concepts through which the mind and body
serve to fashion the disciplined self.[54]

The ideals credited to Islam that inspire women to activity are important for the understanding of civil society processes. One value
through which action is initiated is the biological and psychological differences between the genders. One of the several motivating factors the
founder struggled to provide a shelter for women is the conviction of
inherent gender differences: "It is an unnatural situation for women to
be on their own. Women have to be protected, so for a woman to be all
on her own is unbearable. She needs to be allowed a place to rest. Unfair burdens should not be placed on her. Men are the providers. Men
can manage, but women are different." The organizational leader seeks
women's empowerment from abuse, starvation, poverty, and lack of access to basic well-being because women are viewed as the weaker sex
and their plights are understood to be a consequence of their not receiving the appropriate protection as females. She situates her argument
within rights, language of a patriarchal framework in which a woman
has the right to well-being, dignity, and protection by a man because
men have the role as providers. What is natural for women is not autonomy and independence from the male gender.

As women's right to well-being is interpreted via a traditional discourse in which the Qur'anic verse, "Men shall take full care of women with the bounties which God has bestowed more abundantly on the former than on the latter, and with what they may spend out of their possessions"[55] is cited, among supporting *hadith,* the "sexual contract" is reified. Ensuring the continuity of the "sexual contract" does not, however, mean the women involved are disempowered. Practically speaking, many of the women who are provided shelter, food, security, emotional and psychological counseling have left traumatizing and abusive situations. Most of the women activists reject struggle against patriarchy and view this "western" quest as individualistic and the source of moral and social decay. For them, identity means family, community, or tribe. Understanding the desires women have in their differing sociohistorical context to the liberal and secular trajectory that presupposes a universal and innate drive for freedom from patriarchy enables us to situate these women's process of empowerment as "divinely inspired" in their discursive tradition.

Though empowerment is experienced in several examples of women's participation in Islamic-oriented associations, some aspects of their work lead to disempowerment. With morality as a major theme in the Islamic discourse, a woman's happiness can become sidelined to save society from a narration of its decline. Not all women who have put on a *hijab* feel greater empowerment when as a result they are then treated less favorably in terms of career opportunities. If a solution is sought to deter a man from marrying another woman, it is placed on the woman herself. She must do everything possible to keep her husband's gaze on her by beautifying herself and attending to his needs and desires within the home. In all, the woman is responsible for the upkeep of a healthy and moral society, putting tremendous pressure on the woman to accept responsibility for her husband's actions and the preached moral decline of society. In the case when the married woman is advised to accept a polygamous relationship, the situation, in most cases, is emotionally and economically disadvantageous for her. Some of the participants would extend counseling services or financial help to women who were the first wives and whose husbands' attention and finances (as generally happens) go to the subsequent wife/wives.

Power For: Provision of Services

Through these associations participants were able to better the conditions of society at large. Techniques for responsiblization of individuals in the welfare of members in society are anchored in Islamic discursive traditions. For example, a *hadith* women referred to that was used as a motivator for giving charity could merely mean a smile. Hence, visiting the sick, providing counseling services, or, as was very common, sitting with persons who are lonely or need to talk about their oppressive situations was charity that serves to alleviate one's emotional and psychological pain. Participants visited the sick in hospitals, if only to let the patients know that someone cares by listening to their complaints. Participants visited poor schools and provided clothes and presents. Other forms of help included collecting money for the poor, especially the *bedoon* (without any citizenship), or those who needed money for an operation, orphans, school fees, etcetera. Their modes of action included collecting money from sponsors, contacts, friends or relatives, holding garage sales, bake sales, or coordinating projects with local businesses in which items are donated and sold to raise money for the charitable projects. The cultivation of selves that take on responsibility for the welfare of society has significant consequences for civil society development.

By alleviating poverty and addressing the concerns of individuals in society, the associations are, thus, enabling a redistribution of power. By attending to the structural oppressions within society, whether as a result of government policies, capitalism, or social stratification within what many interviewees referred to as a caste system, the associations play an important role in bettering the conditions of people who seek the services offered by associations, whether these services are provided formally, or as in many cases, informally. Listening to one's grievances or giving advice can have a tremendous liberating effect on the receiver.

Several participants, furthermore, searched together for strategies that would help needy individuals realize personal potentials so that self-reliance and autonomy could be achieved. Hence, a neoliberal governmentality occurs in which the needy were provided tools to govern their own development. Education is one example. Some children or even adults were given money to get an education. Schools were funded to provide education for those who could not pay. Employment was found for several individuals. Language and computer lessons were offered to facilitate employment, sometimes for a minimal charge. Such strategies enabled an empowerment, even if on a small scale, that could not be taken away.

By providing needed services, an empowerment process is realized. A large proportion of those requiring charitable services, if not most, have no other recourse. The persons are *bedoon*. Hence, the associations that risk helping such persons in need are also challenging an oppressive system in which those who need help the most would be placed in even worse conditions were they to seek help through state legitimized avenues for charity. They might, for example, face deportation to countries that are poverty stricken, war torn, do not recognize their right to citizenship to begin with, or where repression was a factor for their fleeing to the UAE.

A further consequence of fashioning productive, responsible, and caring selves is the self-empowerment and self-achievement these women derive. The women learn they can make a difference in their environment and often witness tangible results. Hence, happier and satisfied subjectivities evolve from the activism in which the participants involve themselves when they help others.

CIVILITY

Civility through Trust

Civility was elucidated in terms of trust, reciprocity, cooperation, and tolerance. Studying how the participants develop these norms, through various "technologies of self" and acts in the pursuit of other interests, helps us understand how their capacity to contribute to the formation of civil society in the UAE emerges. This chapter refutes essentialist charges that Middle Eastern forms of organization are typically uncivil. Rather, these organizations foster subjectivities largely productive of civility.

Trusting, and dependable selves evolved through the practices in which participants engaged. While some associations directed their lessons, advice, and modes of being and practicing from different points along a spectrum of conservative to liberal, for example, trust was exemplified among participants, regardless of their proficiency in adhering to the group view. In a few cases, Christians participated in Islamic organizations. As a general observation, the associations demonstrate civility through the welcoming of all women. Civility is demonstrated within the interaction of individuals whose idea of a common good does not preclude the participation of a woman because of a particular lineage, ethnicity, class, or ideology. In this view, a generalized trust is enabled that bridges to stronger civility, a necessary condition for the expansion of civil society, as the associations are located within a sharply stratified society.

Importantly, trust in an authoritarian environment involves sometimes taking great risks due to the consequences of breaching trust. Every association and *halaqa* demonstrated deep levels of trust with information that if used in an unintended way could possibly cause participants to suffer repercussions. In one of the *halaqas* the leader made clear to the attendees at the first meeting that the *halaqa* was to be kept a secret (it was illegal). Throughout the lesson, she reminded the attendees of this message and that all subjects discussed throughout the *halaqas* could not be divulged to anyone outside the circle, even husbands. The amount of trust that the teacher expressed, through this expectation, toward her students was striking. Help was needed in another association to deal with some issues that required some secrecy for the protection of those already involved in particular projects. Participants were, nonetheless, informed of the situations of, in an example, some needy families who arrived by boat illegally from one of the Arab populated Iranian islands. In several associations money was collected for various projects aimed to support people or children in great financial need, usually *bedoon*. The collection of funds for purposes that are not in the interest of the state could lead to legal repercussions. Yet, despite a real threat, participants continue to collect funds in trust that all those involved will not divulge such acts. Most associations do not have legal permission to collect money from the public for any purpose. Furthermore, participants are well aware that Islamic associations are being closed down, as observed among several of the charity organizations. Moreover, participants are often convinced spies are in their organizations. Yet, participants in most Islamic-oriented associations will still collect money.

Civility through Reciprocity

Sharing and giving were all qualities implanted within the Islamic subjectivity. There is a general feeling of compassion expressed by participants when they learn that a member or someone outside the association is in need. Participants are quick to pool their resources together to give assistance, emotional support, and advice. Participants used previously learned skills to benefit others, continued to learn skills within the association, and gave back to members of the association the tools and abilities they learned. Such included managerial, social, communicative, interpersonal, language, and educational skills, to name a few. Indeed, acts of reciprocation were defining components of the kinds of subjectivities fashioned through these associations.

A *hadith* repeated in lectures that was chosen to inculcate an empathizing subjectivity was, "If one organ hurts, the rest of the body will also suffer." A participant illustrates the embodiment of the injunction when she explains, "The first and most important part of working together is that we feel closer to one another. If one of us is not fine, we're all not fine." The *thawab* (blessings) that could accrue to an individual in this life and the hereafter was a technique generously applied within lectures and within conversations of participants to motivate one another to help and give. As such, resorting to the multitude of *ahadith* and Qur'anic injunctions that spelled out these rewards in calculable or visualizable terms formed the pillars of these techniques. Moreover, members were responsibilized with symbolic notions, such as that one is responsible for members of the *ummah*, and so to dispense one's knowledge among one's sisters would strengthen the capabilities of active members of the *ummah*.

As such, a generous self could be produced by values developed through a discursive tradition integral to the participants' worldview. It can, as well, be a product of the desire to achieve what has been generally agreed upon among Islamic activists as a "common good."

Civility through Cooperation

A cooperative self was assessed from different aspects among the case study participants. The women's propensity as cooperative subjects manifested through observable acts between them and male activists, internally among Islamic associations, and externally among the Islamic associations and a multitude of international Islamic forms of collaboration.

A feature of Islamic women's activism is cooperation with men. Despite a sanctioned norm of segregation, women will seek support and help from men to achieve a particular aim. Being attached to a men's wing in the majority of associations meant that women could address common problems with men in their respective organizations. Many forms of patriarchy were rarely placed on any agenda for activism. Instead, organizational leaders placed *dawa*, contesting the Other, dress, and morals as overriding concerns through techniques of frames and language. Because these concerns were discursively organized as goals among both men and women, collaboration, following the norms of proper conduct between the sexes, was made possible.

Cooperation among participants within their respective associations was high. Participants cooperated on various projects, by for example, coordinating who would take specific roles to accomplish a task, or assisting in a role different to a participant's usual or specified role. A participant attests, "Teamwork is magic. You cannot achieve anything on your own. When I try to find a solution the best we can find is by brainstorming together. You will always find a way." Cooperative subjectivities were fashioned through sheer practice of overcoming personal wishes, agreeing on things, and compromising to achieve what is framed by the organizational leaders as a common and overarching goal. The overarching goal would oftentimes be categorized and sanctioned as "Islamic." Hence, because the goal, being associated with something Godly, is bundled with various meanings of superiority, purity, and resultant blessings, working toward the achievement of the project could often involve little conflict. A participant explains:

Volunteer work is not like a job because a group of people are coming together to do something they believe in. So people have to come to a meeting point with others. What you personally want will not necessarily happen. Not everything will go your way. It is a learning process. You learn how to interact with others. You persevere though because what you do becomes a passion. Working for Islam is a passion for me.

Though cooperation between Islamic-oriented associations was not necessarily high, due to some obstacles, the younger generation of activists, as found among university Islamic clubs, have proved high levels of interorganizational cooperation is yet possible. It is expected that these activists will take their experiences and expectations with them when they leave university and so champion social capital formation among other associational activity in society.

The cooperation that the Islamic-oriented associations of this study sought among international organizations was among other Islamic groups, educational institutes, organizations, or communities. Hence, cooperation was to exchange learning experiences or acquire educational guidance, strengthen solidarity of specific groups, facilitate the funding of various projects, such as the building of mosques and basic infrastructures, facilitate charities to poor communities outside the UAE, and aid the distribution of Islamic materials and resources between other countries and the UAE.

Civility through Tolerance

Typically, the shaping of tolerant subjectivities resulted from the practices related to inclusivity and toleration. Practices in which tolerance could be developed as part of the participants' subjectivation were displayed to various peoples within and outside the Islamic-oriented associations. Tolerance could also be observed toward opposing views.

Tolerance as understood to encompass inclusivity was observed when individuals from diverse groups or classes were included in the organizations. Despite a proclivity among participants to choose associations in which problems germane among specific cultures or ethnic groups were more readily addressed, organizations and *halaqas* were rather diverse in ethnic and racial makeup. Nonlocal interviewees still expressed antagonistic remarks about locals in general. However, what was strikingly different to the testimonies of nonlocal interviewees in the federation of women's associations and UAE women's clubs was that no contention was expressed toward locals within the Islamic-oriented associations themselves. Therefore, tolerance toward those of different ethnic backgrounds is much greater among Islamic-oriented associations. As further elaborated within the above section, no participant was excluded from participation based on class, though preferences among participants are inevitable. In other words, what had placed a line between women in the government-run women's associations and clubs and what is in UAE society a striking factor to segregate women into separate groups was overridden in Islamic-oriented associations. Table 4 in the appendix presents the general diversity among associations not only in ethnic background, but job or career backgrounds and age.

What is of importance in confirming tolerance in these terms is that women of different backgrounds would not be met with discrimination or their roles subordinated to that of others based on identities or social status. In fact, women would emphasize they partook in organizations in which hierarchies dissolved under a form of sisterhood. In voking the language of sisterhood enabled many forms of stratification and hierarchy to seem to disappear. Hierarchy, rather, was accorded to the knowledge of Islamic sources a woman proved to possess.

Tolerant selves are also produced when women learn to debate and contest opposing views or competing religious interpretations in a civil manner. The participants ground their arguments in particular discursive traditions and modes of reasoning to convey their ideas or work. It does not mean that the odd association will never resort to tactics to undermine its competitors. Examples of such techniques were observed through the case study as exists even in a developed civil society. However, the dominant mode of contestation was through civil means. Given that associations, such as many of this study, advance their interests predominantly through civil modes of action within an environment in which silencing, exclusion, and elimination of dissenting voices increasingly comprise the governmentality of the powerful, these women contribute essential social capital for the growth of civility.

IMPLICATIONS FOR THE CIVIL SOCIETY CONCEPT

Islamic-oriented organizations are contributing to civil society in the UAE in a number of respects. In fact, the Islamic women's associations have a number of advantages that enable them to contribute to the building blocks of a civil society. These include increased participation levels, a higher volunteerism ethos, stronger mobilization strategies and greater autonomy from the state. These advantages are achieved as Islamic-oriented associations provide opportunities for the assemblage of powerful techniques of organizational governmentality. It is through these various techniques women come to embody the desires and "technologies of self" that shape the kinds of subjectivities transformative of society.

Most associations maintained grassroots level initiations that proved to flourish both vertically and horizontally. Associations developed out of an idea of one or more founding members, and programs were gradually added. Participant numbers increased in all associations. Thus, the associations and *halaqas* grew in size. Participants attest women, in particular, are more active, "because men come here to work, and so have no time to improve themselves religiously. Men do the minimum, which is prayer, so they are weak, not active." Women's advantage in activism is, therefore, attributed to a division of labor, in which women's oftentimes privately oriented actions contribute to development on the public level. A form of neoliberal governmentality in which participants acquired a sense of responsibility toward their actions constructed productive and ethical subjectivities. As a participant explains, "God will ask me about them [the people she helps] at the end. I am responsible for them."

The associations are either semi-autonomous or completely autonomous from the state. Their autonomy is supported by the fact that most participants were not paid for their work. In many other kinds of organizations leaders and administration are appointed by ministries, thereby ensuring programs reflect government interests. Volunteerism in the Islamic-oriented associations was at an exceptionally high level. Thus, with high volunteerism levels, grassroots interests continued to be ensured. Moreover, as they are generally not controlled through government funding, they need not acquiesce to government agendas.

Including empowerment as an index for civil society growth in a developing country is revealing of important developments for civil society. When the women's actions were analyzed within a contextually grounded framework that enabled the study of their power as *power to, power with, power from within,* and *power for,* a wealth of forms of empowerment could be discovered. Aside from the many forms of services and help extended to members of society, women found the ability, strength, confidence, and resources to attain skills and education important for the enhancement of the virtuous self. Women were provided the means to knowledge formation through Qur'an memorization, courses, and lectures. Women could find resources to deepen their understanding of the scripts and other areas. They also learned how to use their inner resources, such as patience, to pursue *jihad* of the *nafs.* The communicative, oratory, and debating skills learned, coupled with a wealth of knowledge about the *din* and the embodiment of particular teachings of the *din* enabled each individual to pursue reform. Concentration was on the societal level through engaging and contesting competing views, and penetrating society with a particular view of morality, well-being, and mode of living discursively enabled through the polity of the *ummah.* Associations honed the skills and abilities for self-reform of participants, and in the process, both intentionally and unintentionally, served to build better skilled and endowed civil society actors.

The associations, furthermore, proved to develop the kinds of subjectivities conducive to a healthy civil society in terms of an ethos of civility they cultivated. The associations provided atmospheres welcoming to individuals irrespective of nationality and ethnic background. Other qualities of civility were observed, such as reciprocity and cooperation. Women cooperated within associations and with other associations to achieve goals and advance shared interests. They further collaborated with men to achieve common Islamist goals. Besides sacrificing their own funds, they sacrificed time, despite the fact that most lead very busy lives with work, study, or family. Cooperation and reciprocity were possible as the underlying quality that bound participants together in activism was a strong sense of trust and vision. Civic virtue, defined by Michael Walzer as "the moral and political qualities that make a good citizen,"[56] is a byproduct, though also a goal attained by participants and attendees.

Both (nonviolent) Islamist groups and Islamic organizations function in the same manner. Both Islamist and Islamic activists comprise those, as Dale Eickelman and James Piscatori describe, whose consciousness has been objectified and who are "committed to implementing their vision of Islam as a corrective to current 'un-Islamic' practices."[57] They form forums where ideas are contested, and some are advanced over others. Al-Oraimi's findings support these findings: "[T]he Islamic-oriented women have linked themselves to the Islamic groups in the UAE—they work together as an integrated body and have never been separated by gender or any other social aspect."[58] Both categorizations of activists have the same value for expanding or hindering civil society in the UAE. Both are active in framing the Islamic cause by imbuing society with Islamic symbols according to whichever way each group understands them and contributing to the betterment of social conditions on the societal level.

This investigation also found convergence in the discourses in many circumstances between actors among Islamic-oriented organizations or Islamist groups and the state. Both attempt to imbue society with symbols and meanings often resorting to the same discursive tradition and techniques of language framing to deal with the effects of globalization. In this context, Islamists will promote those state initiatives that coincide with their agendas in their discourse and actions, and state actors will tow a line between allowing Islamists to do "their work" and constraining activities that might wind up delegitimizing their authority and claims to authenticity. In effect, an Islamization of society is achieved from the bottom up and the top down, in which the stricter interpretations invariably serve to sediment a patriarchal framework. Such is supported through consensus between the authority of the state and the legitimacy of religious institutions and scholars.

The danger in the actions of Islamic-oriented associations, Islamist groups, and the women's government-run associations altogether posed to civility is some aspects of their ideological politics. These aspects include their fixation on nationalism/*ummah* nationhood and the superiority of class based on ethnicity among locals or superiority based on the possession of the "right" Islam among Islamists and Islamic activists. Edward Shils, however, clarifies:

It has not been the substantive values sought by ideological politics which have done such damage. Rather it has been the rigidity, exclusiveness, and the extremity with which particular values have been sought. There is nothing evil about loyalty to one's community, national or ethnic or cultural, nor is there anything wicked in the appreciation of equality or the devotion to any particular ideal. What is so malign is the evaluation of one value, such as equality or national or ethnic solidarity, to supremacy over all others, and the insistence on its exclusive domination in every sphere of life.[59]

To assume that civility entails complete eradication of ideologies is utopian and impossible. Unity is a necessary condition for development and progress, and has been the reason for the successful establishment of the UAE in the first place. A sense of nationhood or conception of *ummah*(hood) may serve to bind individuals together for a sense of identity, which is, at times, useful for individual/group survival. Shils underscores, "Civil society requires compromise and reasonableness, prudent self-restraint, and responsibility."[60] What can become problematic for civil society growth anywhere, however, is that specific values are placed over others to such an extent ideology then serves to justify uncivil acts against competitors.

To varying degrees, the teachings and actions of the associations and *halaqas* are based on patriarchal assumptions and, thereby, reproduce patriarchy. Participants engage discourses that uphold this structure in different ways. The result of their actions can, consequently, range from producing greater autonomy and self-reliance for women to entrenching dependency. But as Asad has argued, Islamic actors should not be constituted through the lens of a Western model of secular modernity in which they are portrayed as traditional in many of their practices, and their traditions are within a stage of social development naturally toward modernity, but evaluated on their own terms as evolving and shaping through their discourse.[61]

Though activism among the organizations looked at in this chapter are, indeed, embedded in ideological politics and patriarchy as framed in the Western discourse, the purpose here is to illustrate that activism has much more consequences to the individuals and society. If civil society studies fail to recognize and invest upon the rich articulations for the good life, then such studies are guided by an ethnocentric bias and are failing to assess civil society developments adequately.

In understanding the effect of the associations on civil society, one must also bear in mind the gap left between the state and society in which no political society is allowed to function as a mouthpiece for citizens to express their opinions and claim rights. Thus, those individuals pushing for change can find no other avenue except through government positions and associations in which people gather to pursue their interests. Women's Islamic-oriented associations have political charge for upsetting set modes in which state politics are exercised. They are the forums for dissenting opinions, and because of their relative independence from the state, the seeds for political mobilization for the future.

As a concept, civil society is challenged to include processes that lead to notions of individual and societal well-being that fit ill with liberal progressive and secular ideals. This challenge becomes painful when, in the balance of things, these associations also form the medium through which some aspects of civil society growth is frustrated. However, the idea of embracing such civil society formations is not so difficult if we contemplate that nowhere is a pristine civil society to be found. Moreover, civil society analysts have come to recognize that the concept of civil society has taken on different meanings and references, not only dependent upon the interests that have driven the idea, but also dependent upon the differing challenges that groups within particular societies have had to struggle with/against. Civil society is a process and not merely an end in itself. Therefore, if we situate this study's activism within the process of civil society formation, it should become clearer, as well, that the participants are making notable contributions within a continuum. Their work cannot be comprehended from a snapshot. As a participant attests: "We are attaining our objectives to a certain extent. Not all goals are being addressed, but consider the organization as a first step. Until now we have been very effective in the social part and the community support. This is very important and at least that is there. Teaching needs to be addressed more. There is yet a lot to be achieved."

CHAPTER 5

WOMEN'S ACTIVISM THROUGH
NETWORKING

INTRODUCTION

Like chapters 5 and 6, this chapter investigates aspects of women's activism and their impact on civil society. It looks past the NGOs—the concept of civil society that has come to be signified by this form of collaboration—and asks if networks of individuals serve to contribute to a civil society in the UAE. The civil society concept has become synonymous with organizations dedicated to an aim, but that function primarily as a bulwark against the state. Such a concept, coupled with the expectation of change that will be guided from the top down, excludes actors and their actions, and this becomes more problematic in authoritarian, undemocratic environments in which changes are taking place. Because the actors in such a process are tangential, such changes cannot be documented as such.

This chapter is divided into eight sections. The first describes networking activity in the UAE. The section emphasizes a vast array of networking activity that produces effects on the political and societal arenas. The second section explains the indices used to investigate the activism of networkers in civil society. The third presents the profiles of participants. The fourth presents the case study on women's networks. The discussion of this chapter is developed around networks of gooddoers, in general, and importantly, human rights activists. It will be argued that the development of a civil society in the UAE is steered by this sector of civil society actors. The fifth section examines their impact through the variable of empowerment. The sixth examines the variable of participation and the seventh section studies the variable of civility. In the eighth section, I discuss how women's networking impacts civil society through its various advantages over other forms of collaboration.

Networking is a form of activism that has advantages over all other forms of activism in countries with small populations and the rentier effect. The advantage of networks, especially in repressive environments, has been recognized by an increasing number of studies.[1] Formal organizations have limited capacity to tackle sensitive issues, especially human rights issues. Governments in countries with very low populations can monitor organizational activity more easily because fewer organizations exist. Organizations are more easily co-opted due to the generous funding provided by such governments in an endeavor to steer and contain the organizations' agendas. I shall argue in this chapter that amongst all the civil society actors in the UAE, this sector is making the greatest strides in building a foundation for civil society.

The concept and function of networking has been closely tied to social movement theory. Much theorization has also revolved around structures and strategies of recruitment into social movements through social ties and the influence of friends for participation.[2] Scholars focus on a multitude of forms of network participation, from extremist to peaceful interest groups. However, despite the breadth of analysis and the various aspects of networking examined, the overwhelming majority of studies frame the function of networks as protest oriented and especially state centered. While many networking activities, also identified in the case study, address government, many of the networkers' actions are embedded within other power structures.

Works on the Middle East are sometimes more helpful in expanding the scope for comprehending networking as being more than state centered, since they recognize the embeddedness of these networks in a sociohistoric system that supports informal collaboration for a variety of interests. For instance, Asef Bayat proposes the "quiet encroachment of the ordinary" in describing the agency of the poor in a case study on Cairo's poorest areas and the individuals' slow but effective impact on state resources.[3] His case study on Iran similarly shows how the poor utilize networks as a survival strategy.[4] Diane Singerman, too, exposes the agency of Cairo's poor in networking to attain greater economic access and services and to influence politics.[5] Janine Clark adopts a different focus from the many works on Islamist movements that accentuate the activities of fringe Islamists in terror organizations and elaborates instead on mainstream Islamist networks that contribute to development. Her study on net-

works within the Islamist movement in Cairo, Yemen, and Jordan
links the concept of networking to development, predominantly of
the middle class; thus, she shatters the assumption that the activities
of the Islamist groups are directed at providing services mainly for
the poor.[6] Guilain Denouex's work shows that networks can be used
for both political stability and urban unrest.[7] And although
Sangeetha Purushothaman's work is not Middle East-based and focuses primarily on the impact of actions on the state, her study on
India illustrates the function of networks in advancing women's interests and rights.[8] This study reveals that the concept of networking
is especially applicable to civil society theorization in authoritarian
contexts.

I position this argument in the idea of agency of actors in the production of meaning. As David Snow and Robert Benford argue, actors are not merely carriers of extant ideas and meanings that have
resulted from structural arrangements, unanticipated events, or existing ideologies; rather they engage in the production and maintenance
of meaning.[9] A structuralist approach to social movement theory will
view networks as embedded in identities. Structuralist approaches
emphasize identities, values, and social networks as determining factors for participation. Rationalist approaches emphasize the role of
human agency. As discussed in the previous chapters, desires and
the formation of particular selves are attached to a historical context.
Thus, while "rational" decisions are made according to the cost of
participating on an individual basis, actions within network activism
cannot be viewed as disconnected from the discursive traditions to
which meanings are attached and from which an individual's worldview has been fashioned.

The objectives of the case study networks vary and change according to circumstance and needs; however, the major foci are human
rights empowerment, public benefit, and charity attained through
what makes up the most grassroots-level strategy of collaboration,
that is, networking. These networks were found to bridge various ideologies, as indicated through the collaboration of individuals whose
identities belonged to different ideological groups. As such, discourse
was, in most respects, not limited to Islamic or Islamist goals or na-
tionalistic aspirations. Concerns articulated in their talks did include
Islamist concerns on morality and globalization, but as these themes
have already been discussed in the previous chapter, they will not be
covered here. Of all the forms of collaboration studied, human rights
issues were articulated only among networks. Thus, studying the transformative capabilities of networks within an authoritarian rentier-based

environment is crucial to a discussion of civil society in similar environments.

I argue that the discourse is grounded in Western discursive traditions on human rights and Islamic orthodoxy. The discourse of the women on human rights violations and human dignity opens new opportunities for activism and mobilization that have an important impact on talks about human development and rights. Thus, I query how such networks impact on civil society expansion by analyzing their discourses and modes of action. The chapter also asks how the networks of "good-doers" contribute to the empowerment of the marginalized, and how their work may expand a civil society. It queries, too, how the networks that form to create better opportunities and access for participating members also involve an empowerment process and develop norms of civility.

FORMS OF NETWORKING IN THE UAE

In defining networks, Mario Diani suggests beginning from the conventional view that refers to networks as "sets of nodes, linked by some form of relationship, and delimited by some specific criteria."[10] Nodes have been used to mean individuals, organizations, and other entities, such as neighborhoods or even states. They have, moreover, referred to events linked by persons or elements of speech.[11] Nodes may be linked directly, as, for example, when two individuals form explicit modes of interaction and interdependence. Modes may be indirectly linked, for example, when two separate organizations overlap in activities without direct collaboration. Nodes may be linked differentially according to terms of contents, emotional intensity, and strength.[12]

Networking in the UAE is a form of organization for individuals to advance specific interests and has its historical roots in traditional tribal society before the advent of modern associations. Individuals networked based on the tribal affiliations to which their identities were attached. Their sense of belonging to a group based on tribal lineage was the basis upon which action to help one another and pursue interests was motivated and guided. Most civil society theorists do not view such forms of organization as part of a civil society, correctly so in the modern context, since tribal affiliations as currently practiced, serve primarily to strengthen internal ties to the exclusion of others and results in greater discrimination based on one's heritage or lineage. However, seen in historical light, networking through tribal cohesion was a necessary and practical means for survival that fostered values of civility between and amongst some of the other tribes. Yet it is hard to recognize such a system as a forerunner for civil society activism because of an ethnocentric bias that has also trained us to recognize civil society activity as urban based and the source for state-centered activism. The networks outlined here also stem from this historical setting and have continued to grow and take on added value due to the political environment. The present forms of networking have variants, some of which, I maintain, form the most effective means for civil society expansion and growth among alternatives, though some forms of networking will be at war with civil society. Most studies linking networks to civil society activity or social change discuss the effectiveness of networks by analyzing their structures.[13] By elucidating the spectrum of networks through a few examples (see below), I attempt instead to delineate, in terms of civility and purpose, which forms are, or are not, conducive to a civil society.

Networking is not inherently an act that is virtuous or civil. In the context of the UAE, it is also used by extremist groups to collect funds and recruit members for resistance initiatives abroad and, furthermore, is used by mafia groups in the UAE to smuggle women and children into the country. For instance, one mafia group networked with prominent individuals within the UAE, in the surrounding region, and with countries in Eastern Europe to smuggle teenage girls and young women into the country for forced prostitution. While the group's activities could also be referred to as organized crime, the people they worked with enabled their interests to be achieved, since a web of connections was formed with people who had an interest in benefiting from the actions of the group. In this sense, all parties involved were able efficiently to smuggle a large number of young women into the country through networking abilities. Another mafia group smuggled toddlers and small children to be used as camel jockeys into the UAE and surrounding region on a large scale from the poorer neighboring countries of Southeast Asia. Mafia members and wealthy and prominent persons cooperated to form a network over borders to make this happen. And, as previously discussed, extremist Islamists are recruiting and collecting funds to fight what they refer to as the "occupiers of Iraq." Networking can involve criminal acts and acts of terror; therefore, it can work against civility and freedoms.

Networks can comprise horizontal ties or vertical collaboration. Horizontal network ties, that is, ties between nodes within the public sector (such as civil organizations or participants of relatively equal rank), are generally hailed as the means to the formation of social capital. In the literature, vertical collaboration often refers to ties of patronage, including ties to state actors or any person in a higher hierarchy of influence.[14] The phenomenon of *wasta* may be included in this understanding. *Wasta* refers to the person who mediates or intercedes, as well as the act of mediation or intercession.[15] Historically, *wasta* in Arabic literature described mediation on one's part in a dispute between individuals or a group. It could also be for a cause, that is, when an individual served as the referrer of a potential bridegroom or bride to a searching family. Today, it has taken on the intercessory meaning of a link between two or more persons, often of lower and higher ranks, by which a person, usually (though not always) of a lower rank, can achieve some personal benefit, such as a job position. In the UAE, this link is typically based on tribal or familial affiliation, or on friendships between individuals. In lay terms, *wasta* has come to substitute for "connection" or "influence."

Wasta has been widely recognized as the cause of unfair treatment. Inequality in access results when a particular individual or group has the strongest *wasta,* and other capable persons or groups find a barrier to resources, opportunities, or upward mobility. Consequently, *wasta* has also been credited for economic sluggishness. Thomas cites the problem created by *wasta* when daughters of the elite in the UAE pose as an example of success. To her these women are masking the reality of the struggle faced by less privileged women to achieve success in a business career.[16] Speaking about the dangerous ramifications of *wasta* and favoritism, Hadeel Qazzaz notes, "There is an intricate relationship between corruption, favoritism, and WASTA, as they all create an atmosphere of mistrust because people will depend on personal and familial ties instead of qualifications and expertise in assuming public jobs."[17]

So, for example, the al-Nahayan, with other members of the family's Bani Yas tribe, control the most important positions in Abu Dhabi's emirate and federal government, including the military, the Abu Dhabi National Oil Company (and related companies) and the Abu Dhabi Investment Authority, with 14 members of a total of 17 on the Executive Council and eight out of eleven members on the Supreme Petroleum Council board.[18] As Van der Meulen notes, this means the effective control over the federal and provincial governments is exercised by a tribe that represents less than 10 percent of all nationals across the UAE, and 30 percent of nationals of the emirate.[19] The Dhawahir tribe is taking prominence over other tribes previously closer to the al-Nahayan and with their appointments make up 16 out of the 17 members on the Executive Council and ten out of 11 members on the Supreme Petroleum Council.[20] Thus, through the forging of a new network of loyal supporters the al-Nahayan tribe ensures the strengthening of its political and economic position. Such examples illustrate how competitors are deprived of the right to equal access, while the elite achieve firmer control of economic and political power. Networking through *wasta* based on familialism undermines civil interaction and further weakens civil society.

Though scholars argue that intercessory *wasta* furthers a person's interests, and so harms the collective interest, Robert Cunningham and Yasin Sarayrah have pointed out that among Middle Eastern states intercessory *wasta* is the norm, and that it functions as insurance for an individual's social, psychological, and economic well-being.[21] *Wasta* is a major part of life in the UAE. On one hand, networking through *wasta* occurs mostly with a lack of sense of social responsibility. On the other hand, Individuals network through *wasta* for a variety of reasons beyond mere self-interest. Good-doers often require the help of individuals in important or strategic positions. Since *wasta* is, in effect, the norm, civil society work must sometimes be achieved via networking with those who can exert influence.

Networking is used as a means to attain what some individuals hold to be a good thing and others a bad thing. For example, unofficially two separate interest groups formed through the networking of individuals, one wishing to see women retire after 15 years of service, and the other not wishing to see women leave public life so quickly. The idea began with a small number of upper-class women who discussed the idea and brought it to the attention of the ruling family, apparently in Dubai initially, but then with support from women in Abu Dhabi, Ajman, and Sharjah, after which it was officially taken up within the women's GONGO associations. Women who opposed the idea, though fewer in number, entered the discourse and attempted to advance their position by writing letters to the amirs, or by telephoning talk shows and radio programs. Networking is used for competing ends.

Networks that comprise the case study for activism in civil society development in the UAE normally include the nodes that represent individuals. As such, we speak predominantly of networks of individuals in which individuals are loosely tied to one another. In other words, persons will maintain regular means of communication and interaction to produce a desired effect or attain a specific goal that the participants share. At times, the nodes represent individuals connected to groups or organizations, but in this chapter nodes do not comprise organizations collaborating with other organizations. Social movement networks whose activities fall outside the scope of civil society, such as those that advocate any form of violence, are not situated within this case study.

INDICES OF CIVIL SOCIETY ACTIVISM

The indices used to determine the effectiveness of the women in this study were empowerment, participation, and civility. As with the investigation of the previous forms of collaboration in this study, empowerment is a crucial component for making sense of the impact these networks have on civil society development. Women produce empowered selves when they share information, pursue education, and take action together to challenge an oppressive structure. This includes participants seeking to better the conditions of others, or simply advancing their individual positions financially. Power is exercised and distributed throughout society when participants seek improvement, better conditions, happiness, or a greater good in collaborating either for themselves or the marginalized.

In studying the actions of the women, the chapter uses a model that differentiates strategic interests from practical interests to explain how the various interests can motivate women toward participation. Whereas feminist literature generally differentiates the two forms of interests and "hierachializes" strategic over practical gender interests, this chapter argues that both modalities of action are equally important for understanding civil society processes. Some activities involve responses to immediate needs, or women may pursue practical interests, such as sharing information or resources to improve their economic positions. Other activities involve actions that are strategically aimed at bettering the conditions of a particular group (for example, women, children, laborers, etc.) by more consciously addressing the sources of oppression.[22]

To assess the impact of the activities of these women on civil society development, it is necessary to investigate whether these networks contribute to civility. Such an investigation is determined through analyzing the main values of civility—tolerance, trust, reciprocity, and cooperation. It is crucial to determine civility as a variable among the case study participants, since a civil society expansion cannot be put in motion without people dealing with each other with dignity and respect.

PROFILE OF INTERVIEWEES

The women who took part in the interviews for networks are categorized in table 5 in the appendix. While 20 women were interviewed using the schedule of questions for networkers, the data is used from a net sample of 48 women, most of which also took part in Islamic associations and some in the government-run associations. Further-more, data was also gathered through interaction with dozens of peo-ple outside the case studies who were also involved in various other networks.

As can be seen from table 5, the proportion of locals to nonlocals is 15 to 85 percent. The mean age of 43 is significantly higher than women who participate in associations of this research at around 29. There are two points to be made in this regard. One, university stu-dent activists were not included in this sample. Including all partici-pants of the Islamic oriented associations and GONGO associations who were found to network reduces this age difference substantially. As seen from the table, a pool of 48 women in total make up the case study participants used here. Two, the women who were most out-standing in the communities across the emirates of Dubai, Sharjah, Abu Dhabi, and Ajman were, apart from locals, women who lived longer in the Emirates and, in most cases, had made the UAE their home, irrespective of original citizenship. Among the most vocal and resourceful participants within the networks are women who are es-tablished in the UAE. A higher proportion of nonlocal women com-pared to those in associations, 25 percent, were also married to locals. The mean number of 2.4 children distributed among all 20 intervie-wees, including those without children, is much higher than the two other case study samples. Age might account for the higher number of women married and the higher number of children. However, if we exclude women without children, we have 3.2 children for each woman, which is still high, and what is remarkable is that the category of networkers comprises the women who, I have argued, are the most active. Having a larger number of children does not negatively impact participation levels amongst women in the UAE as nearly all the net-workers within the core sample had at least one maid to free their time from housework and provide care for the children.

Of the participants, 60 percent held jobs or owned a business (20 percent or four women had their own business). This figure roughly compares to the employment level of Islamic-oriented participants at 63 percent. Despite over half of the participants holding positions of employment, 85 percent volunteered their time in at least one more network or association. Participants did not receive any financial benefit from networking. With altogether 2.4 children and over half working in paid employment, women were, nonetheless, normally in-volved in more than one avenue for activism. Women who network do not, as a rule, allow two seemingly major obstacles to activism to get in their way—family and work. Again, together with high levels of motivation, house help is indispensable in this regard. Networks comprise, furthermore, the most resilient and courageous activists, as will be argued in the section on human rights activism.

Of all women, 70 percent had at least a B.A. degree, which is slightly lower than the percentages for women in the two other case study samples. All women, except one, nevertheless, had attended a postsecondary institution. Moreover, 30 percent or six out of the 20 women had attained an M.A. level, and five percent or one person a law degree in addition to a B.A. Two women had attained a Ph.D. and one with an M.A. level was close to completion of a Ph.D., making the overall number of those with graduate degrees half! Ten of the 20 women or 50 percent received some level of postsecondary education in universities located in Europe or North America. This is considerably greater than the percentage of Islamic activists and GONGO associations. A Western education seems to be a factor in the greater participation levels of networkers and the way they approach activism. A higher education might be pointed to as a reason, but all participants with postgraduate degrees except two received their educations in a Western university. Of those with postsecondary educations, 35 percent had degrees in social sciences (language, history, sociology, or law), 30 percent in business, management, or computer science, 5 percent in science, 5 percent in fine arts, 15 percent in medicine, and 10 percent in Islamic theology.

A Western education or experience in volunteerism in the West as a factor in higher activism levels is supported, moreover, in women's narrations on which skills enabled them to be active. While most interviewees understood the question on motivating factors to mean managerial skills, communication skills, friendliness or patience, respectively, 15 percent or three of the 20 women answered the knowledge they had gained from the West played a role in their present activism. Two participants, one American and one Emirati, named a profound understanding of what volunteerism means in America. The two had gained experiences participating in associations and with their general knowledge derived from their experiences sought to implement the concept of activism in any way they could in the UAE. The third participant, a British born Pakistani raised in Holland, named the basic willingness of people (in the West) to smile at others and offer help as a source of motivation to her activism in the UAE. All three participants dedicated hours daily to various forms of activity. Activism and volunteerism are clearly concepts that are part of the Gulfian heritage and modes of interacting. However, such testimonies coupled with the fact that the case study group with the highest level of activity has by far more individuals with Western educations points to a Western influence as a factor in elevated activism levels among networkers. Several more interviewees stated or alluded that the concept of volunteerism was a Western concept that members of society would eventually come to understand, though some interviewees asserted that society has forgotten what volunteerism means because people have forgotten their religion. In this regard, these women looked at their goals of reaching higher standards of human rights and dignity for the oppressed as understood in the West through awakening the consciousness in Islamic terminology. This process was expected to be incremental through education, with an acute understanding of Bedouin heritage and recent rapid technological development, but at times needed to be sped up by bringing in media attention for further reflection. That noted, however, the motivating factors to secure justice and greater well-being, described later, also indicate that not only the concept of volunteerism, but also a human rights perspective has its variants deeply rooted in the Islamic tradition. The concept volunteerism, as having been largely one-on-one, or justice in the Islamic tradition is not fixed, but rather changes due to the new challenges in the local context.

UAE Women's Networks

The participants for networking focused on a wider range of activity than the associations discussed in this book, though they worked along much the same lines. Their focus was on human rights issues, collecting funds, and providing charity. The categories of activism found within networks included the following: providing medical care; provision of shelter for men, women, and children; struggling to free persons from situations of oppression; giving voice to the oppressed; and contesting opinions or views through various forms of discursive space; regularly sharing/giving of time, comforting unrelated individuals; providing food, clothing, household items, money, toys, etcetera; providing various forms of education or lessons, or funding education; and counseling (professional and nonprofessional). If a person is unable to fulfill a particular role, such as performing an operation, the person will call on the appropriate person within her network or request the help of a friend.

The participants seek to accomplish such tasks sometimes on an individual basis, with just two persons, a handful, or dozens. Thus, it is not possible to give the precise number of networks that became part of this study. For example, a handful of women together would call friends/contacts to collect money and clothes for some very poor school children, some of them orphaned, and a few who were saved from camel jockeying. All visited two schools[23] with gifts and clothing, particularly during the Eid celebrations, and on such occasions would need the help of peripheral participants. Even so, a few individuals from the network would visit the schools on their own on a more regular basis, having collected goods and money from other networks they were connected to, to give the children more time, affection, and attention. Even though the network was regularly nurtured through the activism of a handful of women, most participants participated in one large Islamic organization and could request help for this project, among others, through affiliation to the organization. A few members participated regularly in another organization and were able to build contacts there. As such, the network's goals can be followed through by one person and can easily involve dozens of individuals at any given time. Consequently, a network is fluid among other networks; it also shrinks and grows, or requires fewer or more members, depending on the type of activity at a given moment.

EMPOWERMENT

A Human Rights Discourse: The Silence Broken by Networks

Whereas discussion of human rights problems was generally absent in the formal associations, discourse among networks includes human rights issues. No other form of collaboration was brave enough to articulate human rights abuses or confront the sources of these abuses in the way women's networks did in the UAE. Thus, I will argue that gender is a factor in the shaping of selves conducive to pushing for greater rights and freedoms. In many of the networks, a somewhat defiant self was constructed when women learned to stand up to oppressive structures and forms of dominance. From such a production come women who play a pivotal role in advancing civil society values by breaking a silence over human rights abuses. Consequently, the women are in the process of slowly enabling a discourse among individuals, state actors, and media in which human rights concerns may be articulated.

Women are viewed as more active in civil society. When 16 individuals, men and women, local and other Arab, were asked in a group setting whether they felt gender made a difference in activism level in the region, the overwhelming majority confirmed that gender played a pivotal role and that women dominated activism. Explanations ranged from, "women have more time" to the most exemplary of the views, "women have a bigger heart; they feel more for the people." The few who differed, Saudis themselves, pointed to restrictions imposed on women's mobility in public in Saudi Arabia, a different context from the UAE. As such, there is the sociological expectation in the UAE that women will lead the way in extending help to the marginalized and poverty stricken.

Women demonstrated that they lead the way in taking risks to confront rights issues affecting especially women and children. An interviewee tells how she took a risk to assist a woman affected by laws that disadvantaged a woman and her children:

I helped a woman get over the border of Oman. I was on . . . [name of station] TV and I was talking about myself. I had them put my phone number on satellite TV while I was talking for any networking possibilities. I always think, maybe I can make a difference. Networking, that is the best way to do things. I got calls from Tunisia, Germany, etcetera. I got a call from a woman in Abu Dhabi. She was married for 13 years. She had two kids of her own and two other kids. When she arrived she found her husband acted totally different. He became harsh and cold. The minute she got off the airplane he took their passports. He was always out. Then he announced he had another wife. She ran away from him after he beat her and went to the police for help. She was arrested and put in prison for five days. She was only allowed to call her husband. He came and got her and took her back to their apartment. He was mean and abusive to her. She called me. She told me she had a travel ban. This was on the day before one of her sons' passports was to expire. I could not get her out. I could not hide her. Her husband was going into surgery that morning. We were going to take a huge risk. We called the ambassador in Oman. He said he could not help her until she was at the embassy. They could not get her over the border and they could not drive her to the American embassy from the border either. She would be helped only once she arrived at the embassy. I drove her to the Omani border and I could not go further with her. So, I had to drop her off with her two small children. The problem was getting her past the police. At the border you need to have stamps for insurance and have the passports stamped. She came into the UAE with a UAE passport [the woman and children, thus, needed to have the same passports to exit the country, but only had American passports]. If I took her over, we would all get arrested. I told her to walk behind the police and behind a taxi car. She had to first walk to Masafi. She walked with her sons. It was so tense. And then it was such a horrible sight to see her walking away with her two small kids. I did know if they would make it. I called the ambassador in Muscat. The Ambassador waited. It took her six hours. The ambassador said they arrived safely.

In such examples, women are taking practical steps to defy laws that govern women's lives until human rights organizations can be permitted to operate to confront endemic problems more systematically. The literature on rational choice articulates the view that people will calculate the cost of activism and opt not to participate in an activity that will cost them too much.[24] Such works are unhelpful in explaining participation in collective action in high risk activities.[25] However, works that have pointed to the embeddedness of individuals in specific identities may contribute more insight. Doug McAdam argues the most important variable in participation studies that is largely ignored is gender.[26] The collective experience and recognition of marginalization may result in higher activism levels among women who tackle gender specific discrimination. However, what functions as a motivator is probably a combination of gender solidarity, a religiously held or moral obligation, or what Mara Loveman refers to as "prosocial" collective action and identity after Martín-Baró, in which commitment to community or greater good outweighs individual needs.[27]

The above interviewee identifies the systemic problems of discrimination against women. She points to an accumulation of harsh precedents made mostly by Egyptian and Sudanese judges with regard to cases filed against abusive husbands or by women wanting a divorce. She also notes how the police have handled cases of domestic violence. Through these, together with the traditions and mentalities that regard women as the property of men, such a structure of inequality is maintained and institutionalized. The consequence of a mentality that views women as the property of men is shown in a fatal case. In winter 2004, a Jordanian woman in Ajman had poured gasoline over herself in the desperate hope that her husband might be shocked at the expression of her suffering after years of physical abuse. Instead, when he entered the house he lit a match and threw it on her, killing her in front of their two young children. According to interviewees, just before her death she had again gone to the police to plead for protection after her husband had beaten her, only to be returned to her husband. Reportedly the most the police did was to admonish the man not to do such things.

The structural forms of oppression experienced by women also affect children. As such, the modes of action of networkers to contest oppressions against women and children are similar. Interviewees attest child abuse is a serious problem. One interviewee begged to take children from families who repeatedly abused their children. Interviewees also confirmed that police did not intervene in cases in the UAE in which child abuse had occurred. In her plea, the interviewee based

her position on a well-established system in the Islamic discursive tradition in which the state is interpreted as the responsible structure to
care for individuals when individuals cannot adequately care for themselves. That was not accepted, and the similar argument was applied as
is applied for women in situations of abuse—the children are not the
responsibility of the state; just as the woman belongs to her husband,
they belong regardless to the mother and father if they are alive. The
interviewee then took pictures of the abused children. One toddler
(photographed for an appeal to take him from his family) eventually
had multiple bone fractures and subsequently died. In one instance,
the participant's camera was confiscated by the police. However,
through her *wasta*, a tribal sheikh, her camera was returned.

Because a child born out of wedlock takes on its main identity as a
bastard in the sense that it has lost all rights, including that to life,
babies are left to die out of starvation at police stations, after their
mothers have abandoned them.[28] These situations arise because of a
mentality that has developed from dominant historical discourses, and
has been cemented and further shaped through actors on the ground.
For example, actors include judges who, in effect, establish that a
woman belongs to her husband; and/or the police who confirm the
belonging of one human being to another, and so, in practical terms,
deny the oppressed, whether a woman or a child, the right to protection by a state apparatus.

When pleading to take a newborn baby home with them or to feed
it, the response received by networkers was that such babies were ille-
gitimate. This specific response is, furthermore, symptomatic of a form
of socialization in which rights and freedoms are attached to class,
one's lineage, or a parent's position. While some interviewees said the
police did not know any better and substantiated an inevitably slow
process of education as a means to tackle such issues, such actions on
part of individuals can, however, serve to strengthen a system in which
women and children as a group are repressed and subjected to abuse,
and even death. Other interviewees confronted these issues directly.
When this happens a discourse takes place between the networkers and
those in places of authority, in which themes of rights to human dignity, basic well-being, and life are articulated.

One human rights issue spearheaded by a small number of women
(well before it hit the international media and only recently recording
any notable success along the way) is the trafficking of small children
for use as camel jockeys. Members of the network would pose as
tourists and enter the places where the boys were kept to take pictures
of the children. The women would scour the country to list and locate

the places where children were used. With the proofs and information they had gathered, they would address persons in government, which was the platform on which they struggled through years of debate and protest. One participant would address the mafia directly. Sometimes members simply roamed particular areas looking for children who could escape, and occasionally finding them and taking them to places of refuge, including their own homes. Another network was found to be addressing the issue; however, it was unable to effect changes. These women gathered statistics and data via the countries from which children were taken, and attempted to publish the findings through local media. This strategy proved unproductive as the media refused to have anything to do with the cause. Though the local media (the *Khaleej Times*) did eventually cover some facets of the issue, the local media is nervous about publishing anything that is critical of heads of state or prominent figures, or that may affect the local economy and currency.[29]

Child camel jockeying was highlighted outside the borders of the UAE via a reporter who documented some of its aspects in 2002. Though this was not the first time discussion on the issue had taken place outside the country, the reporter's endeavors began to bring some international attention.[30] Until this point, great secrecy had surrounded its occurrence and networkers were afraid that any outside attention would destabilize their efforts on the ground, and that interventionist strategies would undermine the help they had been extending to some of the children. Correspondingly, when I first witnessed a situation where two severely malnourished children, one brain damaged, had been picked up by members of one of the networks, I was made to promise never to divulge what I had seen or any of the related activities of the participants. This strategy was judged the best route, given the repercussions feared by the networkers and given they felt they were making a difference on the ground that no one else was able to at the time.[31] The strategy of secrecy among the first network changed three years later, as I will explain below.

Children as young as two years old are used as camel jockeys; many are around four years of age. Small children are used because they are very light and when they scream the camels run faster. In this way the camels are trained to run at top speeds. The children frequently fall off the camel. In some instances they are trampled over by another camel, which results in injuries and in a small number of cases, brain damage or death. A few thousand children have been brought in as one of the networkers attests. Another interviewee argued, however, that the numbers were more accurately in the "tens of thousands."

Children will be sold for up to DH20,000 each. The mafia group responsible for trafficking children into the UAE usually comes from the countries from which the children are taken, mainly Pakistan, and its members are dispersed throughout the Arabian Gulf. Some very wealthy Pakistani families also network with the mafia. The children are taken from Kazakhstan, Bangladesh, India, Pakistan, and specifically the Punjab, Baluchistan and tribal areas of Pakistan. They are sometimes kidnapped in their countries of origin, and are less frequently kidnapped within the UAE. They are most often sold by their own parents. Sometimes the parents are told their children will be given a job caring for camels and that their children will receive not only money, but also shelter and food for their work. The children receive no money. They are starved and given little water, so that they remain lightweight. All are physically abused, and several can show where wounds have been inflicted. Several, if not the majority, have been repeatedly molested and raped.

If the children are taken from parents residing in the UAE, the parents are usually more aware of what happens to them. It is normally the father, looking for a meager profit to support an addiction, who sells the child. However, I also spoke to a mother who was responsible for sending her son off to camel jockeying because she could not support her five children, all girls.[32] None of the families where she lived could send their children to schools. It seemed as though some parents were not even aware of the whereabouts of small toddlers who roamed about freely where they wished. Small children, abandoned by families living in dreadfully poor conditions in relatively secluded local villages, easily fall prey either to kidnappers or to relatives who sell them. Some of these villages are close to some of the most beautiful areas in the UAE, with high-rise blocks, shops, and clubs. Others are located in more mountainous parts of the country. Some of the villages are so secluded that the military does not immediately learn of their existence. One rather large village was only discovered by the military when some of its inhabitants kidnapped Emirati children. Because the inhabitants of such villages are illegal, seeking help from the authorities for missing children will entail their deportation. However, the fact that the Emirati children bore the citizenship of the country prompted immediate action.

Another human rights issue that has been pursued by networkers is the trafficking of young women and teenage girls for prostitution. Young women are brought into the country after being told that they will work in various respectable jobs. Upon arrival they find themselves forced to perform as prostitutes in various establishments, including the many that cater to businessmen. The persons who network with the mafia are well positioned politically and financially to traffic the women, some of them as young as 14. Therefore, the risks the women take in opening any discourse on the process and nature of trafficking are high. The mode of action of the networkers is to collaborate with officers and officials to take the women who have been jailed for prostitution and raise funds through networking to send them home. Even collaborating with officers poses many hurdles, as the police do not know to discriminate between women who are being raped and forced to submit to sexual exploitation as a commodity, and the thousands of women, also from Eastern Europe, who have bought their own tickets to the Gulf to work in prostitution.[33] Nonetheless, based on trust, officers have allowed the networkers to rescue several women. Many of the women trafficked are in the UAE on false passports so that if they are ever caught by the police they are not sent to their homes, but to another country where they will be picked up again by the mafia and sent to another country in the Gulf. Thus, when the women who network provide help, support, and counseling and send these rescued women back to their families by buying them tickets and getting them to their destinations legally (through *wasta*), they are defying an elaborate and powerful system of exploitation and abuse in an environment in which not everyone is able to understand the issue as abduction and rape.

Confrontation is not always the best way to tackle human rights abuses. Success in developing a human rights consciousness has sometimes required immense patience and tact on the part of the networkers. So, when a participant could not accept that children were being kept in police stations for several years without any education or adequate care, she had to restrain her frustration and persist with establishing trust with the officers over long periods before she was in a position to do anything. She tells how she had to deal with a prosecutor in the police department who had authority over the children being kept at one of the largest police stations:

I had to first soften her. She was so hardened she simply would not interact with the baby. She does not see the child. I wanted to take Munira.[34] She was abandoned as a baby. She was used as a slave by a relative of hers who would burn her. She lived at the police station for 10 years. I wanted to place her in a family, give her another chance. She deserves an education. She is 12 and does not know how to read. Sultan has also been living at the police station for 10 years. What I want to do is build a shelter for kids where they can experience dignity. It is about time we change the system. I seemed eventually to be able to make friends with her [the officer]. So at last I at least walked out with the girl, Munira. . . . I felt she [the officer] was a hard person. She said to me, "Look at her. She will run away." But I explained to her I treat her with respect and dignity. I started to infiltrate the human rights department. I would spend three hours a day. I would be there every day, studying how they handle their cases. I won their hearts over. . . . They assumed I was there because of *dawa*. . . . I would give *dawa*. I would make little suggestions without intimidating them. I would take over a case having to do with a woman and let them watch. I would mediate situations very successfully most of the time. By the will of Allah through several more cases I took on I was able to calm things down. So, I got their respect. The director felt threatened at some point. I made differences there not according to his rules. So I had to step back. But then, the officers would automatically call me. Because they would keep calling me without their boss knowing for my help I became validated. So, in front of the Sheikh my cases come from the police. I am being called because they believe in me. They would slip my phone number to the women [women in various situations at the police, though mostly allegedly prostitutes who are really trafficked]. They do the same thing in the immigration department. So, I also have back up from immigration. All this validates me. This was my strategy—to gain validation. If I did not get this validation I would have been stopped.

The strategies implemented by many of the women in their networking endeavors include references to Islamic symbols. Establishing oneself as a traditional respectful "mother," who is taking her place as a protector of Islamic symbols is less confrontational, less threatening to the established order. Such expression to secure legitimacy is crucial in a patriarchal society if a woman expects to push change. Validation can only be achieved if the participant is able to demonstrate that she understands the language of the power holders she is dealing with. Crucially, the subtle message she must get across is that she wants to help her society, not correct how things should be done. In other words, she must work from the inside, not from the outside. In this manner, participants place themselves strategically in the most advantageous position from which they may exercise power.

Dominant discursive traditions can change only incrementally through actors who link their frames to orthodoxy. Charles Tilly describes the effect of ongoing conversations that occur between social movement actors: "Conversation in general shapes social life by altering individual and collective understandings, by creating and transforming social ties, by generating cultural materials that are then available for subsequent social interchange, and by establishing, obliterating, or shifting commitments on the part of participants."[35] As such, a human rights discourse is also constructed within the Islamic discursive tradition.

Adoption according to most Islamic scholars is forbidden. Mainly it would erase the lineage of the child if by adopting the host family's name the child is prevented from learning its roots and take resources away from natural children, a device to protect families. Although several orphanages exist, taking unrelated children into one's home, however, is also illegal according to UAE law. A child is a *yatim* (orphan) even if its mother is still living. Based on this definition, children who are without both parents or without a father, the latter viewed as the breadwinner, have a right to be supported by the community according to dominant religious interpretation.

A group of Islamists (among the *Ikhwan*) has opened their homes to children who cannot be cared for by their parents, so that they are given care, love, education, and importantly, an Islamic upbringing. If a child is found to need a home, a member of this network will activate the link to find an appropriate home. A group of Islamists are helping both groups of children—those who have no parents at all and those who only have a mother. This group of Islamists also makes some changes in the definition of a *yatim* according to their practice. In a few instances, the father is a local and alive, but pays no support to the divorced wife. In these circumstances the wife is a foreigner and so has been denied legal rights and cannot support the children.[36] Lack of citizenship can entail deprivation, even if one's children are local. Thus, not only are the actions of these Islamists a means by which women and their children's oppressions can be alleviated, but they are also a means by which a wider sense of responsibilization of the "Islamic community" is reached—here taking on what in other countries would also be a form of social services provided by the state.

First, these Islamists are defying laws that forbid taking children into private homes. However, in their actions, this network of foster parents alters the definition of a *yatim* by also caring for children whose fathers are alive and well. The view of the state, based on chosen Islamic referents, is that children are the responsibility of the father. However, the discourse on who should be considered an orphan and the rights of an orphan is of crucial importance because rights-based articulations reverberate within a number of interconnected discourses having to do with oppressive structures and resistance within a strictly socially and economically stratified society. Thus, even though adapting the definition of *yatim* might not seem very significant to a Westerner, all practical changes on the ground influence the way a particular group is viewed through discourse framing, and consequently treated. The change that is occurring in this example has been fashioned within the Islamic discursive tradition due to changing dynamics locally that bring about new dilemmas.

However, given that half the case study networkers had received a Western education, and that some interviewees said their activism was influenced by their experience of volunteerism while living in Western countries, the local discourse is also adopting and absorbing frames from the West. Women's testimonies (refer above to profile of interviewees) confirm that not only are they motivated by a dignity agenda or sense of obligation to their community through nationalist sentiments and Islamic referents, but also that a subjectivation to Western frames of justice has profoundly elevated their sense of responsibility toward others. The skills they acquired in the West has contributed to the emergence of productive selves, as they affirm. Several of the networkers were Westerners themselves married to local men. There is the view that nonlocal women cannot be committed to development of the country. As some of the most vocal women were Western women married to locals this assumption is unfounded. They felt a responsibility to use their worldviews to develop a society in which they felt strongly a part of and in which their own children were rooted. Through their husbands' family names, lineage, or government position, many (not all) were provided resources to vocalize their understanding of a fairer society, basic rights for all and visions for development.

While this observation may be viewed as a natural occurrence, given the strength of Western globalization, it is, indeed, interesting that a Western discourse related to rights and access is synthesized within predominantly local frames. Some of those who use rights talk are not only Western (born or educated) but Islamist. They are fully aware of Western sentiments locally, among their own circles. Several Islamist interviewees made it clear that the vast majority rejected any Western philosophical or ideological constructs. Yet, an Islamist networker wanted to adopt a small boy who had been used as a camel jockey. She took him into her home and gave him the love and material things she gave all her children. When she referred to the boy, she used the terminology "adopted." However, she had also asked an Islamic scholar to supply her with alternative interpretations that would sanction the adoption—as a child raised as a member of her family as opposed to the form of foster care typically provided by those sheltering others in their homes and differentiated from their own children—if she was confronted by authorities. Those women were, thus indeed, motivated by a human rights agenda alongside a sense of duty or obligation.

Furthermore, networks are concerned with the abuse of laborers and maids. A women's network provides laborers with food, as their conditions are considered by networks to be poor. Often the conditions under which laborers work involve long hours of physical work in the heat.[37] Abuse includes being fed two buns, soup, and water as a day's food ration, as stated in interviews with some laborers, whose pay was only DH450 a month (£65 or $140 US).[38] Abuse also includes living in tiny makeshift metal compartments that reach extreme temperatures in the heat, and with no toilet. Abuse, furthermore, includes working under dangerous conditions, in which lives are threatened, and hundreds have actually been lost, if one counts two recent accidents in one of the emirates, which no official was allowed to discuss.[39] To help improve their living conditions, networkers call in the press to cover these observations, and these issues are increasingly being covered by the media. For example, networkers called the local press to cover the company that made their workers sleep in "tin cans" in the heat. The situation was remedied as a result, and the laborers were provided with more adequate shelter. Thus, women's networks address the deprivation and abuse of laborers in various ways. In doing so, they bring awareness to situations of oppression, while at the same time mitigating the oppressions on the ground.

The discourse on maids in the UAE is attached to the destructive and negative influences they have on the children they look after. Most other forms of articulation regarding the issue of maids are attacked for exaggerating their victimization. Awareness of the abusive situations of some maids is led by a female academic in the UAE who gives lectures and seminars on the problem. However, no research on maids in the UAE has to date recognized their proactive actions to network together to mitigate oppressive conditions and locate advantageous opportunities. This is a project by itself, but what I argue here is that the situations of abuse or oppression experienced by many maids are not only addressed by good-doers outside the class circle of the maids, but mostly by the maids themselves in whatever capacities they are able to assume.

In one case, two maids working for the same employer would be yelled at and at times slapped on the face. They were new to the country and could not imagine speaking up directly for themselves. They asked another maid to come to the house where they worked to stand up for them. The maid who was called in had previously worked for the employer and had been in the Gulf for nearly 20 years. Given her language skills and elderly status she was able to intervene on the two women's behalf and "talk back" to the employer, warning him never to do such a thing again. According to her, her plea was respected.

Another Filipino maid eventually married a local and started up a business with him that included the running of a large cafeteria. Most of the employees were maids who had run away from their employers. At the time of interview, six maids were being given shelter and a place to earn money until they could find work by this woman and her husband. All six maids had reportedly suffered physical abuse. Because they all belonged to a network to which this woman and her husband were connected, they were in a position to find help. In another case a maid was severely abused. She was not allowed to eat anything from the fridge, had only six hours a day off her job to sleep, and was repeatedly physically abused by her female employer. Her condition was worsening. Another maid observed what was happening through the windows of the house in which she worked. With her employer's support, the observer pulled the maid from the house and later passed her to her network to be cared for. Such small-scale collaboration sometimes translates into larger networks. For example, a church in one of the major cities has become a nodal point for several maids' networks because of the dedication of a woman churchgoer and her husband to the cause of helping abused and runaway maids and laborers in desperate conditions. Through this couple, several maids have been able to find shelter and emotional support, they have been able to return home through the funds raised.

Whether they are struggles for personal freedom or for the freedom and dignity of others, these forms of networking are central to the study of civil society actions. Each form of oppression raised as a concern by the networkers enables the development of a discourse on rights. An expansion of civil society is occurring through the various strategies by which individuals attempt to effect change. When people defy dominant views and confront those in power positions through such acts, they eventually change practices and laws. Such acts are on the ground, are not in any sort of "limelight," and are rarely in the media. However, networking to educate, to debate, to save the lives of innocent children and babies, to raise children who would otherwise be severely disadvantaged because of lack of rights, or to liberate women in abusive situations or from forced prostitution must be considered as some of the most effective modes of challenging a system that is not being dealt with by other sectors of a civil society.

POWER FOR: BETTERING THE CONDITIONS
OF THE DEPRIVED

Charity and "doing good" to others was a major focus among networks. Networkers' participation was largely characterized by philanthropic work which involved collaboration with one or more persons to alleviate pain or suffering of others. Not only funding would be provided, but also nonmaterial care, such as counseling. Networkers were also active in the provision of resources for learning development. Such education could include Islamic *dawa*, language lessons or the possibility for children to enter schools by paying school fees. Networks of good-doers help in various ways to develop the individual self. Such work not only serves to better the conditions of individual persons but challenges systematic forces of oppression and engages contesters over meanings and symbols. As such, these women contribute to civil society.

A participant's narration of her philanthropic work illustrates the various modes of participation individuals networks can typically sustain:

It doesn't matter who I help. I am genuine about that. I help mostly women, but also some men. If someone has medical problems—cancer, kidney problems, etcetera, I provide the medical care I can. I come to know about them through friends. I am not in direct contact with the people who ask for help. In other situations I help financially. Maybe I give clothing. . . . I help the . . . [name of Islamic organization]. I give lectures and help out in other activities. I give lectures on anything—the *sahaba*, the Prophet's life, the battles, history, a social topic. These are for boys under ten; the age group is seven to 10 and girls seven to 12. . . . With friends we hold a tea party or coffee morning once a week. The host will have me give a 10 minute lecture. I used to go to hospitals. Since seven months I am not. A friend and I would go to the children's ward and take goody bags and *zamm zamm* water. For the staff we bring cookies. We go to each room and talk to the patient's parents, just talk. I have also helped a few patients financially with a small amount. A sister launched a magazine, . . . [name]. It covers topics having to do with the family, youth, women, children. I helped her out. I collected funds. I have written articles for it. I help distribute it here in the UAE. . . . I have been here 18 years. I started to do this kind of work seven years ago when I reverted back to the *deen* [religion]. Before that I would help friends—if someone was sick I would cook food, go the market for her, etcetera. But not for Allah. I was also helping, but we have to make the *niya* to please Allah. I please a person so that Allah is pleased with me. The thought never comes to me not to help. Even if I do not want to, I push myself for the sake of Allah.

The participant's narration demonstrates that her mode of participation is not narrowly conceived to address a single problem or advance a specific idea. Her activism is directed to a number of issues and various persons. While activism that addresses particular issues may also contribute to civil society growth and development, the resolve to simply "do good" is a superior form of activism as such demonstrates a commitment and a responsibilization of the self for the common good of society in general, not a specific strata or internal group. Such an activist will not desist from participating when a project has been completed or a particular task becomes challenging.

Participants sought to better the conditions of the deprived on a number of counts. For example, one network would distribute charity among the laborers. Together with the food they cooked and empty Gulfa water bottles they filled with cold water they would go out to construction sites. They would distribute the food and water every day. Another group of friends would bake and make various crafts. These local women would gather at a woman's house each meeting and sell their goods. They would use the proceeds for local families in need that depended on constant help to survive day to day expenses. A group of university students would network to collect money or clothes for the disadvantaged. Some of the needy were local families that also depended on continued help; some were people outside the country, such as in Iraq or Palestine. Another group of ten women would meet every Monday and hold a party at which each woman would contribute DH300. With the money they buy various items, such as an air conditioning unit for a school, Islamic cassettes to distribute, clothing, gifts, etcetera. Another such example was among a few women who would host over 200 women at either of the two homes usually three times a year, such as during Ramadan. They would provide a lavish dinner for which entry tickets would be purchased, usually for DH100. Women were encouraged to bring jewelery and fashionable dresses to be auctioned off. The money collected would be used for various charities specifically for women.

Civil society expansion is achieved in these women's activisms on two fronts. The first is the empowerment process the good-doers sustain and nurture when they extend the various forms of material and nonmaterial benefits to deprived men, women, and children. The networks are contributing to the empowering of marginalized groups that have no other recourse to aid and help. When networkers contribute to the dignity, respect, health, and lives of individuals, a crucial empowerment process occurs. Women who struggle for practical goals, such as better economic status, also contribute to self-empowerment and em-powerment of those they support. Participants in networks pursue various interests that forms a process in which self-sacrifice begets self-satisfaction. As such, when women collaborate together to empower others, they effect a cumulative process that leads to their own em-powerment. When women collaborate together, share skills and expe-riences, and enter a learning process together, women "discipline the self" to be productive agents of civil society. Women, moreover, strengthen themselves as a cohesive group, and with their solidarity establish a stronger voice to contend with. Hence, they are a more powerful force as civil society actors.

The second is addressing systemic problems that no other form of organization in the country is capable of or willing to. The issue of workers having inadequate living quarters or food provided by their employers is addressed by these networks, even if the majority of net-works tackle the problem by providing food or medical care. As a 19-year-old female interviewee tells,

I did not receive my pay for four months. We all did not get paid. Four months is too much. I only received my pay the first three months, DH400 and we had to buy our own food. . . . My father needs that money. I prom-ised my father I would send money [back to her home country in Sri Lanka] for my brother and my sister every month. . . . They go to school with this money. Now my father is very upset. . . . Mr. Hameed [named changed for boss] is supposed to be in jail for not paying workers. He has made so many workers run away and get into trouble. But he is never in any trouble. He lies about the workers. . . . None of us can talk to him. His position is so high up. . . . If he finds out where I am he will have me deported right away. . . . I ran away with eight others. He will say that I ran away. He gets away with not giving us our pay. He will not get into trouble. I will.

By extending help to the workers, habitually calling the local press to investigate or some participants writing articles themselves as journal-ists, greater awareness is achieved and a discourse has evolved which frames the treatment by some companies of their employers as abuse. Addressing laborers as the poor, demonstrates that those in need of help easily expands to low-level workers in the UAE. Framing a sector of those employed in the Gulf as deprived is the initial step to dis-courses on human rights issues related to employment. The support of local families on a regular basis in the UAE by some of the net-works studied demonstrates a systematic problem of bias in the distri-bution of wealth partially alleviated through the acute awareness of the particular situations on the ground. As stated above, the Ministry of Labor eventually had to decree a new law in 2006 to address some of the problems these networkers have long been addressing.

WHY DO WOMEN NETWORK?

As can be noted from table 5 in the appendix, the participation levels among networks exceeds that of both the GONGO women's associations and Islamic-oriented associations of this study. This section seeks to determine the variables that contribute to higher participation levels and greater impact networks have on social reform. It is important to understand what the driving factors are for women's networking. It is also important to understand what value systems furnish their participation. Apparently, participation is driven by both immediate interests and existentialist goals. The former is important to stress as located within civil society activism, however, as the women seek to alleviate the effects of discrimination and gain greater force. The section will then argue the advantage these forms of collaboration have over the formal modes of collaboration in contributing to civil society and social reform.

Even though networks focused on here are female based, women in the UAE do not network as a women's group might with a conscious identification as a group, "women," nor strategically with conscious feminist goals. Some activities involve responses to immediate needs. Women may pursue practical interests, such as sharing information or resources to better their economic positions. Several participants provided charity, shelter or food for needy women, men, and children in an attempt to alleviate poverty. They may work consciously to mitigate oppressive structures in which women and children fall more easily victim. Some participants counseled abused women and sought to provide them the skills to survive traumatic experiences. None of the women interviewed called themselves feminists. Yet, what is deemed politically relevant in much of the literature includes strategic feminist goals. All the goals the women of the networks here pursue, whether practical or objective-oriented is significant action for the evaluation of civil society. Much of their actions serve to mitigate inequalities and help themselves in some cases and others in most cases in their quest to rise above oppressive structures. These women stand out from other civil society actors, importantly however, because whether they are practical- or strategic-oriented, they assume a responsibility toward themselves and others that enables changes to occur within the social and political arenas.

Literature on the practical concerns pursued by women attempts to cover the activities of poorer women to compensate academics' focus of politically relevant action placed on state actors and people in publicly influential positions. The networking activities of domestic servants in the UAE should also be considered in the same vein. Like anyone else in the region, they flock to the Gulf because of the financial advantage to salaries in their home countries. However, the predominantly Filipino, Indian, Sri Lankan, and Ethiopian maids, respectively, do not make enough money in the vast majority of cases according to UAE law to have family members accompany them. As maids are normally live-in, allowing family members to join is logistically not possible. Nearly 60 percent of all the maids interviewed outside the case study sample had to leave children with relatives in their home countries—normally for several years. Most of the women are either lonely, suffering under depression or are overworked, if not all three. But, they form networks of support to cope with their challenges.

For example, networks are formed between maids of the same social status and between people who enjoy greater freedoms in the UAE. Members are usually bound together through a common ethnicity. Such networks are support for a woman when she suddenly loses her job. If a maid runs away from her employer, as happens frequently, she is often connected through her network to women in another city where she can move more freely. If a member of a network is in need of money to send home for a sudden emergency, among various reasons, she is able to quickly collect money from her network. The network is nurtured through keeping contact with members by phone on a regular basis, the frequent giving of gifts, if merely a special dish and constant reminders that one is available to help in any situation.

Despite the need to illustrate the activities of poorer women as relevant to civil society when they pursue practical interests, one should not assume that only the poor attempt to better their conditions or status through practical oriented activities. For example, the practice of forming *jamayat* is an old Arabic practice exercised by upper, middle, and lower classes. A *jamayat* was formed by a group of local female professors. Each member would pitch in an amount of money each month and a rotation was followed in which a member would collect from the pool of money and buy something for herself. When asked what sorts of items the participants would purchase, a participant named items, such as a house. Networks, as such, are created for personal advantage. However, including such forms of activity into civil society action for the empowerment of women is important. As Marilyn Carr, Martha Chen, and Renana Jhabvala argue, "economic empowerment" involves changes in power relationships in both the economic sphere as an input and in the social and political spheres as an output.[40] *Jamayat* that serve to provide a group of women more financial power, thereby serve to empower women with more financial decision-making power and freedom. And with an empowerment process occurring here, civil society expansion is closely linked to issues concerning the "quality of life"[41] and remedying of the financial disparity often found between the two genders.

Women take part in networking due to several motivations that of which also includes nonmaterial rewards. As a participant explains, "I do this for the *ajr* [blessings]. I need blessings for my son. . . . I would never work for money. I do it for charity, for *ajr*." This participant hopes that by helping people, Allah will help her mentally handicapped son and that perhaps one day he might talk or walk. Her activism started when she says she realized that she was actually blessed with all the physiotherapy and professional medical care to which her son had access and of which others were deprived. She then began to visit hospitals and comforts any patient, especially those who do not have many family members visiting and parents of young patients, whom she tries to support and give advice to from her own experience. Among numerous activities, she cares for deprived children in her own home, set up programs for poor and orphaned children in her home country, and fights against highly sensitive human rights abuses in the UAE. Another participant illustrates the existential aspect that has conditioned the kind of giving self she has become:

There is a verse in the Qur'an [3:92] which says, "You will not enter heaven [sic. attain righteousness] if you did not pay from the things you love." Once you do this you know you will go to heaven. The Prophet taught us as well. If you are keen for things in this life then you do not feel the *Akhira*. But if you help the oppressed you will be closer to God. Live well but do things for people. Each person has a good thing to do in this life. We are not here for our own enjoyment.

Another participant said, "I give charity through the co-ops. But when I give directly to the person in need, I feel the difference I have made. I feel I am doing something when the person smiles. This little money then makes you feel like helping more . . . You feel happiness in helping." Other women network to focus on other things besides themselves, as a participant says, "We get together and want to do something besides raising kids and being focused on ourselves." Most of the participants in networks collaborated for nonmaterial reasons. Their goals were pursued typically in hopes of receiving some form of blessings, or for humanitarian reasons.

Some women articulate more overt political motivations for why they are involved in such activisms. A woman explains, "My motivating force is this: I am interested in the Palestinian-Israeli conflict because it is the longest ongoing unjust situation of the last century. It is the number one issue fuelling terrorism because of the unintended reaction of policy." This participant operates on varied modes of action to tackle issues through collaboration in a number of networks. Through a few different networks she strives to alleviate poverty, such as by selling crafts and toys in the UAE children in Palestine make. But also importantly, she lectures on the danger of Israeli policies in aggravating terrorism. Collaborating with like-minded individuals, women and men, she has nearly completed a bold documentary covering the internal politics of Palestine and Israel, the plight of Palestinians, and an endangered future of the Israeli state from a Jewish perspective.

It is important to recognize what motivating factors and value systems furnish the kinds of subjectivities conducive to greater levels of participation but not to cast these motivating reasons in terms of specific ideals, so when they do not fit, important actions that empower individuals and serve to expand a civil society are deemed irrelevant and consequently marginalized. The motivating factors that enable women to participate include compassion for humanity and value systems ascribed to Islam, such as striving to attain mercy, blessings, or good deeds for the afterlife, for example. Thus, examples prove that civil society is not always linked to institutions that are by definition secular. This observation has been supported by a growing number of scholars.[42] Moreover, though some women articulated awareness of oppressions of women and awareness of traditions within society that deny the rights of women, none of the women expressed that a feminist epistemology was followed in their activism. Because oppressive structures in an authoritarian environment are found by many participants to affect men in much the same ways as women, women's interests cannot be narrowly construed. Women have a variety of practical-oriented interests. This analysis does not discriminate whether these women *intend* to act in a way that will strategically alleviate the oppressions of women; nor can the analysis risk misconstruing representation of effective actors based on a simplistic notion that religiously based or motivated action cannot form a part of civil society. What is of significance to an evaluation of civil society expansion is what action can translate into greater civility, power, freedoms, and voice for the marginalized and oppressed, additionally what actions and discourses contribute to change for a perceived common good.

The Advantage of Networking

Through networks, individuals promote their views and pursue their goals. Their mechanisms for mobilization and communication enable activism to have impact in an environment in which formal structures are endangered from becoming co-opted or heavily scrutinized, hence, less able to provide avenues for civil society work. I argue that networks are the superior form of civil society collaboration due to their structural ability to challenge oppressive structures, the flexibility of participants to pursue various goals through such form of participation, the efficient means of communicating interests and needs, and the optimum utilization of experiences and skills of participants.

In his study on the Salafi movement in Jordan, Wiktorowicz explains the Salafis make networking a strategic choice that is informed by evaluations on the tactical efficacy of formal organizations. He argues networks have the same functions as formal forms of organization, although they are more effective in evading regime repression and constraints because of the fluidity and multiplicity of networks.[43] Organizations in the UAE are not only unable to challenge repressive power structures because of external restraints but also because of internal constraints. Some networkers choose not to direct their energy into the state-run charity organizations because they find these places do not help people in the UAE who are in need. As an alternative they utilize networks to achieve their aims. An interviewee said:

The Bait al Khair Charity, the Red Crescent—these are a big joke. They only help people in the UAE who are UAE nationals holding the citizenship. Why would anyone of these people need help? They have a hospital card; they have land, etcetera. They will not give anyone help who is in real need. So where are the funds all going? There are lots of people in desperate need and terrible situations. But these organizations are there to help 0.01 percent of the people here. Why aren't they building schools, hospitals, playgrounds, etcetera? The Red Crescent's warehouse is full. Their bank account is full. But desperate people can't get help from them because they do not have a resident visa. Many people are stateless, Somali victims of war, Palestinians, etcetera. If you are stateless, a widow with children as stateless, if you are hungry, isn't that a priority? People are in urgent need of operations, poor people are suffering, tired, have no money, no one to help take care of their children. They are only to be told they are not eligible. They are told to bring this, and bring that, etcetera.

Networking becomes a central avenue to address pressing issues, many stemming from poverty and oppressive conditions. As this participant points out, those who are suffering are mostly women and children who have no access to help because they are stateless or have no legal rights in the UAE. Those who participate in networking, women and men, are partially filling a gaping hole in the system that is supposedly meant to help those in need. In other words, networks are contributing to the real issues within UAE borders that organizations are only proposing to address. In their actions these participants are circumventing an unfair and inefficient system.

Women, moreover, choose to network over participating in organizations because they find their activism is used to its full potential in networks, whereas participating in organizations has hampered their abilities. A networker explains what other interviewees have similarly pointed out:

You do not get anywhere in organizations. People are in organizations for the prestige, for the positions they are bestowed, for the money. Someone created that position a person takes as chairperson or manager. It is someone's friend or relative who gets the influential positions. A person does not get into an organization because of some heartfelt compassion. If you are passionate you will not get to such positions. People are sitting in organizations for the money. You are supposed to start with an activist—people who push and fight should be made the chair. But I have seen people all over the place who are here today and gone tomorrow because their pockets have been filled.

This participant's mode of action is to utilize contacts and friendships to "make a difference." Because of *wasta* and clientalism, organizations are prone to becoming inefficient and unproductive. People are most often in paid positions within NGOs because of contacts they have forged. *Wasta* practiced as such obstructs civil society activism because it hinders the advancement of persons to positions of influence who have zeal and experience to pursue a vision for the betterment of society. Individuals are rather promoted who are pursuing personal interests at the expense of goals of the larger population. As discussed in chapter 3, the ministries appoint the directors and managers through networks to women's government-run associations based on ethnicity and relations among specific families. A participant attests, "Networking is especially important because the official women's organizations do not want volunteers." Hence, women who struggle to make a difference in society often work from within networks.

Conversely, as a strategic mode of action, some women choose to include organizations in their networking mostly because of the legitimacy some organizations enjoy. Of the case study sample of 43 women who networked as a strategy of participation, 6 or 14 percent continued to participate in the Red Crescent, though more women had at some time previously either worked for or volunteered in the charity organization. A participant who volunteers in the Red Crescent confirms the organization does not address the needs of children in police stations because of the residency permit specification. To improve the situation of the children she networks with a few other women who were concerned about the issue, and she is struggling to open an organization that addresses the policies and legal obstacles that hinder the help of orphans in the UAE. However, she keeps her position with the Red Crescent for legitimacy and as an avenue to help those who she can legally help. Another participant affirms the importance of working through the Red Crescent to help people in other countries because of the legitimacy it has internationally. A further participant explains her mode of action to help Palestinians cannot be effective through any organization linked to Palestinians. She points out, "Everyone is paranoid. What people are doing in these [Palestinian] organizations is not violent activity. But when I want to get anything done or anything through to Palestinian parts, I go through Jewish organizations because no one can accuse them of being terrorist organizations."

Networks are also the foundation of associations. Associations often develop out of an idea some friends or individuals express and then attempt to realize through grassroots initiatives and networking. A networker tells how she established two organizations; one is a *dawa* community center that she started in her own home. It began with a handful of women who wanted to connect with other women and were interested in Islam, including herself. It grew so large over the years that she could no longer hold the meetings in her home and handed the organization over to one of the women who took part in it and registered it officially. The other association developed out of her initiatives with like-minded individuals for counseling people in desperate need of support has been established as a nonprofit organization for psychiatry and counseling with highly skilled professionals in areas such as clinical, transition, marriage, special needs, occupational, speech, early intervention, yoga, and breathing therapy. The persons who work in this organization continue to network by providing people who need such help free of charge. Members sponsor workshops in schools for teachers and other places. Their work extends overseas. Locally, members counsel and advise in places such as in a major hospital and the police station. Both establishments have become very large and well-known centers due to the initial struggle of this one woman together with friends. The latter establishment has been so successful it has an impact not only on the societal level through individual and group initiatives, but on how persons in government handle various cases due to their consultation with the organization.

As noted under "Profiles of Interviewees" in the appendix, nearly all participants collaborated through more than one network. Collaboration through more than a single network indicates a higher level of activism. Instead of limiting oneself to participation in an organization in which roles may be attached to specific descriptions, one is enabled to take on different roles according to various needs, interests, and a participant's differing capabilities. Participating through more than one network enabled that an individual multitasked. If one goal was in process and nothing could be done in the meantime, a participant was better able to utilize her time by pursuing another goal through whichever activities necessary to its achievement. One participant illustrates the advantage of networking as a civil society sector:

I receive daily around 15 cases. People call me up for all sorts of help. At the . . . association I meet over 100 people there. They request help. If I do not give money, then maybe I give food for some cause, or basic things. If I or anyone else can't, then a contact is provided for someone who can offer something. For example, I know someone who owns a rice factory. I have asked him to help when I have been asked to donate food. At the . . . [other] association we collect and distribute donations. We do this also together with other associations. Among my calls today, someone asked me to help an 18 year old who needs an operation. . . . I had contacted people and found sponsors to raise enough money for the operation. A 38 year old woman in depression with a 9 month old baby needed help. I spent two hours with her. A man called for psychiatric help. I called . . . [other woman this participant always networks with] to give him counselling with his wife. This evening I will attend a meeting with the . . . association. I network between this association and [narrator names a number of associations, some secular, some Islamic and a church]. For all these places and among them I refer people and connect people.

Because networking is supported through a structure of social ties and informal modes of recruitment, greater levels of participation can be achieved quickly. The incentive of opportunities for socialization is a technique implemented by some networkers to get women involved in charitable work. So, for example, the ladies who put on a dinner to raise funds for charity purposes enable women at the same time to socialize. Outward social ties are crucial for a network's growth. As Roger Gould has argued, "If there are obstacles standing between sympathizing and participating, or between feeling neutral and sympathizing, a social relationship with someone who is already a participant helps to overcome them."[44]

However, participatory encompassment is enabled through a number of techniques. Persons within a network do not necessarily know each other. Funds, for example, are collected through personal contacts, but also the contacts of those personal contacts can be called upon. Participants are motivated to action through word of mouth, by phone, or frequently by mobile phone text messaging (SMS). Word of mouth includes persons discussing a problem or expressing the need to collect funds to solve a problem. Friends or a core network of individuals will widen their circle of contacts to people they trust or people they have contacted previously for help. Contacts are maintained for future utilization and, hence, a larger network of individuals is established. Often when a person agrees to participate in some effort his or her contact will be put into a database as on a mobile phone and consequently added to a network to be updated on future projects. Such informal modes are effective because people need not make a conscious decision to choose a particular organization to participate, yet remain connected through an oftentimes impersonal lifeline that can be activated by core members at any time for whatever pressing issue that arises. During times of natural disasters in countries, such as the earthquake in Bam, Iran in 2004 or the tsunami that hit many countries late 2004, individuals were extremely efficient in collecting funds, clothes, and blankets via SMS, phone, and e-mail. Networkers recognize the use of various forms of technology to achieve goals quickly. As one networker remarked, "We are connected to the world through internet. We have access to a lot of information, and we can share our experiences quickly."

Evolving technologies play a role in providing lifelines to which individuals may be easily connected to share views, problems, challenges, and eventually goals. Networking through "blogging" is a newer mode of action executed by numerous networks in the UAE. They are used by networks of women to advance Islamic ideology, or simply enter discussion on a variety of issues. Typical topics some networks of Emirati women's blogs cover are *halal/haram*, Ramadan, *dua*'s/prayer, international news, shopping, stories, poetry, beauty, cooking, cars, games, and tunes for mobiles.[45] Blogs set up by groups of local women do not address issues of an overtly political nature. Any blog directly discussing politics set up within the UAE is quickly deleted or if set up outside the UAE is soon censured and blocked by the ministry through the two existing internet providers.

The significance of these blogs, however, is that they offer women a discursive space to discuss issues of importance, even if a large part of their focus is cars, mobiles, and hair and beauty tips. One of the blogs states at the top of its page, "Subscribe with us. Your freedom of speech is guaranteed." Implied in the statement alone is that freedom of speech is curtailed in the UAE, and a forum for women to express themselves is desired. Although overt political statements are usually avoided, when major events occur members jump straight into discussion and ideas are shared. So when Ahmed Yassin was assassinated, the "invasion of Iraq" began, and Sheikh Zayed died, lively discussion hit the blogs. Moreover, ideas and perceptions are shared; thus, a shaping of identity is achieved through blogging. In one of the blogs a subscriber asks if it is *haram* to chant "Allah" in groups as do Sufis. Answers to the question confirm the Salafi position among others that Sufism falls outside mainstream Islamic practice. In the same blog the *niqab* is defended under the section for "debates." A male asks if it is banned for a man to get to know a woman over the mobile, a debate endemic in many discussions in the local *halaqas,* and a position taken by most religious sheikhs as *haram.* The question evokes various responses among the women ranging from it being a bad thing, a sign of no religion on part of the two persons, a matter of intention, to it being "a part of globalization . . . a part of life. [So] get over it!"[46]

Networks utilize the resources participants bring with them. Because the person is not seeking to fulfill some job specific duties, the participant relies on all experiences and skills for the various goals she might have. Relevant experiences and skills to achieving goals interviewees named included educational backgrounds (i.e., media studies, communication, business, linguistics, computer, or Islamic degrees), speaking publicly, being a good listener, writing, memorization of the Qur'an, etcetera. For instance, one participant uses her organizational skills to network. She has a database with the names of the women she knows of who are needy and whose information she collects through contacts. She furthermore collects the names of businessmen. She explains how:

I feel I am a businesswoman. I have to be sincere and do everything with sincerity. . . . I am trying to understand the needs of women. . . . I have a database on women who are needy. I also do a financial part to it. I do research of the Muslim men who might be willing to give money. I plan appointments with the men and tell them what is happening. I contacted, for example, . . . [name of a company] and spoke with . . . [name]. Now he gives some portion of his charity for me to distribute. I register all the cases in the database and keep a clear record.

Networks are a more efficient and advantageous means of collaboration. First, networks are "the lifeline of the community" because they can become dormant when a project has been completed and activated within one day for the next project because individuals remain connected. The temporary inactivation of networks is especially useful if and when some action on part of its participants has drawn unwanted government attention. Projects involve little bureaucracy and organization in comparison to official organizations. Second, networks are especially efficient also because anyone can begin and nurture a network. This is significant because one need not be a citizen to establish a forum where individuals can vent their frustrations and discuss strategies to reach a particular end. Third, because of the grassroots level of activism, networking is flexible, and means of action can be tailored according to specific circumstances. A participant explains, "I feel you must study each different case to have an idea about the suffering of the people. People have differing needs according to many factors. You will find each case is different." Fourth, because of the loose structure of networks, directly addressing sensitive issues related to human rights and freedoms is made a greater possibility than through the use of associations that are either co-opted or scrutinized. Networks are at such grassroots levels they fill the gaps most efficiently. They do not require papers to provide help; in fact, many networks target especially those who are *bedoon*. Networks in an environment, such as the UAE, are a central civil society sector. Through networking women contribute to civil society expansion in the most efficient and productive means.

Civility

Civility through Tolerance

Civility was analyzed through the observance of tolerance, trust, cooperation, and reciprocity. The networks, I argue, are key mechanisms through which norms of tolerance, trust, cooperation, and reciprocity are nurtured and developed. Civility is demonstrated in terms of behavior exercised between members. Thus, an ethos of civility is inculcated in the self when its norms are repeatedly performed.

Tolerance is greater among women who network than among any other form of association. Greater tolerance was displayed in women's collaboration across economic and social class barriers, ethnicities and of differing faiths, despite the tendency of internal religious and ethnic forms of collaboration in the UAE. Most networks comprise individuals from specific religious groups, and so each pursues interests that are most pressing to a specific community. A great deal of what Putnam refers to as "the accumulation of internal human capital" is achieved through activism on strict ethnic and religious lines. This situation arises in great part because of rigid ethnic stratification as an important element in defining class divisions in the UAE. However, several of the case study networks were able to overcome the barriers of internal group or network activity. Network stratification was evident when compared to organizations. Only in one of the associations was I able to identify a few participants who were Christian, which was among one of the Islamic associations. In the networks was some collaboration between Christians, Jews, and Muslims, mostly Sunni, but also Shi'a. In six networks studied, Christian and Muslim women collaborated for various interests. A participant tells, "I do not make any difference between men or women. I also do not differentiate between people of different religions—Hindu, Christian, Muslim. I will visit a sick man. I do not go near fanatical political people."

Several networks also existed in which women differed as to what extent they followed mainstream and dominant religious practice in dress codes among Muslim participants. In the interest of helping others, women did not focus on the moral aspirations of ideology as did the organizations. The interest of several networks was illustrated as for the common good over ideology because the frames utilized between members shifted to persons in need, rather than what the women themselves presented and how they should present knowledge. In many instances the construction of knowledge took place within discourses on the elevation of people to better opportunities, standard of living, or fair access to resources and rights. The emphasis on the themes of human rights and personal freedoms of the oppressed illustrates wider civil society capabilities or in Shils' words "civil politics" than organizations studied.

Men were also connected to networks. None of the networks made men their objective, even though some participants made mention of difficulty in getting men to take their concerns seriously. On the whole, women would not carry out activities physically close to unrelated men as a regular part of their networking; however, if a man could fulfill a needed role, he was not excluded based on his gender or a norm of segregation. So, for example, men would be called by telephone or SMS to collect money, collect and bring food-stuffs or clothes to the needy, provide a needed operation, and to provide further links or a contact in an influential position. Indeed, collaboration with men was strongest among networks than other forms of collaboration. Such inclusivity enables greater efficacy and efficiency.

Civility through Trust

A notable degree of trust was found in terms of to what extent partic-ipants could rely on one another with secret information, or rely on others to fulfill their agreed upon roles. Some issues the participants were active in addressing were highly sensitive, and if any information leaked outside the network circle, some members could be in trouble with the law/government or in trouble with mafia groups, for exam-ple. Yet information is shared within networks so that members can successfully work together on an issue. As with Islamic associations, issues of concern included provision of shelter, food, clothing, and general assistance to stateless persons or *bedoon*. So, when the location of *bedoon* families has been provided, confidence in the secrecy of their whereabouts is expected without its verbalization.

This trust is built between individuals who have together agreed that to report these families to the authorities is unjust and to help them in secrecy is virtuous. A socialization process occurs through these networks in which new participants are introduced to an ethos that places value on human rights and freedom from oppression. This process is achieved though framing the situation of these people they help within language that attaches meanings of oppression and injus-tice. Margaret Somers explains this framing occurs through the use of symbols, rituals, or narratives that build and solidify identities among these actors.[47] These actors find themselves embedded in a structure that creates or solidifies political consciousness toward a given is-sue.[48] This solidified consciousness and solidarity cannot be created without a structure built on trust. Already existing identities form a partial basis for this trust even when the social ties are weak. As such, women would speedily commit to networks because they trusted the network's members shared the same ideological perspectives toward particular issues. Similarly, women who had aspirations for advancing human rights causes could readily join a network that fought along these lines because there is an implicit trust that working together for such noble causes is worth the risk.

Civility through Reciprocity

Sharing and giving were qualities encouraged and self-disciplined among networkers. Reciprocating takes different shapes depending, however, on the goals of the networkers. When the terms of productivity and success in establishing a good or a moral order have been established together, the production of empowered selves may be attained. Goals among good-doers are often directed externally as opposed to internally. As such, sharing or giving is to benefit others outside the network circle. When such networkers direct their activisms away from their circle, they receive the empowering feelings and sense of existential reward derived from extending help to others. Sharing in struggle against systemic forms of oppression, whether embodied in state laws or poverty, also establishes closer friendships among those persons networkers participate with closely. As such, standing together, especially taking risks together, in struggle against shared notions of oppression, produces rewards and fulfillment from which empowered selves emerge.

This, however, does not mean that empowerment and civility cannot result from participation that is directed inwardly. This is particularly true for networks whose focus is on practical issues that directly affect the participants themselves as a group. So, for example, the maids who directed their efforts to establish links among themselves and others in positions of strategic importance would make reciprocity a goal in itself. An ethos of reciprocity would be aimed for to build the structure of a network and define who is in. Who gives, shares, and receives forms part of the network. The gift giving, sharing of crucial information, such as which local will find a sponsor for a runaway maid or which immigration officer will provide a residency permit for a maid that has gotten into some kind of trouble forms this network. By consciously establishing an ethos of reciprocity, the lifeline to access to various material and social benefits is ensured. As such, reciprocity is valued as a crucial means for survival and benefit.

Civility through Cooperation

Cooperation defines the mode of action of networking. Networks are established and bound by the ties individuals establish through their resolve and commitment to cooperate to achieve goals together. The achievement of goals rests squarely on modes of collaboration among the participants.

One of many cases noted illustrates the source of networking. Because she is a medical doctor, a network participant's attention was called to a small orphan boy (his father had died and his mother did not have adequate funds for his support) and needed immediate medical attention. While playing with explosives the boy severely burned his face. She did not have the means to treat the boy so she presented the case to a few network participants. One of the participants called a doctor who she knew regularly treats patients who have no money to pay for medical care. Meanwhile another participant hurried to collect the boy from a poor village outside city limits. The doctor gave the immediate attention required, until another network participant, also a doctor, could use more invasive methods. Each participant played a role to her/his capacity in this coordinated effort to give medical care to a child who was *bedoon* and consequently could have no medical insurance.

Participants who cooperate together on such cases do so without usually ever knowing who they are helping personally. In this configuration of networking, cooperation is directed to public benefit, not internal solidarities. With the resources available to the networkers and their embeddedness in a network that could be activated to respond to an immediate problem, networks are able to achieve numerous goals. As such, cooperation is such a key feature of networking and, thus, a notable variable in their civil society activism.

THE IMPACT OF WOMEN'S NETWORKS ON UAE CIVIL SOCIETY

Due to the structure of networking, women are able to expand a civil society more efficiently and forcefully than any other form of organization within an authoritarian environment. "Where the state is unresponsive, its institutions are undemocratic, or its democracy is ill designed to recognize and respond to citizen demands, the character of collective action will be decidedly different than under a strong and democratic system."[49] Networks function efficiently in a small monarchic state in which *wasta* determines access to resources and bargaining power. In a rentier state in which interests are secured through remittances, an organized force that can only survive and function off of generous financial and material support is automatically weakened as a contester over issues in which the state has an interest. Accordingly, a civil society cannot be state fostered in an authoritarian environment. Organizational forms of collaboration in which an association operates legally through its registration with government cannot effectively tackle issues that might be interpreted to threaten major actors in government or actors in powerful positions. Networks, having no legal basis, can only be traced back to individuals. To obstruct the activism of individuals in collaboration through networking is more difficult as networks are harder to detect and dismantle than establishments. These can be easily shut down.[50] It does not mean that individuals are not associated with a particular association, as most of the case study networkers do participate in organizational activity. However, the most sensitive issues are not pursued in the name of an organization, even if they are spearheaded by associational leaders. Networks, therefore, are the only avenue through which members of a public can contest issues, especially those related to human rights violations, governance, and state policies. Consequently, such a dense and vibrant form of collaboration must be acknowledged as an essential part of civil society if the concept is to have meaning for any context of an authoritarian polity.

The most effective means for tackling human rights issues in the UAE has been through networking. Even though three groups of individuals were working toward the establishment of human rights organizations, no human rights organizations have been allowed to function. As one of these groups includes women participants, women have been the most active in addressing highly sensitive issues. Obviously, dealing with issues of a sensitive nature in which people in powerful positions or in mafia groups are involved poses danger to the activists not only in terms of legal repercussions, but also in terms of criminal terrorization. One participant's life was threatened by a mafia member if she did not cease her activities. She threatened back that she would never stop. The same participant received a warning from her *wasta,* a close family friend of many years in a government position, informing her that she was being monitored and to stop her activities or else she would be soon thrown out of the country. She asserted, "I am not afraid. Who else will do this for them? Even if I am thrown out tomorrow I have to." The same participant was jailed and interrogated for five hours after she presented some information the researcher passed on to her to a member in government. Eventually, this participant's defiant and open mode of action to debate with persons in positions of power was rewarded when she received at least assurance that her concerns were taken seriously in her plea against human rights abuses from another state actor she approached.

Networks become the most important avenue for struggle in a sparsely populated monarchic form of rule because their structure facilitates collaboration between civil society actors and state actors. Networking, in fact, affords actors a means through which defiant acts can be expressed because networking involves not only collaboration between horizontal relationships, but also avenues for vertical collaboration and bargaining. Because as several interviewees attested, "nothing can be done without *wasta*," a mode of action that takes advantage of this system which in most cases hinders equal access to rights, power, and commodities, is, nonetheless, indispensable. A participant curtly asserts how she is able to network to help people in various oppressive situations: "I know a lot of people and I have *wasta*." Organizations are banned from any political activity, broadly defined, and so cannot pose as lobby groups. Individuals can make changes through the contacts they have forged or maintain through family, friends, or acquaintances in government positions. The change networks can achieve by pleading, bargaining, or debating with state actors also demonstrates that vertical interaction involves actions on part of the state actors that serve to reconfigure the entity of state and allow political liberalization.

Networking allows for relations and contacts to be established between several forces with power leverage. Establishing nodes of one's network among players situated in different localities is a strategy that gives the network greater strength and abilities. The relationships networks in the UAE can forge to pursue a specific interest that includes connecting to media, institutions in the West, or other actors. The defiant modes of action found in networks were illustrated through links beyond state actors. In dealing with the same human rights abuse of child camel jockeying, another participant was able to receive assistance from her own *wasta* in government, who even mobilized the police to her aid. But when her *wasta* was suddenly replaced by a person unconcerned about her struggle, she changed her initial strategy of secrecy and patience. She took her human rights case to the media after a long fight of several years in the spring of 2005. She called in the BBC to investigate the situation of children jockeys. However, with the leverage the network proved to be in a position to tap into and the influence its participants sustained with members of government, along with the assiduous struggle of others, a major change occurred a few months later. The network was granted full backing of its activities, and the government declared to all parties involved and the countries from which the children were taken its sincere support for the complete eradication of the enslaving and kidnapping of child camel jockeys into the UAE.[51] Besides continuing their endeavors to save the small children from such terrible abuse, the next phase of

these networkers' challenge is how to rehabilitate, adequately counsel, and send the children back to their "rightful" homes, when, in a
lot of the cases, the children were sold by their own parents. Given
the risks the network participants have taken in addressing such issues, these women are, indeed, the most indispensable members of a
civil society. Hence, I argue that women who network to alleviate suffering and harm of the oppressed are the champions of civil society
expansion in the UAE.

Comparisons across the developing world indicate that the structure of civil networks can strongly influence their effectiveness. Remonda Kleinberg and Janine Clark cite other examples of networking,
such as in Nicaragua, Indonesia, and the Philippines, that mitigated
human rights abuses after which a refiguration of the political field
proceeded.[52] Further examples include Argentina and Chile in which
women's networks were instrumental in opening a human rights discourse and bringing justice to human rights abuses, first through horizontal networking and then through linkages forged with media and
northern NGOs.[53] Maryjane Osa has argued, in fact, that civil society
did not just suddenly appear in Eastern European countries but grew
through the force of networks that substituted for organizations and
media in a public sphere that was replaced by an "official one."[54] It is
important that civil society forces are not equated with organizations,
as "[d]iffering domestic political configurations present different obstacles and opportunities for civil associations."[55] Networking can have
greater force and impact in some environments.

What the sample reveals is that networks have efficient ways of collecting and distributing funds, various forms of aid, and information
through a web of contacts and links. Moreover, networkers have direct
contact with many of the needy and the people they try to help. They
do not need to go through bureaucracy, in which there is suspicion
that funds may get lost, goods may pile up and waste, or money may
get distributed among employees. Thus, when the several charitable
associations in the UAE were shut down or the actions of those remaining came under stringent scrutiny after 9/11, the lifeline of networks continued to supply what the needy relies upon. Wiktorowicz
explains networking is not a new innovation. It is simply an indigenous
model of mobilization adopted that fulfills the same function as organizations.[56] However, as I hope is already sufficiently apparent, networking has greater functionality in an authoritarian environment. I
argue that it has even greater functionality in a rentier based authoritarian environment due to the added mechanisms of governmentality
to weaken civil society through remittances and the usually oil-backed

vertical encompassment of civil society institutions and actors. An interviewee explains the functionality of networking: "United together for a good cause is the most effective way to get things done. . . . Very little is being done to tackle problems. And we cannot do anything through organizations. They are all being thrown out."

The dominant role women's networks play in tackling women, children, or human rights issues is important to underscore because they are making differences for a common good that no other form of collaboration is able due to practical, legal, and even cultural constraints. Laws are not a neutral agent and reflect dominant relations in society.[57] Therefore, while women did not feel they were pursuing strategic feminist goals, some participants identified and struggled against power structures. This is evident with the example of court cases involving domestic disputes, in which decrees are male dominated and in effect establish the notion that women are the property of their husbands. Such actions on part of the networkers are contributing to awareness of human rights discriminations, and in the future this awareness will aid in the development of strategies pursued in a discourse channeled through to women and men cross culturally struggling for the eradication of parallel discriminations and abuses. Already one network had made contact with a Western feminist institution that struggles against domestic violence, so that the networkers may collaborate in educating themselves further about the phenomenon and bridge experiences and strategies. As Boutheina Cheriet points out, because human rights issues and empowerment of women and marginalized groups forms such contested discourses, as found in international forums, such as the Beijing conference, empowerment must be demanded and pursued from within, forged in debates, in conflict and consensus if social change benefiting women is to be achieved.[58] Because local associations are handicapped or state run and international organizations are mostly suspect of cultural imperialism, the only practical, legitimate, and functional alternative to pursue women's interests are women's networks, whose participants are keenly aware of issues and events as they unfold on the ground.

If the networkers collaborate together to reach common goals in a civil manner and the consequences of their struggles entail greater civility within society, they are fostering the civility component. Because the women's collaboration involve the acts of sharing, reciprocity, participatory norms, and a high degree of trust, social capital is generated that, as Robert Putnam argues, is essential to civic participation and the building of democracy.[59] Unlike organizations, networks are much more fluid, as they reach across lines of ethnicity, class, and norms of segregation much more effectively than any other form of collaboration. This is essential, especially in a sharply segregated society, as "bridging social capital can generate broader identities and reciprocity, whereas bonding social capital bolsters our narrower selves."[60] Empowerment results and human dignity is restored when reciprocity, sharing, and respect for the Other is fostered between the socially disadvantaged and those ranked by society as above others. In setting aside differences to collaborate with others for a common good, networkers of this study are contributing to civility in the highest sense, for "[t]hey participate in many collectivities and they are also individuals. They participate in many collective self-consciousnesses and they also have their own individual self-consciousness, but in a civil society, they participate in, they are parts of, the collective self-consciousness of society. The image of the common good is inherent in the nature of collective self-consciousness."[61]

Placing our Western construct of the public/private divide and our theories of political institutions and behavior can only provide inaccurate conclusions on civil society and political change. As a growing number of political theorists have recognized, the rentier state theory is too static, plus it does not take account of the developments that take place due to civil society activisms. Especially the activisms of women become marginalized and/or misconstrued. Therefore, it is pertinent that women's networking achievements are assessed in the functionality they have in their specific environments. Networks are formed between housewives; sometimes their discussions or actions take place in the home around a women's party. Women strive together to alleviate burdens or strive to better their status within their own homes. Domestic servants produce networks of trust and reciprocity for basic survival. All such acts must be considered for an assessment of civil society action. It is irrelevant whether women collaborate within a Western constructed *feminine* role. If women are circumventing policies, laws, traditions, or reigning religious interpretations that serve to disempower or disadvantage women and the marginalized they care for, then they are expanding civil society in their actions. These women who assume a social responsibility on part of the oppressed and marginalized attain numerous achievements through their individual-based networks. What they attain is truly phenomenal.

CHAPTER 6

WOMEN IN CIVIL SOCIETY: PROSPECTS FOR THE UAE

WOMEN'S PARTICIPATION IN UAE CIVIL SOCIETY

In the goal of contributing to a better theoretical understanding of civil society and the role of women, this book has explored the role of UAE women in civil society. To determine and analyze civil society growth, it has focused on three key forms of association: state-run women's organizations, Islamic-oriented organizations, and women's networks. Studying these different forms of women's organizing has enabled a more nuanced and comprehensive understanding of women's participation and the way in which subjectivities are fashioned. This project has produced some important observations, namely (1) GONGO women's organizations play a central role in governmentality; (2) Islamic-oriented women's organizations contribute to civil society formation despite their ideological motivations and some problematic formulations of justice; and (3) women's networks can be the most vital elements for civil society development. On a theoretical level, such findings make the argument more pertinent that the civil society concept, among related theories, be reexamined in contexts other than that in which it has been historically fashioned.

The following elaborates on these conclusions in more detail. UAE women's GONGOs proved to play a central role in facilitating the state's domination over civil society. State domination is maintained and extended due to the mechanisms of governance that are implemented through these organizations. One, they impact society on a large scale through their extensive branches, large amount of government funding, and the legitimacy they derive from being under the auspices of the sheikhs and sheikhas. Two, their programs are formulated by state leaders and their wives and monitored by state appointed supervisors within the associations. Three, their participants are almost exclusively paid either by the association or by a ministry. As facilitators of the Emiratization plan, they have been instrumental in securing and widening cleavages along ethnicities and class and gender lines. Because state interests involve squashing competing voices through the mechanism of state-run women's organizations, the women's role in civil society serve largely the encompassment of civil society.

Despite this significant function, these state-run women's organizations also play a role in societal and individual development. First, while these organizations present the most effective form of governmentality, they pose simultaneously as an avenue through which some participants feel they may influence government "from within" or influence society through their activism according to principles and beliefs. Second, these state-run associations contribute to the state's development projects. Contributions to development have been most pronounced within literacy programs, health awareness programs, and religious instruction. Individuals benefit from such educational programs, often in ways that enhance their quality of living.

This study has also demonstrated that despite the ideological motivations that guide most actors within Islamic-oriented organizations, these organizations are civil and have substantial impact on the public level. The participants have proven their capabilities in providing the building blocks for civil society in three main ways: one, contributing to participation levels of civil society activism; two, articulating their own needs and goals, engaging and contesting opposing views, and developing modes of being that furnish their empowerment and the transformation of society; and three, contributing to civility through the norms and practices they seek to produce and reproduce.

Incorporating social movement theory, this work was able to uncover networking as a form of civil society activism that has advantages over all other forms of activism in the UAE context. It was found that formal organizations in the UAE have limited capacity to tackle issues of a sensitive nature in a country with a low population and an authoritarian environment. Therefore, when individuals network they become more effective in advancing their interests. Networks are more effectual due to their structural ability to challenge oppressive structures, the flexibility of participants to pursue various goals through such form of participation, the efficient means of communicating interests and needs, and the optimum utilization of experiences and skills of participants. This sector, in fact, is making the greatest strides in building a foundation for civil society amongst all the civil society actors in the UAE.

RESPONDING TO THE DOMINANT CONCEPTUAL TRENDS

The theoretical implications of this study will hopefully be found of value in a number of areas. The main area to which this book has aimed to contribute is in expanding the civil society concept to be more inclusive of activism oftentimes marginalized in the concept's dominant trends. The three matters of concern here were a narrow conception of the civility component of civil society that renders Islamic activism outside the confines of civil society; a private/public divide followed in most scholarly works that impedes analysis of important forms of participation; and the equation of civil society with "organizations" as found in much of the civil society literature. Further areas with which this work has engaged include linking the notion of governmentality with the study of civil society and nuancing rentier theory. Hence, in the following, I respond to the conceptual trends that govern these areas.

With the example of a generally illiberal, though peaceful, form of activism, I address the problem of a narrow definition of civility that is further burdened with biases as to who to include and exclude. Especially the symbols, norms, and practices that run against secular liberal politics are seen as incongruous with the project of civil society. Consequently, Islamic organizations are judged to have little worth in terms of civility. If, as was found, activists can pursue an ideologically based goal believed to be for the betterment of individuals and society, through peaceful action and engagement, then essentially these activists form a part of civil society. As such, the dominant trend that formulates civility to exclude ideologically based activism—chiefly Islamic, needs to be theoretically reworked to encompass such forms of activism that can richly add to civil society dynamism.

Activism that is also excluded from mainstream scholarship on civil society is that which is privately oriented. Such oversight has left important forms of civil society participation oftentimes unrecognizable as components of civil society. This book has studied a sector of civil society that such scholarship conventionally marginalizes because its actors frequently focus on individual and personal transformation with respect to, for example, morality, ethics, and piety. These actors, however, often view individual development as a strategy toward societal development. Precisely because such actors have found that programs that target the authoritarian state are ineffective, they seek change by first transforming society. For them, society cannot experience transformation before the unit of the family and the individual is developed, whichever way they envision development and enhancement. This is also an Islamist agenda, a category of activism squarely placed within studies on the "public." Hence, these findings call into question the presumption of mainstream civil society literature that civil society activism must be squarely publicly oriented. As such, for the concept to have relevance in environments similar to that of this book's focus, it must take into account privately oriented action.

The idea of civil society has been so closely associated with organizations that other vital forms of participation have been sidelined in its mainstream literature. Rather than focusing on participation through NGOs, scholarship must embrace a wider sphere of participatory forms as perhaps central modalities of actions in repressive and authoritarian environments. This endeavor begins with the critical engagement of the literature to examine how the civil society idea has been historically constructed to become synonymous with NGOs (i.e., beginning with the traditions of John Locke, Thomas Paine, and De Tocqueville). The implication this study poses for the civil society concept has been illustrated through a case study in an authoritarian context in which the most valuable form of collaboration among civil society actors was found among networks.

Furthermore, voices significant to civil society activism have been ignored through essentializations, resulting in civil societies judged to be absent. Civil society participation takes different forms according to the different challenges in which actors are engaged and the sociohistorical environment in which they are situated. Essentializing how all men or all women should pursue their interests in a particular environment serves to exclude crucial actors. Women's forms of organizing differ within the same environment and context. It is, therefore, important to begin any inquiry with acknowledging the vast array of variables that influence women's forms of participation, such as interests, needs, beliefs, class, economic status, family, lineage, and the different or shared opportunities, challenges, and experiences women face. Women do not necessarily pursue certain interests because of their gender. This last point can be better understood through recourse to the governmentality literature.

However, the neoliberal governmentality literature cannot be applied to the UAE case. The central argument of the neoliberal governmentality literature is that a decentralization of state power occurs through state-run organizations. The argument is that governments will need to lessen their burden of responsibility through the decentralizing of power by enabling government-created or run organizations to take on some of their functions. The dialectic is that a decentralization of state power corresponds to an empowerment process among actors outside government. But the kinds of subjectivities that state actors have aimed to shape are productive in a way that serve, first and foremost, the legitimacy of the state and the anchoring of truths to which the state strives to construct and authenticate in pursuit of its own interests. Women in the UAE are empowered with these responsibilities and they are empowered in the skills in as much as is necessary to fulfill these responsibilities. For these state goals to be achieved, women were able to acquire skills and practical experiences that enabled them to take a bigger role in the production of the state through the shaping of selves within society to acquire the truths the state constructs.

A state feminism produced more capable subjects in some respects, but in some other major respects shaped less capable subjectivities. For example, women learned and perpetuated the idea that women could not be equal to men in mental capacities and, therefore, could not take on positions of responsibility in government as could men. In this way, the state entrenched their greater dependency and, thereby, that of society to the state. But the state is enabled to bolster its powers through the women's state-run organizations not only by "acting on the choices and self-steering properties"[1] of the women involved, but largely through its rentier governmentality. It coerces subjects to support its goals through the provision of jobs at these associations, positions of prestige within the associations, opportunities to move to other prestigious positions from the associations, and generally large amounts of funding for "women's" activities. Those who do not wish for any of these will never be able to take up larger roles in these organizations. Authoritarian forms of governing do not view subjects as free citizens the way literature on neoliberal governmentality claim liberal governments do.

PROSPECTS FOR FUTURE RESEARCH

This study aimed to contribute to a broadened perspective of civil society. In this endeavor, it has engaged with a number of conceptual issues. It, thus, analyzed the multitude of activities of actors framed as uncivil, too passive, or too repressed to form part of civil society. It also included actors that serve the encompassment of civil society while simultaneously producing subjectivities with greater organizational skills and practical experiences to be able to contribute to society. Such an undertaking can only skim the surface of related matters. There is a great need for fieldwork-based investigation to further query the issues engaged in this book and nuance dominant themes within the literature on state-society interaction, especially in the region most poorly understood and oftentimes misconstrued—the Middle East. Analysis on the Middle East through a civil society lens opens abundant opportunity for further work on related topics. In closing I outline some areas for future research.

First, there is a need to study and compare how different variables shape actors' subjectivities and how individuals respond to and engage the various discourses. Looking at the meaning or impact of different forms of participation has formed part of this project. This work revealed the different avenues through which women can have impact, and the tendencies most pronounced in each form of organization. Activism is influenced by competing value systems, varying socioeconomic contexts, and more broadly, different forms of governance. Analyzing the differing variables would produce insights into the differing ways in which actors constitute and develop a civil society. Such should hopefully broaden our normative notions on how a civil society should develop.

Second, the significance of a gender factor is sorely understated in studies on civil society or network movements. There is further need to investigate the roles women play in civil society, state-society relations, and social movements, in general. From this basis, we can be in a position to identify forms of activism, such as self-development projects, that have impact on the way in which civil society takes root and forms, otherwise missed in state-oriented and male-oriented works. Thus, questions that may lead to fruitful discussion or investigation include: How does gender focus affect the way in which civil society has been historically constructed? How does a gender lens change the way in which we may identify components of civil society? Does gender play a role in how actors pursue interests or choose which issues to tackle? Working with such questions will reveal forms of activisms that have been deemed irrelevant, inconsequential, or have been simply omitted within mainstream literature. Such questions, however, should also reveal that gender as an explanatory power has limits.

Third, because the familial sphere is oftentimes deemed largely inconsequential to the realm of civil society and the political, we learn little about what processes occur on the familial level that promote, shape, or inhibit women's participation in the public. There needs to be more inquiries into how familial socialization facilitates or obstructs women's participating in civil society and the political realms. Moreover, case study analysis is crucial for greater insight into women's actions within the homes. What forms of power matter? What mechanisms do women forge to combat restrictive notions of their roles in society among family members? How does increased awareness of biases between men and women change women's choices in how they participate on the public level?

Fourth, the relationship between civil society and political liberalization needs greater theorization based on country study findings. A better theoretical understanding of the civil society concept will offer researchers a more useful tool for analyzing prospects for political liberalization. Can political liberalization take different forms under differing circumstances and within differing environments? Certainly, if women are able to push for policies and laws, such as those governing the human rights issues discussed in chapter 5, through patron-client relations typically found between state actors and civil society actors in the Gulf, then women may also be playing a role in the freeing of political space. Women may have an impact on political liberalization if they are able to secure better conditions and greater voice for people. Subsequently, what are the reactions of those in powerful positions to their demands? How do different forms of government in the Middle East respond to demands?

Some forms of governance associated with neoliberalism cannot be explained adequately by the neo-governmentality literature that has focused primarily on Western models of neoliberal governance. Authoritarian governance that shows aspects of neoliberalism needs to be better understood. This book demonstrated that the process of neoliberalism is not occurring in the UAE. Studies need to address concepts that are not explaining political processes as described in the literature. What technologies of government are in place in authoritarian governments? How does rentier-based governmentality differ from neoliberal governmentality? Such queries will open up a host of other issues that need to be resolved. Subsequently, when speaking of governmentality who is government to begin with? What forms of power sharing or control are occurring among state actors themselves?

Sixth, the paradigm most salient within literature on the Arab Gulf, rentierism, also cannot explain various political processes in the region. Rentier wealth should be scrutinized further in terms of how it is utilized as a mechanism of control over civil society. It cannot fully explain why rentier money also has limitations in stifling dissent. Other variables need to be addressed to understand the distribution of power. As Abdulkhaleq Abdullah argues, a non-oil perspective is essential in studying the region for a broad and balanced understanding of the regions contemporary politics and society.[2] To avoid essentializing the Arab Gulf region in terms of oil and rentier wealth, one may try to understand the area by searching for other variables that shape the political landscape. What other factors support the tribal elite's stronghold on power besides oil wealth?

As a final point, there remains a lack of understanding in how Islamic-oriented forms of organization can contribute to empowerment or the formation of civil society. Because Islamic groups' interests and goals often run against the (often Western) secular liberal notion of development, they are excluded from discussion on progress and civil society expansion. Studies must continue to engage the literature that formulates ideas of empowerment, civility, modernity, and progress in which Islamic-oriented actors find no place. How has progress been defined? How has civility been conceptualized? What biases in the literature determine particular groups cannot contribute to these notions? How have these biases been effectively translated into language that serves to articulate certain subjectivities cannot be conducive to civility and peace? Indeed, for all the above points there is a critical need to study the concepts we apply to our subjects and ask where they have relevance and where they need "reelaboration" in the different contexts.

APPENDIX

METHODS

The primary technique of data collection was open-ended interviews. This involved the collecting of oral narration and answers to a semi-structured schedule of questions. The interview data was supplemented through observation and sometimes by taking part in the activities over three years of the fieldwork. In most cases using a tape recorder, interviews were conducted mostly in the English language; however, some were in Arabic and translating help was resorted to at the time of interview or else the interview was translated later.

I aimed to provide a profile of women in the official government-run women's organizations, Islamic women's organizations, and networkers from all emirates. The systematic criteria I followed from amongst the government-run organizations (33 in all including makeshift set ups in rural areas) are the following: (1) I included the umbrella association, the main emirate branch and then the larger of the associations under that branch, if present. Each of these would have on average 1000 regular members. (2) I aimed to include the clubs that were also run by the emirate sheikha as they were said to place greater emphasis on sports. Who I could interview was often limited.

To find a sample for Islamic-oriented women's organizations, I developed a list of the existing women's Islamic-oriented associations. Mosques often provided information regarding *halaqas*. There is no categorization for women's organizations under the Ministry of Social Affairs for women's Islamic organizations.

In regards to finding networks, I pursued two main avenues. One, from word of mouth, activists and experts, I was able to make a list of names of activists. Two, after interviewing formally I would ask for names of women who the interviewee judged to be active in the struggle for some societal or political goal, which I would then verify when contacting the person.

Schedule of Questions

Interviews with Participants

1. I would like to know a little about yourself:

   (a) Age (b) educational level attained (c) profession (d) which part of the emirates you are from/village or city (e) what your family name and lineage is.

2. Please comment on the position of women in Emirati society?

3. How does your status differ from your mother's and grandmothers' when they were your age?

4. What are your motivations behind taking part in this organization/group?

5. What are the needs and interests of the women within this group? And what are the needs of the people in the community using the services of this group?

6. What strategies do the participants implement to meet these needs and interests?

7. Do you have any other kind of background that has enabled you to help solve some of the challenges facing women (educational, professional, familial, contacts, interpersonal links)?

8. If the participants and yourself feel that as a group alone you are not able to deal with a particular problem what do you do next?

9. How do you communicate your concerns to important or influential people in government?

10. What skills have you learned while at this organization?

11. Do you participate in any other kind of activity or women's gathering, including those that take place simply in a home?

12. How does this organization make decisions?

    Does the management ask you your opinions?
    What ideas or issues have you brought up?
    Have they been implemented?

13. What do you think of women's struggles for participation in politics in the region, such as Kuwait or Bahrain?

14. Do you feel the work of the organization and the work you do personally makes a change in Emirati society? In what ways?

Interviews with Leaders of Organizations

1. I would like to know a little about yourself:
   (a) Age (b) educational level attained (c) profession (d) which

part of the emirates you are from/village or city (e) what your family name and lineage is.

2. Please comment on the position of women in Emirati society?
3. How does your status differ from your mother's and grandmothers' when they were your age?
4. For what reasons was this organization founded?
5. What are the current activities of this organization?
6. How many people participate in your organization?
7. What are the needs and interests of the women within this group? And what are the needs of the people in the community using the services of this group? How many nonmembers who use your services are there on a weekly basis?
8. What strategies do the participants implement to meet their needs and interests?
9. Do you have any other kind of background that has enabled you to help solve some of the challenges facing women (educational, professional, familial, contacts, interpersonal links)?
10. If the participants and yourself feel that as a group alone you are not able to deal with a particular problem what do you do next?
11. How do you communicate your concerns to important or influential people in government?
12. How were you chosen for your position?
13. What skills have your members brought with them and have learned here?
14. Are there women participating here from well-known families or established lineages and has this made a difference in their participation?
15. How much funding do you receive from donations and what percentage of your source of funding does this constitute? From the government? And from networking (through individuals and other associations)? Any other source?
16. What kinds of demands do some of these sources place on you in terms of what activities or programs to pursue?
17. What are the costs of running this organization?
18. What restrictions does your organization face in its operation (i.e. financial, traditional norms)?
19. What other obstacles exist in Emirati society in meeting the goals of this organization?
20. Do you coordinate any of your activities with men or organizations including men? (If yes) How are the roles divided?
21. How is your organization different from other organizations (women's, cultural)?

22. Do you network with any other organization or institution? (If yes) With whom? How do you coordinate your activities?
23. Do you have a vision for change in the emirates? (If yes) What is it?

Interviews with Those Participating in Networks

1. I would like to know a little about yourself:
    (a) Age (b) educational level attained (c) profession (d) which part of the emirates you are from/village or city (e) what your family name and lineage is.
2. Please comment on the position of women in Emirati society?
3. How does your status differ from your mother's and grandmothers' when they were your age?
4. How did you begin to serve society in this way?
5. For what reasons do you pursue your activities or people come to seek your help and guidance?
6. How many people seek your help on a weekly basis?
7. Have you been able to make a change in their lives/helped them? What strategies have you used in an attempt to assist them?
8. What strategies have you taught them to help themselves?
9. Have these people learned any specific skills?
10. Do you have any other kind of background that has enabled you to help solve some of the challenges facing women (educational, professional, familial, contacts, interpersonal links)?
11. If you feel that alone you are not able to deal with a particular problem what do you do next?
12. How do you communicate your concerns to important or influential people in government?
13. Do you network with other people to reach your goals?
14. Are there any costs involved in your volunteerism?
15. Do you receive any financial help for your activities? Do people who support you financially have any requests on how you should provide assistance?
16. What restrictions do you face (i.e., norms)?
17. What other obstacles exist in Emirati society in meeting your goals through such philanthropy?
18. Do you have a vision for change in the emirates? (If yes) What is it?

ACTIVITIES OF ASSOCIATIONS

Table 1   Women's Official Associations Included in Case Study

Number	Name of Association	Emirate	Ongoing Activities
1	Abu Dhabi Ladies Union	Abu Dhabi	Conferences, courses, lectures, entertainment, festivals, financial support, office for graduates, handicrafts, research
2	Abu Dhabi Ladies Club	Abu Dhabi	Lectures, sports facilities, painting, cake decoration, library, computer courses, nursery
3	Abu Dhabi Women's Association in Bateen	Abu Dhabi	*Durrat Al-Imarat* magazine, family counseling, handicrafts Qur'an lessons, sewing, specialized lessons, lectures, legal dept., school, media center, nursery
4	Umm Al Mu'mineen	Ajman	Café, children's karate, drawing, embroidery, handicrafts, henna, legal dept., marriage office, multipurpose halls, Qur'an lessons, religious education, sewing/stitching, specialized lessons, lectures, sports club
5	Dubai Women's Association	Dubai	Children's karate, family counseling, handicrafts, legal dept., sewing, specialized lessons, lectures, Qur'an lessons, nursery, Sheikha Latifa Award
6	Sharjah Women's Association	Sharjah	Literacy classes, children's karate, children and youth summer camps, Qur'an lessons, sewing, handcrafts, specialized lessons, lectures
7	Sharjah Ladies Club	Sharjah	Café, specialized lessons, sports facilities, swimming pool, children's lessons, nursery
8	Ras al-Khaima Women's Association	Ras al-Khaima	Literacy classes, Qur'an lessons, sewing, handcrafts, specialized lessons, lectures, nursery

Table 2 Women's Islamic-Oriented Associations Included in Case Study

Number	Type of Islamic Association	Activities
1	*Halaka*	Qur'anic recitation, *Hadith*, *Tafseer*, *Tajweed*
2	*Halaka*	Lessons (*Tafseer*, *Hadith*, *Fatawa*, *Halal/Haram*, prayer, contemporary political issues and world events, women's issues)
3	Information and community center	*Dawa*, Women's *Tajweed*, children's lessons (art, drama, Qur'anic recitation, Islamic history/stories), Arabic language, lectures with various speakers, women's shelter
4	Information center	*Dawa*, Qur'anic recitation, *Tafseer*, lectures with invited speakers, lessons
5	Learning center	Qur'anic recitation, *Hadith*, *Tafseer*
6	Learning center	Qur'anic recitation, *Hadith*, *Tafseer*, literacy
7	Women's committee in social development organization	Lessons, activities (mostly for teenage girls), literacy, lectures with invited speakers
8	University student association	*Dawa*, Qur'anic recitation, lessons, activities, charity
9	Women's wing of university student association	*Dawa*, Qur'anic recitation, lessons, activities, charity

INTERVIEWEE PROFILES

Table 3 Background Characteristics of Interviewees for Chapter 3: Women's GONGOs

Percent Local/ Nonlocal	Mean Age	Percent Married	Mean Number of Children	B.A.	Percent Partici- pating Outside	Percent Working Outside	Percent Paid	Sample Size
64/36	30	54	1.6	79	14	0	86	28

Table 4 Background Characteristics of Interviewees for Chapter 4: Islamic-Oriented Associations

Percent Local/ Nonlocal	Mean Age	Percent Married	Mean Number of Children	B.A. in process	Percent Partici- pating Outside	Percent Working Outside	Percent Paid	Sample Size
17/83	28	37	1	50/83	73	53	26	30

Table 5 Background Characteristics of Interviewees for Chapter 5: Women in Networks

Percent Local/ Nonlocal	Mean Age	Percent Married	Mean Number of Children	B.A.	Percent Partici- pating Outside Single Network	Percent Working Outside	Percent Paid	Sample Size	Net Sample Size
15/85	43	75	2.4	70	90	60	0	20	48

Notes

Chapter 1

1. Yael Navaro-Yashin (2002), *Faces of the State: Secularism and Public Life in Turkey*, Princeton: Princeton University Press, 4, 136.
2. See, for example, Timothy Mitchell (1991), "The Limits of the State: Beyond Statist Approaches and Their Critics," *American Political Science Review* 85, 1: 77–96.
3. Jude Howell (2005), "Introduction," in *Gender and Civil Society: Transcending Boundaries*, ed. Jude Howell and Diane Mulligan, London: Routledge, 4.
4. Sheila Carapico (1998), *Civil Society in Yemen: The Political Economy of Activism in Modern Arabia*, Cambridge: Cambridge University Press, 2.
5. Carole Pateman (1989), *The Disorder of Women: Democracy, Feminism and Political Theory*, Stanford: Polity Press, 33.
6. Janine A. Clark (1994), "Islamic Social-Welfare Organizations and the Legitimacy of the State in Egypt: Democratization or Islamization From Below?" Ph.D. diss., University of Toronto, Canada, 35.
7. Nilüfer Göle (1994), "Towards an Autonomization of Politics and Civil Society in Turkey," in *Politics in the Third Turkish Republic*, ed. Metin Heper, Boulder: Westview Press, 221.
8. Amani Kandil (1999), "Women and Civil Society," in *Civil Society at the Millennium*, Civicus, Connecticut: Kumarian Press, 63.
9. Jillian Schwedler (1995), "Introduction," in *Toward Civil Society in the Middle East? A Primer*, ed. Jillian Schwedler, Boulder CO: Lynne Rienner, 16.
10. Marlies Glasius (2005), "Who is the Real Civil Society? Women's Groups versus Pro-Family Groups at the International Criminal Court Negotiations," in *Gender and Civil Society*, ed. Jude Howell and Diane Mulligan, London: Routledge, 224.
11. For a critique of the secular-liberal principles, see, for example, Saba Mahmood (2004), *Politics of Piety: The Islamic Revival and the Feminist Subject*, Princeton: Princeton University Press.
12. Howell 2005, 6.
13. Thomas Carothers (1999), "Civil Society: Think Again," *Foreign Policy* no. 117: 21.
14. See James P. Troxel (1998), "The Recovery of Civic Engagement in America," in *Beyond Prince and Merchant: Citizen Participation and the Rise of Civil Society*, ed. John Burbidge, New York: Pact Publications.

15. For example, Abdulkhaleq Abdullah, Taha Hussein Hassan, and Rashid Mohamed Rashid (1995), *Al-Mujtama' al-madani wal-tahawwal al-dimuqrati fi al-imarat al-'arabiyya al-mutahida* [Civil Society and Democratic Change in the UAE], preface by Saad Eddin Ibrahim, Cairo: Ibn Khaldoun Centre for Development Studies.

16. Sayyid H. Hurreiz (2002), *Folklore and Folklife in the United Arab Emirates,* London: RoutledgeCurzon, 58.

17. See Theda Skocpol (1984), "Bringing the State Back In: Current Research" in *Bringing the State Back ,* ed. Peter B. Evans et al., Cambridge: Cambridge University Press.

18. Richard Norton (1995) "Introduction," in *Civil Society in the Middle East,* vol. 1. ed. Augustus Richard Norton, Leiden: E. J. Brill, 11.

19. Philippe Schmitter (1974), "Still the Century of Corporatism," *Review of Politics* 36, 1 (January): 93.

20. Carothers 1999, 19, 20.

21. Aradhana Sharma (2006), "Crossbreeding Institutions, Breeding Struggle: Women's Empowerment, Neoliberal Governmentality, and State (Re)Formation in India," *Cultural Anthropology* 21, 1: 62.

22. James Ferguson and Akhil Gupta (2002), "Spatializing States: Toward an Ethnography of Neoliberal Governmentality," *American Ethnologist* 29, 4: 981.

23. Barry Hindess (1997), *Discourses of Power: From Hobbes to Foucault,* Oxford: Blackwell, 106; and Mitchell Dean (1999), *Governmentality: Power and Rule in Modern Society,* London: Sage, 17, 18.

24. Dean 1999, 10.

25. Sharma 2006, 62.

26. See Dean's (western) historical account, in Dean 1999, 2.

27. Dean 1999, 31.

28. Ibid., 67.

29. Edward Shils (1992) "The Virtue of Civil Society," *Government and Opposition* 26, 1 (Winter): 3.

30. Centre for Civil Society, "Report on Activities for 2002–05," London School of Economics and Political Science. http://www.lse.ac.uk/collections/CCS/pdf/CCS_Report_on_Activities_2002–5.pdf. I include, however, the struggle among marginalized persons for economic empowerment.

31. Christopher G. A. Bryant (1994), "A Further Comment on Kumar's Civil Society," *British Journal of Sociology* 45, 3 (September): 497.

32. Ibid., 498.

33. Mark Neocleous (1995), "From Civil Society to the Social," *British Journal of Sociology* 46, 3 (September): 398.

34. Ibid., 398.

35. Krishan Kumar (1993), "Civil Society: An Inquiry into the Usefulness of an Historical Term," *British Journal of Sociology* 44, 3 (September): 383.

36. See Alvin A. Gouldner (1971), *Coming Crisis of Western Sociology,* London: Heinemann Educational Books.

37. Burhan Ghalyûn, quoted in Salwa Ismail (1994), "The Civil Society Concept and the Middle East: Questions of Meaning and Relevance," paper presented at the Canadian Political Science Association Annual Meeting, Calgary: University of Calgary, 14.

38. See, for example, Richard Antoun (2000) "Civil Society, Tribal Process, and Change in Jordan: An Anthropological View," *International Journal of Middle East Studies* 32, 4 (November).

39. Bryant 1994, 498.

40. Sami Zubaida (1992), "Islam, the State and Democracy," *Middle East Report* 179 (November-December): 4.

41. John P. Entelis (1996), "Civil Society and the Authoritarian Temptation in Algerian Politics: Islamic Democracy vs. the Centralized State," in *Civil Society in the Middle East,* vol. 2, ed. Augustus Richard Norton, Leiden: Brill, 44.

42. Jeff Haynes (2000), *Democracy and Civil Society in the Third World: Politics and New Political Movements,* Cambridge: Polity Press, 48.

43. Ibid.,169.

44. See ibid., 48, 120, 121, and 169.

45. Sheila Carapico (1996), "Yemen between Civility and Civil War," in *Civil Society in the Middle East,* vol. 2, ed. Richard Norton, Leiden: Brill, 287, 288.

46. Ernest Gellner (1996), *Conditions of Liberty: Civil Society and its Rivals,* London: Penguin Books, 26.

47. Mehran Kamrava (1998), *Democracy in the Balance: Culture and Society in the Middle East,* New York: Chatham House, 226.

48. Ibid., xv.

49. Saad Eddin Ibrahim (1998), "Populism, Islam, and Civil Society in the Arab World," in *Beyond Prince and Merchant,* ed. John Burbidge, New York: Pact, 57.

50. Saad Eddin Ibrahim 1995, "Preface," in Abdullah et al., 1995, 7.

51. Antoun 2000, 441.

52. Mohamed Salim al-Awwa, cited in Ahmad Moussalli (1995), "Muslim Fundamentalist Discourses," in *Civil Society in the Middle East,* vol. 1, ed. Richard Norton, Leiden: E.J. Brill, 106.

53. Norton 1996, 5.

54. See, Chris Hann, in Antoun 2000, 445.

55. Kumi Naidoo and Rajesh Tandon, eds. (1999), "The Promise of Civil Society," in *Civil Society at the Millenium,* Civicus, Connecticut: Kumarian Press, 2.

56. Robert W. Hefner (1998), *Democratic Civility: The History and Cross-Cultural Possibility of a Modern Political Ideal,* New Brunswick: Transaction, 11.

57. Ibid.

58. Rached Ghannouchi (1999), *Muqarabat fi al-'ilmaniyya w'al-mujtam' al-madani* [Papers on Secularism and Civil Society], London: Maghreb Center for Research and Translation, 83.

59. See, for example, Taha Jabir Alwani (1996), *Islah al-fikr al-islami bayna al-qudrat wa al-'aqabat: waraqat 'amal*. [The Reform of Islamic Thought between Capabilities and Obstacles], The Islamization of Knowledge Series, no. 10, Herndon, VA: International Institute of Islamic Thought.

60. Clark 1994, 17, 18.

61. Hefner 1998, 22.

62. Mustapha K. al-Sayyid (1993), "A Civil Society in Egypt?" *Middle East Journal* 47, 2 (Spring): 230.

63. Ibid., 230.

64. Ibid., 231.

65. Ibid., 239.

66. Carapico 1996, 288.

67. Quoted in Carapico 1996, 289.

68. Schwedler 1995, 16.

69. Ibid.

70. Ghannouchi 1999, 81. See, also, Michel Foucault (1980), *The History of Sexuality: Volume One*, New York: Vintage.

71. Foucault 1978, 1989, cited in Mahmood 2004, 17.

72. Jean Cohen and Andrew Arato (1992), *Civil Society and Political Theory*, Cambridge: MIT Press.

73. Antoun 2000, 445.

74. Ibid.

75. Robert D. Putnam (1995), "Bowling Alone: America's Declining Social Capital," *Journal of Democracy* 6, 1 (January): 66.

76. Schwedler 1995, 16.

77. Robert D. Putnam (2000), *Bowling Alone: The Collapse and Revival of American Community*, New York: Touchstone, 338.

78. Chris Hann and Elizabeth Dunn eds. (1996), *Civil Society: Challenging Western Models*, London: Routledge, 22.

79. Naidoo and Tandon 1999, 6.

80. See Cynthia Enloe (1989). *Bananas, Beaches and Bases: Making Feminist Sense of International Politics*, London: Pandora.

81. Parvin Paider (1995), *Women and the Political Process in Twentieth-Century Iran*, Cambridge: Cambridge University Press, 2.

82. Nadje S. al-Ali (2005), "Gender and Civil Society in the Middle East," in *Gender and Civil Society: Transcending Boundaries*, ed. Jude Howell and Diane Mulligan, London: Routledge, 101.

83. Georgina Waylen (1994), "Women and Democratization: Conceptualizing Gender Relations in Transition Politics," *World Politics* 46: 335.

84. Mahmood 2004, 189.

85. Sondra Hale (1997), *Gender Politics in Sudan: Islamism, Socialism, and the State*, Boulder CO: Westview Press, 31.

86. See, for example, Mervat Hatem (1985), "Conservative Patriarchal Modernization in the Arabian Gulf," *Contemporary Marxism*, no.11 (Fall): 96–109.

87. For example. Haleh Afshar (1994), *Why Fundamentalism? Iranian Women and Their Support of Islam,* York: University of York.

88. See, for example, Valentine M. Moghadam (1998), *Women, Work and Economic Reform in the Middle East and North Africa,* Boulder: Lynne Rienner Publishers.

89. See, for example, Mahmood 2004; Hafez 2003; and Christiansen 2003.

90. For a significant contribution to the area, see the volume compiled by Dawn Chatty and Annika Rabo (1996). *Organizing Women: Formal and Informal Women's Groups in the Middle East,* Oxford: Berg. See also Amani Kandil, ed. (1997) *Dalil awwali lil-jam'iyyat al-ahliyya al-'arabiyya* [An Initial Guide to the Arabic Civil Associations], Cairo: The Second Conference for Arabic Civil Organizations.

91. See Catharina Raudvere (2003), "Knowledge in Trust: Sufi Women in Istanbul," *Social Compass* 50, 1: 23–34; Chatty and Rabo 1996; and Diane Singerman (1995), *Avenues of Participation: Family, Politics, and Networks in Urban Quarters of Cairo,* Princeton: Princeton University Press.

92. See, for example, Mary Ann Tétreault and Haya al-Mughni (1996), "Gender, Citizenship and Nationalism in Kuwait," *British Journal of Middle Eastern Studies,* no. 22: 64–80; and Shafeeq Ghabra (1991), "Voluntary Associations in Kuwait: The Foundation of a New System?" *Middle East Journal,* no. 45: 199–215.

93. Singerman 1995, 5.

94. Mohamad A. K. al-Zekri (1998), "Folk Beliefs of Arab Women of Dubai Prior to Oil Discovery in 1966," M.Phil. diss., University of Exeter, UK.

95. Razan Abdul Hamdi Abdul Majeed (2000), "Modernity and Social Problems: Case of Dubai," unpublished MA diss., University of Exeter, UK.

96. Nora al-Zaabi (1993), *Ta'akhur sin al-zawaj wa'atharuh al-ijtima'iyyu: dirasah 'ala mujtama 'al-imarat al-'arabiyya al-mutahida* [The Rising Marriage Age and its Social Effect: A Study on UAE Society], Dubai, UAE: Dubai Women's Renaissance Association.

97. Lootah-Hessah Abdullah (1999), "Unveiling the Mask: Representation of Women on Dubai (United Arab Emirates) Television," Ph.D. diss., Ohio State University, USA.

98. Hind al-Qasimi (1998) *Al-Thabit w'al-mutaghayrah fi thaqafat al-mar'ah fi al-imarat* [The Constant and the Variable in the Women's Culture in the Emirates], Sharjah, UAE: Sociologists' Association.

99. See, for example, Mouza Ghubash (1999), *Al-Teknolojiyya wa tan-miyyat al-mar'ah al-rifiyya w'al-badawiyya bi dawlat al-imarat* [Technology and the Development of Rural and Bedouin Women in the Emirates,1971–1998], Dubai, UAE: Reading for All Publishing.

100. Maytha al-Shamsi and Abdallah Coulon (2001), *Al-adwar al-mutaghayrah lil-mar'ah fi dawlat al-imarat al-'arabiyya al-mutahida* [The Changing Roles of Women in the UAE: A Critical and Analytical Study], Al-Ain, UAE: UAE University.

101. Suaad Zayed al-Oraimi (2004), "Gender and Development: The role of Women in the Formal Economic and Political Spheres in the United Arab Emirates," Ph.D. diss., American University, Washington, USA.

102. Mohamed Mahmoud (1999), *Al-Mar'ah fi dawlat al-imarat al-'arabiyya al-mutahida markazha al-qanuni fi zil al-qawaneen al-Nafidha wa qada' al-naqd fi al-imarat* [Woman in the State of the UAE: Her Legal Status under Effective Statutes and according to the Higher Court of the Emirates.], Cairo: published by author.

103. Rima Sabban (1996), "Broken Spaces; Bounded Realities: Foreign Female Domestic Workers in the UAE," Ph.D. diss., American University, Washington, USA.

104. Pateman 1989, 211.

105. Suad Joseph (2001), "Women and Politics in the Middle East" in *Women and Power in the Middle East,* ed. Suad Joseph and Susan Slyomovics, Pennsylvania: University of Pennsylvania Press, 34.

106. Singerman 1995, 133.

107. Philip S. Khoury and Joseph Kostiner (1990), eds. *Tribes and State Formation in the Middle East,* Berkeley: University of California Press, 5.

108. Hussein Mahdavy (1970), "The Patterns and Problems of Economic Development in Rentier States: The Case of Iran," in *Studies in Economic History of the Middle East,* ed. A. Cook, London: Oxford University, 428.

109. Hazem Beblawi (1987) "The Rentier State in the Arab World" in *The Rentier State,* ed. Hazem Beblawi and Giacomo Luciani, London: Croom Helm, 51.

110. Nazih N. Ayubi (1996), *Over-stating the Arab State: Politics and Society in the Middle East,* London: I. B. Tauris, 227.

111. Michael L. Ross (2001), "Does Oil Hinder Democracy?" *World Politics,* 53 (April): 330.

112. See, for example, Hendrik van der Meulen (1997), "The Role of Tribal and Kinship Ties in the Politics of the United Arab Emirates," Ph.D. diss., Fletcher School of Law and Diplomacy, USA, 54.

113. Ayubi 1999, 229; and Mohammed al-Fahim (1995), *From Rags to Riches: A Story of Abu Dhabi,* London: London Centre of Arab Studies.

114. Liesl Graz (1990), *The Turbulent Gulf,* London: I. B. Tauris, 178.

115. Ayubi 1996, 227.

116. Michael Herb (2002), "Do Rents Cause Authoritarianism?" Paper presented at the Middle East Studies Association Annual Meeting (November).

117. Robert E. Looney (1997), "Diminishing Returns and Policy Options in a Rentier State: Economic Reform and Regime Legitimacy in Saudi Arabia," *Political Crossroads* 5, nos. 1 & 2: 32.

118. Eva Bellin (2005), "Coercive Institutions and Coercive Leaders," in *Authoritarianism in the Middle East: Regimes and Resistance,* ed. Marsha Pripstein Posusney and Michele Penner Angrist, Boulder: Lynne Rienner, 37.

119. Gwenn Okruhlik (1999), "Rentier Wealth, Unruly Law, and the Rise of Opposition: The Political Economy of Rentier States," *Comparative Politics* 31, 3 (April): 308.

120. John Clark (1997), "Petro-Politics in Congo," *Journal of Democracy* 8, 3: 62–76.

121. Herb 2002, 19, 20.

122. Ibid., 19.

123. Jill Crystal(1995), "Civil Society in the Arab Gulf States," in *Toward Civil Society in the Middle East? A Primer*, ed. Jillian Schwedler, Boulder: Lynne Rienner Publishers, 62.

124. Michael Herb (1999), *All in the Family: Absolutism, Revolution, and Democracy in The Middle Eastern Monarchies*, ed. Shahrough Akhavi,. New York: University of New York Press, 4.

125. Mouza Ghubash (1997), "Social Development in the United Arab Emirates" in *Perspectives on the United Arab Emirates*, ed. Edmund Ghareeb and Ibrahim al Abed, London: Trident Press, 286.

126. Brooke Ackerly (1997) "What's in a Design? The Effects of NGO Programme Delivery Choices on Women's Empowerment in Bangladesh" in *Getting Institutions Right for Women in Development*, ed. Anne Marie Goetz, London: Zed Books, 141.

127. Ann Bookman and Sandra Morgen eds. (1988), *Women and the Politics of Empowerment*, Philadelphia: Temple University Press, 4.

128. Rowlands, quoted in Elsa L. Dawson (1999), "Gender: Assessing the impact," in *Gender Works: Oxfam Experience in Policy and Practice*, ed. Fenella Porter, Ines Smyth, and Caroline Sweetman, London: Oxfam, 126.

129. Barbara Einhorn and Charlie Sever (2005), "Gender, Civil Society and Women's Movements in Central and Eastern Europe," in *Gender and Civil Society: Transcending Boundaries*, ed. Jude Howell and Diane Mulligan, London: Routledge, 24, 25.

130. Quoted in Schwedler 1995, 5.

131. Norton 1995, 213.

132. Schwedler 1995, 6.

133. Antoun 2000, 456.

134. Singerman 1995, 50.

135. Adam B. Seligman (1992), *The Idea of Civil Society*, New York: Free Press, 182.

136. Edward Shils (1997), *The Virtue of Civility: Selected Essays on Liberalism, Tradition, and Civil Society*, ed. Steven Grosby, Indianapolis: Liberty Fund, 335.

137. Seligman 1992, 182.

138. Shils 1997, 25, 26.

139. Seligman 1992, 165.

140. Augustus Richard Norton (1993), "The Future of Civil Society in the Middle East," *Middle Easzt Journal* 47, 2: 214.

141. W. Andy Knight (2000), "State-Society Complexes and the New Multilateralism: Creating Space for Hierarchic Governance," in *Global*

Institutions and Local Empowerment: Competing Theoretical Perspectives, ed. Kendall Stiles, Houndmills: Macmillan Press, 41.
142. Quote in Janine A. Clark and Remonda Bensabat Kleinberg, eds. (2000), "Conclusions: Politics of Democratization—the Force of Civil Society," in *Economic Liberalization, Democratization and Civil Society in the Developing World,* New York: Macmillan Press, 1.

CHAPTER 2

1. CIA World Factbook (2002), United Arab Emirates. http://www.odci.gov/cia/publications/factbook/geos/tc.html (accessed 23 April 2004).
2. Naturalized citizens do not have the same rights as "original" Emiratis. Furthermore, a naturalized citizen's children will further be categorized as naturalized, thus, not fully integrated. Omanis, Qataris, and Bahrainis are eligible for citizenship after three years of residency. Foreign women married to locals must undergo an often protracted administrative process to attain citizenship.
3. "UAE" as an adjective will also be placed before "woman."
4. Mohammad al-Murr (1997), *Amal wataniyya: maqalat fi hubb al-imarat* [National Hopes: Essays in the Love of the Emirates], Sharjah: Dar al-Khalij, 105.
5. Theoretically, each UAE citizen has the right to a home subsidized by the state. However, the distribution of wealth is not uniform across the emirates. Men originally from the Abu Dhabi emirate have the greatest entitlements, having been given separate gifts from the local government of residential, agricultural, and commercial property, plus a grant at the time of marriage towards a house. Citizens of Ras al-Khaima and Umm al-Quwain sometimes live in visibly poor conditions.
6. U.S. Department of State 2006. "United Arab Emirates: Country Reports on Human Rights Practices 2005," released by the Bureau of Democracy, Human Rights, and Labor (March 8), http://www.state.gov/g/drl/rls/hrrpt/2005/61701.htm
7. CIA World Factbook (2005), "United Arab Emirates." www.cia.gov/cia/publications/factbook/geos/ae.html (accessed 23 June 2006).
8. U.S. Department of State (2005), "United Arab Emirates: Country Reports on Human Rights Practices 2004," http://www.state.gov/g/drl/rls/hrrpt/2004/41734.htm (accessed 23 June 2006).
9. CIA World Factbook 2002.
10. U.S. Department of State 2006.
11. According to the CIA *World Factbook* of 2005, age groups 0–14 years constituted 25.3 percent (male 331,269, female 317,977); 15–64 years, 71.1 percent (male 1,115,826, female 707,058); and 65 years and over: 3.6 percent (male 66,404, female 24,678); see CIA World Factbook (2005), "United Arab Emirates."

12. U.S. Department of State 2005.

13. Sayyid H. Hurreiz. 2002. *Folklore and Folklife in the United Arab Emirates,* London: RoutledgeCurzon, 26.

14. Cited in Frauke Heard-Bey (2001), "The Tribal Society of the UAE and its Traditional Economy," in *United Arab Emirates: A New Perspective,* ed. Edmund Ghareeb and Ibrahim al Abed, London: Trident Press, 100.

15. Heard-Bey 2001, 98.

16. Several subtribes of the Bani Yas tribe of Abu Dhabi have names such as Al-Mazrui, Al-Qubaisi, or Al-Hamili.

17. Heard-Bey 2001, 99.

18. It becomes clear that the image of the *harem* was overexaggerated to the extent that it created colossal misconceptions of the reality of women's lives in the Arab Gulf. Heard-Bey says that, "the *harem* is largely a symbol of the position of women within society: they are not members of the community as much as they belong to the private lives of the man on whom they depend most at a particular state in their lives. Women are protected from the male world by the institution of the *harem*." Heard-Bey 1982, 144, 145. Soffan and Lienhardt challenge the image presented earlier. Linda Usra Soffan (1980), *The Women of the United Arab Emirates.* London: Croom Helm, 68 and Peter Lienhardt (2001), *Shaikhdoms of Eastern Arabia,* ed. Ahmed al-Shahi, New York: Palgrave, 34.

19. Ibid.

20. "Women in the UAE," *Arab Women Connect.* www.awc.org.jo/english/uae/downloads/WOMEN%20IN%20THE%20UAE.doc (accessed 3 November 2003).

21. It was not uncommon for succession of rule to take place through the death or removal of the family member ruling. See Michael Herb (1999), *All in the Family: Absolutism, Revolution, and Democracy in The Middle Eastern Monarchies,* ed. Shahrough Akhavis, New York: University of New York Press for detailed accounts.

22. Malcolm Peck (1986), *The United Arab Emirates: A Venture in Unity,* Boulder, Westview Press, 85.

23. Ibid.

24. Lienhardt 2001, 62.

25. Soffan 1980, 68.

26. Heard-Bey 2001, 103–113.

27. Rima Sabban. 1996. "Broken Spaces; Bounded Realities: Foreign Female Domestic Workers in the UAE," Ph.D diss., The American University, Washington, 43.

28. Sabban 1996, 43.

29. Mohammed al-Fahim. 1995. *From Rags to Riches: A Story of Abu Dhabi,* London: London Centre of Arab Studies, 56.

30. Ibid.

31. Ibid.

32. Ronald Codrai (2001)., *Faces of the Emirates: An Arabian Album. A Collection of Mid-20th Century Photographs*, Dubai: Motivate Publishing, 83.

33. Ibid, 84.

34. Heard-Bey 2001, 99; and Soffan 1980, 42.

35. Heard-Bey 2001, 99; and Paul Dresch (2005), "Debates on Marriage and Nationality in the United Arab Emirates," in *Monarchies and Nations: Globalisation and Identity in the Arab States of the Gulf*, ed. Paul Dresch and James Piscatori, London: I.B. Tauris, 138.

36. Soffan 1980, 43. Soffan indicates that a stigma has developed and interviews with divorced local women confirm it.

37. Ibid.

38. Hurreiz 2002, 23.

39. Peck 1986, 65.

40. Ibid.

41. In terms of natural gas reserves, the UAE, with around 6.1 trillion cubic meters, ranks fifth after Kuwait, Qatar, Iran, and Saudi Arabia. In 2000, proven oil reserves were 98.8 billion barrels. Mohamed Shihab (2001), "Economic Development in the UAE," in *United Arab Emirates: A New Perspective*, 250. Abu Dhabi accounts for 92.2 billion (94 percent); Dubai has approximately 4 billion; Sharjah 1.5 billion; and Ras al-Khaima 100 million barrels.

42. Library of Congress, Country Studies: United Arab Emirates (1993). http://lcweb2.loc.gov/cgi-bin/query/r?frd/cstdy:@field(DOCID+ae0033) (accessed 12 February 2005).

43. Ibid.

44. Sabban 1996, 48.

45. The Emirates Center for Strategic Studies and Research, http://www.ecssr.ac.ae/system.html (accessed 12 February 2005); and Hendrik Van der Meulen 1997, "The Role of Tribal and Kinship Ties in the Politics of the United Arab Emirates. Ph.D. diss., Fletcher School of Law and Diplomacy, 283. Mohamed Shihab estimates that at its current production rate the UAE can produce oil for another 122 years. Mohamed Shihab 2001, 250. This prediction is confirmed by the CIA *World Factbook* 2005, United Arab Emirates and Wikipedia Encyclopedia, Economy of the United Arab Emirates at http://en.wikipedia.org/wiki/Economy_of _the_United_Arab_Emirates (accessed 12 February 2005), the latter predicting that at 2.3 million barrels per day (in 2003) oil reserves would last 150 years.

46. Before schools were opened for modern education there were gatherings of (mostly male) students to learn and memorize the Qur'an in what is called the *kuttab* or classroom.

47. Ibid., 58.

48. Abdulkhaleq Abdullah; Taha Hussein Hassan; and Rashid Mohamed Rashid (1995), *Al-Mujtama' al-madani wal-tahawwal al-dimucrati fi*

al-imaraat al-'arabiyya al-mutahida [Civil Society and Democratic Change in the UAE], prefaced by Saad Eddin Ibrahim, Cairo: Ibn Khaldoun Centre for Development Studies.

49. "Women in the UAE," *Arab Women Connect.*

50. See Ibid.

51. "Women in the UAE," *Arab Women Connect.*

52. The 1835 Treaty of Maritime Peace in Perpetuity was in effect until 1971.

53. Sheikh Zayed was born in Al-Ain, capital of the Eastern Province, in 1918, the son of Abu Dhabi's eighth ruler, Sheikh Sultan, and grandson of "Zayed the Great," the fifth ruler from 1855 to 1909. His mother, Sheikha Salima, belonged to the Qubaisat Tribe. In 1966 Zayed, with the support of family members, replaced his brother, Shakhbut, who was then the ruler. Hence, Zayed won the loyalty of the local tribes. From 1946 to 1966 he lived exclusively with the Bedouin and shared their poverty. As the eleventh ruler of Abu Dhabi, with the support of the head of the family council and oil money, Zayed immediately set progressive initiatives in motion.

54. Jane Bristol-Rhys (2005), "In the Other's Words: Historiography of the UAE," paper at the *American Anthropological Association Meeting* (November): 17.

55. Fatma al-Sayegh 2000, "Diversity in Unity: Political Institutions and Civil Society," in *A Century in Thirty Years: Shaykh Zayed and the United Arab Emirates,* ed Joseph A. Kechichian, Washington: Middle East Policy Council, 37, 38; and Library of Congress, Country Studies: United Arab Emirates, 1993.

56. Al-Sayegh 2000, 39; and Library of Congress, 1993.

57. Abu Dhabi and Dubai had appointed eight members each to the FNC, Ras al-Khaima and Sharjah six members each; and Ajman, Al Fujairah, and Umm al Quwain four members each.

58. Van der Meulen 1997, 44.

59. Philip S. Khoury and Joseph Kostiner 1990, 6–7 and Van der Meulen 1996, 38.

60. Cited in Christopher M. Davidson (2005), *The United Arab Emirates: A Study in Survival,* Boulder: Lynne Rienner Publishers, 65.

61. Van der Meulen 1997, 8.

62. See Nazih N. Ayubi, (1999), *Over-stating the Arab State: Politics and Society in the Middle East,* London, I. B. Tauris, 244.

63. Saad Ahmed al-Hajji (2000), *Al-Jam'iyyat al-nisaa'iyya al-ojtima'iyya bedu w'al-majlis al-ta'awun ledu wa al-khaleej al-'arabiyya* [Women's Social Associations in GCC Countries]. Kuwait: published by author, 17.

64. Al-Fahim 1995, 56.

65. Al-Hajji 2000, 17.

66. Ibid.

67. Ibid.

68. Ibid.
69. Ibid.
70. Ibid.
71. Ibid., 63.
72. UNDP-POGAR, cited in Davidson 2005, 270.
73. Davidson 2005, 270.
74. Abdullah et al., 1995, 63
75. One group tried to establish itself as the UAE Human Rights Society and a second the Emirates Association for Human Rights.
76. Mehran Kamrava (1998), *Democracy in the Balance: Culture and Society in the Middle East,* New York: Chatham House, 42.
77. Davidson 2005, 77.
78. Christopher M. Davidson (2006), "The Emirates of Abu Dhabi and Dubai: Contrasting Roles in the International System," paper presented to conference on *The Global Gulf,* Institute of Arab and Islamic Studies, University of Exeter (July): 11.
79. Ayubi 1999, 245. The term, "consociationalism" was coined by David Apter.
80. Sulayman Khalaf, cited in Ayubi 1999, 263.
81. See Davidson 2005, 263.
82. Ibid., 78.
83. Sa'id Abu 'Athira, quoted in ibid.
84. Davidson 2005, 78.
85. Ayubi 1999, 247.
86. Ibid.
87. Davidson 2005, 79.
88. Ayubi 1999, 235.
89. Ibid.
90. Davidson 2006, 12.
91. Martin Hvidt (2006), "Governance in Dubai: The Emergence of Political and Economic Ties between the Public and Private Sector," Centre for Contemporary Middle East Studies, University of Denmark, Working Paper No. 6 (June), 10.
92. Davidson 2006, 11.
93. "Women will enrich FNC says Hind," *Gulf News* (1 December 2002) http://www.gulf-news.com/Articles/news.asp?ArticleID=70782 (accessed 13 December 2004).
94. "Fatima Sees Promising Future for UAE Women," *Gulf News* (8 November 2002) http://www.gulf-news.com/Articles/news.asp?ArticleID=67882m (accessed 13 December2004).
95. Khatib, however, indicates that the demand was in terms of the care women would give their soldiers. She also states that the majority of women who do enter the military are naturalized locals. Maha K.Khatib, (1994), "Beyond the Mysterious and Exotic: Women of the Emirates (And I) Assess Their Lives and Society," Ph.D. diss., Brown University, 231–233.

96. In a major reshuffling of the ministries, the Ministry of Labor and Social Affairs was split into the Ministry of Social Affairs and Ministry of Labor.
97. United Arab Emirates Zayed Centre for Coordination and Follow-up (2000), *Feminine Issues in the United Arab Emirates: Perspectives of a Visionary Leader,* Dubai: Zayed Centre, 9.
98. "Women in UAE," http://www.uae.gov.ae/Government/Women.htm (accessed 3 November 2003).
99. "Women in UAE," http://www.uaeforever.com/Women/ (accessed 3 November 2003).
100. "Women in the UAE," *Arab Women Connect.*
101. Davidson 2005, 74.
102. United Arab Emirates Zayed Centre for Coordination and Follow-up 2000, 11.
103. Mowza bint Mohammed bin Butti al-Hamed (2002), *Zayed. The Millennial Legend,* Dubai: Bin Dasmal, 262.
104. Ibid.
105. Dresch 2005, 24.
106. See also Haya al-Mughni and Mary Ann Tétreault (2005), "Political Actors without the Franchise: Women and Politics in Kuwait," in *Monarchies and Nations: Globalisation and Identity in the Arab States of the Gulf,* ed. Paul Dresch and James Piscatori, London: I. B. Tauris, 207.
107. The national man is granted up to DH70,000. Because of exorbitant dowries men were increasingly turning to marriage to nonlocals. Mass weddings have also been encouraged and supported by the fund on a large scale.
108. Dresch 2005, 148.
109. The UAE and Qatar do not have a personal status law. Badria Abdullah al-Awadhi (2005), "Women in the Gulf and Globalization: Challenges and Opportunities," in *The Gulf Challenges of the Future,* Abu Dhabi: Emirates Center for Strategic Studies and Research, 434, 435.
110. They may possibly be able to confer citizenship in case of divorce, widowhood, or if the father is unknown. Dresch 2005, 144, Sabban 1996, 55 and informal interviews with locals. Children of Emirati women born to foreign fathers are stripped of all rights of nationals, such as free schooling, and as is typical for all Arab Gulf countries, are also not allowed to inherit. See al-Awadhi 2005, 434. However, there have been instances where mothers have received special permission for their children to be granted citizenship.
111. According to the Dubai Court of First Instance, statistics for the Dubai emirate alone show that in 1999, 73 national females married nonnationals, an increase from 42 cases in 1998 and 54 in 1997. The figure for 1996 was 76. See Razan Hamdi Abdul Majeed (2000), "Modernity and Social Problems: Case of Dubai," M.Phil. diss., University of Exeter, 36–39. However, it seems that most local women who have married

non-GCC men do not register their marriages, so that their passports show no evidence of marriage. In the field estimates by local women of the percentage of local women married to nonlocals, ranged from two to ten percent. A likely figure would altogether be five percent (16,000 national women), as quoted by the majority of women who discussed the issue. This number is also supported by the slightly more conservative figure of 15,000 national women proposed by Christopher Davidson, University of Durham, UK, Personal communication, July 2006.

112. "Women in the UAE," *Arab Women Connect*.
113. See, Amnesty International. 1997. "United Arab Emirates: Imprisonment and Flogging for Marriage across Faiths—the Case of Elie Dib Ghaleb," http://web.amnesty.org/library/Index/ENGMDE250031997?open&o f=ENG-ARE (accessed 7 April 2006).
114. See for example, in Qatar the case of Hamda Fahad Jassem Ali al-Thani, a member of Qatar's ruling family, who married an Egyptian in 2003 and petitioned Amnesty International in December 2005 for help. After marrying her Egyptian husband she was reputedly abducted, then transferred and confined to a family home in Qatar. Amnesty International, "Stop Violence against Women," http://web.amnesty.org/actforwomen/ qtr-221205-background-eng (accessed 7 April 2006).
115. The first order to ban women from marrying foreigners was issued on 19 December 1996 from the Presidential *diwan* to the Ministry of Justice, and stated, "if she wishes to marry then she loses her citizenship." The second order was on 25 January 1997, and specified that GCC members were not included as foreigners in the decree. The order has been implemented in practice. For example, a woman from a well-known Abu Dhabi tribe (whose mother was Indian) married her maternal cousin who was nonlocal and the couple were forcibly retrieved from Bahrain to where they had fled. They were then obliged to dissolve their marriage. Dresch 2005, 151. However, there have been hundreds of instances of a woman marrying a maternal nonlocal cousin in the UAE. Dubai in particular has ignored the decree altogether.
116. "Women in UAE," http://www.uaeforever.com/Women/ (accessed 3 November 2003).
117. U.S. Department of State Human Rights Reports for 2000, February 2001, "The 57th Commission on Human Rights," http://www .humanrights-usa.net/reports/unitedarabemirates.html (accessed 3 November 2003).The increase differs from emirate to emirate, with Abu Dhabi, the richest in oil, having the lowest rate.
118. However, a much greater percentage of males study abroad.
119. Interview with Mona al-Bahr, December 2002, Al-Ain, UAE.
120. U.S. Department of State, Human Rights Reports for 2000.
121. Ibid.
122. Ibid.

123. In fact, the Ministry of Justice, Islamic Affairs and Awqaf proposed an amendment in 2004 in which a man could bar his wife from working even if a premarital agreement had been made which allows her to take employment. Amnesty International (2005), "United Arab Emirates: Covering Events from January–December 2004," http://web.amnesty.org/report2005/are-summary-eng (accessed 27 April 2006).

124. See also, al-Awadhi 2005, 436.

125. State policy dictates that a divorced foreign woman without citizenship (commonplace because of lengthy administrative procedures) does not have an automatic right to residency. Hence, she requires a *kafeel* (sponsor), who is often her own minor child. See Dresch 2005, 144, 145. Such policies aim to establish an identity based on local Arab lineage. Non Muslim nonnationals have no legal rights to custody. Even in the case of the death of the husband, the children are automatically placed under the legal custody of female members of the deceased husband's family. Ownership of property is also granted wholly to members of the deceased husband's family if he was married to a nonnational (and if children exist, their inheritance is placed with their relative on the father's side until they are of legal age), even in the event that a will had dictated a portion of his wealth to the nonnational wife.

126. Many court procedures contemplated by a woman are not even begun. The families of national women usually dissuade them from filing for divorce. However, according to a lawyer in Dubai, the greater difficulty is faced by nonnational women wanting to divorce national men, due to practical, especially financial barriers, along with lengthy divorce procedures. Interview, March 2004, Dubai.

127. The judiciary brings many judges from other Arab countries and draws its sources from tribal laws, British, Egyptian, and Iraqi law, but emphasizes *shari'a* (Islamic law). According to informal interviews with locals, the UAE court system often includes both "written" laws and "unwritten" laws. It is the unwritten laws, usually understood from precedents through tradition or discriminatory religious interpretation that take primacy. For example, if someone kills a person by mistake, the killer's tribe (*al-'aqelah*) will have to pay a *diyyah* (ransom) to the dead person's family. Although this is part of the *shari'a*, it is an "unwritten law." Around 40–45 percent of the judiciary is made up of expatriates; see Freedom House (2005), "Freedom in the World Country Ratings: United Arab Emirates."

128. Interviews with Maryan Sultan, December 2002, Al-Ain, UAE; and female Emirati acquaintances, Sharjah, UAE. Some stated that the nature of multiple marriages differed according to the different ethnic backgrounds. For example, the Ajam people do not normally take part in this practice. However, many Ajams adhere to the *shi'a* school of thought that allows men to marry a woman for a predetermined period

of time (*muta*); however, the practice is more prevalent among the youth. What also exists is the *misyar* marriage, which allows the *sunni* man to marry another woman who lives outside his area of residence (which could mean that she lives in another emirate or country). This form of marriage was sanctioned by prominent scholar, al-Qaradawi, for the Gulf region, and has thus acquired legitimacy.

129. "Divorce Survey to Begin Soon" (November 12, 2002), *Gulf News* http://www.gulf-news.com/Articles/news.asp?ArticleID=68212 (accessed 2 February2003). According to a Dubai lawyer, a woman has the right to file for a divorce in the UAE if she has been physically, mentally, or verbally abused. Interview, March 2004, Dubai.

Chapter 3

1. Nikolas Rose (1999), *Governing the Soul: The Shaping of the Private Self,* 2nd ed. London: Free Association Books, 217.
2. Yael Navaro-Yashin (2002), *Faces of the State: Secularism and Public Life in Turkey,* Princeton: Princeton University Press, 132.
3. Rose 1999, xxi.
4. "Verticality" refers to the state as an institution that is somehow "above" civil society, the community, and family. State planning consequently will be top down and state actions directed to manipulate from above, whilst grassroots actions are contrasted with those of the states, because they are initiated from below. With the idea of "encompassment" the state is located within an ever-widening ripple of circles, starting with family and local community and ending with the system of nation-states. James Ferguson and Akhil Gupta (2002), "Spatializing States: Toward an Ethnography of Neoliberal Governmentality," *American Ethnologist* 29, 4: 982.
5. Nikolas Rose (1996), "Governing 'Advanced' Liberal Democracies," in *Foucault and Political Reason: Liberalism, Neo-Liberalism and Rationalities of Governmentality,* ed. Andrew Barry, Thomas Osborne, and Nikolas Rose, Chicago: University of Chicago Press, 46.
6. The ways in which the state represents itself as a reified entity with particular "spatial" properties through specific sets of metaphors and practices. Ferguson and Gupta 2002, 981, 982.
7. Mitchell Dean (1999), *Governmentality: Power and Rule in Modern Society,* London: Sage, 145.
8. Mehran Kamrava (1998), *Democracy in the Balance: Culture and Society in the Middle East,* New York: Chatham House, 54.
9. Sayyid H. Hurreiz (2002), *Folklore and Folklife in the United Arab Emirates,* London: RoutledgeCurzon, 59.
10. Ibid.
11. Frauke Heard-Bey (2001), "The Tribal Society of the UAE and its Traditional Economy," in *United Arab Emirates: A New Perspective,* ed. Peter Hellyer and Ibrahim al-Abed, Bookcraft, UK: Trident Press, 255.

12. Although typical of the clubs, the Dubai and Ras al-Khaima associations included more nonlocals in their programs.

13. Estimate from 2003, "UAE Women," www.uaewomen.net (accessed 28 October 2005).

14. Rose 1999, 213.

15. Haya al-Mughni (1997), "From Gender Equality to Female Subjugation: The Changing Agendas of Women's Groups in Kuwait," in *Organizing Women: Formal and Informal Women's Groups in the Middle East,* ed. Dawn Chatty and Annika Rabo, Oxford: Berg, 195–209.

16. Suad Joseph (1997), "The Reproduction of Political Process among Women Activists in Lebanon: 'Shopkeepers' and Feminists," in *Organizing Women: Formal and Informal Women's Groups in the Middle East,* ed. Dawn Chatty and Annika Rabo, Oxford: Berg, 57–80.

17. Valentine M. Moghadam (1997), "Women's NGOs in the Middle East and North Africa: Constraints, Opportunities, and Priorities." in *Organizing Women: Formal and Informal Women's Groups in the Middle East,* ed. Dawn Chatty and Annika Rabo, Oxford: Berg, 23–55.

18. Roger Owen (2000), *State, Power and Politics in the Making of the Modern Middle East,* 2nd ed. London: Routledge, 229.

19. See Suad Joseph and Susan Slyomovics eds., *Women and Power in the Middle East,* Pennsylvania: University of Pennsylvania Press.

20. Several interviewees did not see that their goals were any different from the state's official apparatus, the Ministry of Social Affairs, on either a practical or a theoretical level.

21. Al-Mughni 1997, 147.

22. Rose 1996, 57.

23. Dean 1999, 67.

24. Suaad Zayed al-Oraimi (2004), "Gender and Development: the role of Women in the formal Economic and Political Spheres in the United Arab Emirates," Ph.D. diss., American University of Washington, 316.

25. James Ferguson (1994), *The Anti-Politics Machine: "Development," Depoliticization, and Bureaucratic Power in Lesotho,* Minneapolis: University of Minnesota Press, 18.

26. Lovenduski, however, explains that state feminism is also defined in terms of referring to feminists or femocrats in government and government institutions that push a feminist agenda through the state. Joni Lovenduski (2005), *State Feminism and Political Representation,* Cambridge: Cambridge University Press, 10–12.

27. Rose 1996, 49.

28. See also al-Oraimi 2004, 314–316.

29. Informants gave examples of prominent women who had achieved a special and personal decree from Sheikh Zayed to marry nonlocals. Another organizational manager explained that this unwritten law had recently been changed and that (two years prior to his passing) Sheikh Zayed had requested a list of all women who were facing this issue so that they and their families could be granted citizenship.

30. Navaro-Yashin 2002, 2.
31. Samar Kanafani, "Child-raising Should Come First: Sheikha Fatima Gives Her View of a Woman's Place," *Daily Star*, http://www.lebanonwire.com/news/02021816DS.htm (accessed 14 December 2004).
32. See *Gulf News,* "Sheikha Fatima Urges Women to Join Council," (March 10, 2002) http://www.gulf-news.com/Articles/news.asp?ArticleID=64620 (accessed 14 December 2004).
33. Paul Dresch (2005), "Debates on Marriage and Nationality in the United Arab Emirates," in *Monarchies and Nations: Globalization and Identity in the Arab States of the Gulf,* ed. Paul Dresch and James Piscatori, London: I.B. Tauris, 151.
34. In June 2003 there was a two day state of emergency in Ras al-Khaima. Tanks (from Abu Dhabi) were positioned in various streets to monitor and contain protesters as Sheikh Khalid was stripped of his entitlement to succession by his father, the world's longest-ruling sovereign (having ruled Ras al-Khaima since 1948). In steadily worsening health, Sheikh Saqr Mohammed al-Qasimi decided, at the age of 86, to strip his eldest son of his title after meeting with Sheikh Zayed, and instead gave the title to one of his younger sons, Sheikh Saud. See Susan Bisset, "Emirate Prince Ousted in Women's Rights Row," *Daily Telegraph* (15 June 2003), www.telegraph.co.uk/news/main.jhtml?xml=/news/2003/06/15 (accessed 9 September 2005).
35. A reliable source discussed the problems that affect average residents or citizens, as well as those in elite positions, who are forbidden to criticize state officials. The example cited was of a sheikha in Dubai who at the time of interview was held under house arrest because she had openly criticized the ruler of Dubai. Her palace had a military guard and all windows were ordered to remain closed. The source described the horrible effects of these measures on the hostage.
36. Al-Oraimi similarly finds these associations have little commitment to gender issues. Al-Oraimi 2004, 321.
37. Personal correspondence with member of WLUML, December 2004.
38. These include a law that puts the burden of a rape case on the woman, thereby making it extremely difficult to prove rape. If rape cannot be proven through four witnesses of the crime, then the accuser will be charged with adultery. UAE law has made this a crime against the state. For previous cases in the UAE, see Women Living under Muslim Laws at http://www.wluml.org (accessed 17 September 2006).
39. Initiatives concerned with women's issues are begun by elite women in the associations or some other source. A participant explained how: "The Ministry of Justice drafted a law concerned with custody rights and gave it to us to review each article. Other review committees were also formed of scholars, people from the courts, people specialised in *shari'a*." The issue that brought custody rights to the attention of the courts came from

within the context of how different Islamic schools of law resolve this matter. In Sharjah, which follows the Hanbali *madhab* (school of Islamic law), women would leave the emirate, if they had custody of a child, before it reached the age of seven, going usually to Dubai where, under the Maliki *madhab*, as elsewhere in the UAE, a mother keeps her child until it reaches the age of nine.

40. Hurreiz 2002, 95.
41. Elizabeth Fernea (1998), *In Search of Islamic Feminism: One Woman's Global Journey*, New York: Double Day. I also wish to acknowledge an anonymous reviewer for pointing out the significance.
42. "Women in the UAE," *Arab Women Connect*, www.awc.org.jo/english/uae/downloads/WOMEN%20IN%20THE%20UAE.doc
43. Ibid.
44. Al Oraimi 2004, 223.
45. See Marilyn Carr, Martha Chen, and Renana Jhabvala eds., (1996), *Speaking Out: Women's Economic Empowerment in South Asia*, London: IT Publications, 215.
46. Munira Ahmed Fakhro (2005), "The Changing Role of Women in the Gulf Region," in *The Gulf Challenges of the Future*, Abu Dhabi: Emirates Center for Strategic Studies and Research, 411.
47. Amy Gutmann, quoted in Robert D. Putnam (2000), *Bowling Alone: The Collapse and Revival of American Community*, New York: Touchstone, 346.
48. Literally "non Arab," but in the UAE those of Iranian decent
49. According to informal interviews with new graduates seeking employment at Dubai Media City, Emirati citizens could expect a monthly salary of not less than DH12,000, other Arab nationalities DH5,500–7,500, and Indians DH1,500–3,000.
50. Al-Oraimi 2004, 317.
51. Rose 1996, 48.
52. Dean 1999, 145.
53. James D. Sidaway (2005), "Geographies of Postdevelopment," paper presented to the Inaugural Meeting of Nordic Geographers, Lund, 10–14 May, 13.
54. Michel Foucault (1997) defines biopolitics as "the endeavor, begun in the eighteenth century, to rationalize problems presented to governmental practice by the phenomena characteristic of a group of living human beings constituted as a population: health, sanitation, birth rate, longevity, race." Quoted in Dean 1999, 91.
55. Michel Foucault (1988) in Dean 1999, 134.
56. Dean 1999, 145.
57. For detailed analysis of structural constraints, particularly within administration of UAE women's associations, see Aaisha Ahmed Abdullah (2002), *Al-mara' wa idarat al-'amal al-ahli fi dawlat al-imarat al-'arabiyya al-mutahida: dirasa mukarana bayna gamayyat al-nahda al-*

nissaya bi dubai wa jamayat wa reyayat al-abhath bi dubai [Women and Voluntary Work Administration in the UAE: A Comparative Study between the Women's Association in Dubai and the Guidance and Welfare of Juvenile Delinquency in Dubai], unpublished M. A. thesis, School of Political Science and Economics, Cairo University, Egypt. See also Fakhro 2005.

58. Navaro-Yashin 2002, 135.

59. Armando Salvatore and Dale F. Eickelman eds., (2004), *Public Islam and the Common Good,* Brill: Leiden, 19.

60. Haya al-Mughni (2001), "Women's Organisations in Kuwait," in *Women and Power in the Middle East,* ed. Suad Joseph and Susan Slyomovics, Pennsylvania: University of Pennsylvania Press,182.

61. Joseph 1997, 59.

62. Aradhana Sharma (2006), "Crossbreeding Institutions, Breeding Struggle: Women's Empowerment, Neoliberal Governmentality, and State (Re)Formation in India," *Cultural Anthropology* 21, 1: 68.

63. Wendy Brown (1995), "Finding the Man in the State," in *States of Inquiry: Power and Freedom in Late Modernity,* Princeton: Princeton University Press, 167.

64. Deniz Kandiyoti (1996), *Gendering the Middle East: Emerging Perspectives,* London: I.B. Tauris. See also Deniz Kandiyoti (2001), "The Politics of Gender and the Conundrums of Citizenship," in *Women and Power in the Middle East,* ed. Suad Joseph and Susan Slyomovics, Pennsylvania: University of Pennsylvania Press, 54, 55.

CHAPTER 4

1. Ruth Wodak and Michael Meyer (2001), *Methods of Critical Discourse Analysis,* London: Sage, 6.

2. Nikolas Rose (1999), *Governing the Soul: The Shaping of the Private Self,* 2nd ed., London: Free Association Books, 4.

3. Ibid., 192.

4. Ibid., xxvii.

5. Michel Foucault (1991), "Governmentality," in *The Foucault Effect: Studies in Governmentality,* ed. Graham Burchell, Colin Gordon, and Peter Miller, Chicago: University of Chicago Press, 102.

6. See James Ferguson and Akhil Gupta (2002), "Spatializing States: Toward an Ethnography of Neoliberal Governmentality," *American Ethnologist* 29, 4: 994.

7. Foucault 1991, 102.

8. Jo Rowlands (1998), "A Word of the Times, but What Does it Mean? Empowerment in the Discourse and Practice of Development," in *Women and Empowerment: Illustrations from the Third World,* ed. Haleh Afshar. New York: St. Martin's Press, 14.

9. Sherine Hafez (2003), *The Terms of Empowerment: Islamic Women Ac-*

tivists in Egypt, Cairo Papers in Social Science 24, 4, Cairo: American University of Cairo Press.

10. Joan Wallach Scott (1988), *Gender and the Politics of History,* New York: Columbia Press, 36.

11. Hafez 2003, 48.

12. Talal Asad (1986), *The Idea of an Anthropology of Islam,* Washington, D.C.: Georgetown University Center for Contemporary Arab Studies, 14.

13. Ibid.

14. John R. Bowen (1993), *Muslims through Discourse: Religion and Ritual in Gayo Society,* Princeton, NJ: Princeton University Press, 10.

15. Mark Woodward (1988), "The *Slametan*: Textual Knowledge and Ritual Performance in Central Javanese Islam," *History of Religions* 28, 1: 87–88.

16. See, for example, Anthony Johns (1975), "Islam in Southeast Asia: Reflections and New Directions," *Indonesia* 19: 33–55.

17. Richard T. Antoun (1989), *Muslim Preacher in the Modern World,* Princeton, NJ: Princeton University Press.

18. Saba.Mahmood (2004), *Politics of Piety: The Islamic Revival and the Feminist Subject,* Princeton: Princeton University Press.

19. Katherine P. Ewing ed., (1988), *Shari'at and Ambiguity in South Asian Islam,* Berkeley: University of California Press, 6.

20. Aihwa Ong (1988), "Colonialism and Modernity: Feminist Representations of Women in Non-Western Societies," *Inscriptions* nos. 3–4 (October): 90.

21. One can hardly differentiate between the thinking of the Ikhwan and Salafis in the Gulf, given the themes they adopt in their mosque lectures, *halakas,* seminars, and their stand on major political issues.

22. Abdulkhaleq Abdullah, Taha Hussein Hassan, and Rashid Mohamed Rashid (1995), *Al-Mujtuma' ul-madani wal-tahawwal al-dimuqrati fi al-imarat al-'arabiyya al-mutahida* [Civil Society and Democratic Change in the UAE], preface by Saad Eddin Ibrahim, Cairo: Ibn Khaldoun Center for Development Studies, 125.

23. Site Institute, "Al-Qaeda in the United Arab Emirates and Oman Issues Ultimatum to the U.A.E. to Remove Jews and Christians from the Country within 10 Days," *The Search for International Terrorist Entities* (3 August 2005) http://siteinstitute.biz/bin/printerfriendly/pf.cgi (accessed 9 July 2006); Stephen Ulph (2005), "New Qaeda Threats to the UAE," *The Jamestown Foundation, TerrorismFocus* 2, 15 (5 August), 6; and Stephen Ulph (2006), "Declassified Document Outlines History of al-Qaeda Threat to the UAE," *The Jamestown Foundation, TerrorismFocus* 3, 11 (21 March): 3.

24. Interview with Suad Zayed al-Oraimi (Al-Ain, Abu Dhabi, June 2005), who during the time of interview was working on a project that focuses on the networking strategies of Islamists in the UAE.

25. Salwa Ismail (2003), *Rethinking Islamist Politics,* London: IB Tauris, 170.

26. See Leila Ahmed (1982), "Western Ethnocentrism and Perceptions of the Harem," *Feminist Studies* 8, 3: 521–534.
27. Robert D. Putnam (2000), *Bowling Alone: The Collapse and Revival of American Community*, New York: Touchstone, 76.
28. Mai Yamani (2000), *Changed Identities: The Challenge of the New Generation in Saudi Arabia*, London: Royal Institute of International Affairs, 115.
29. Rose 1999, 217.
30. Quoted in Melissa Finn (2005), "Media, Security, and Semiotics: A Theoretical and Qualitative Approach," M.A. Thesis, University of Calgary, 86.
31. Myra Marx Ferree and David A. Merrill (2000), "Hot Movements, Cold Cognition: Thinking about Social Movements in Gendered Frames," *Contemporary Sociology* 29, 3 (May): 456.
32. Francis Fukuyama (1999), "Social Capital and Civil Society," paper presented to IMP Conference on Second Generation Reforms.
33. Interview al-Oraimi, Al-Ain, June 2005.
34. Marta Mercado (1999), "Power to Do: and to Make Money," in *Women and Power: Fighting Patriarchies and Poverty*, ed. Janet Gabriel Townsend et al., London: Zed Books, 110, 111.
35. Connie Carøe Christiansen (2003), "Women's Islamic Activism: Between Self Practices and Social Reform Efforts," in *Modernizing Islam: Religion in the Public Sphere in Europe and the Middle East*, ed. John L. Espositio and Françoit Burgat, New Brunswick: Rutgers University Press, 150.
36. A scholar who received his Ph.D. in Islamic Studies in a Western university.
37. Christiansen 2003, 151.
38. Doctors in the UAE give percentiles of young women suffering from depression, mostly out of loneliness, ranging from a striking 50 to 70 percent for both local and nonlocals. One medical doctor interviewee estimated that half the expatriate women about to give birth at her hospital, one of the largest in the UAE, were unable to contact a relative or their husbands to accompany them.
39. Ira Lapidus (1975), "The Separation of State and Religion in the Development of Early Islamic Society," *International Journal of Middle East Studies* 6, 4 (October): 383.
40. Ibid.
41. Mehran Kamrava (1998), *Democracy in the Balance: Culture and Society in the Middle East*, New York: Chatham House, 19.
42. Abdullah et al., 1995, 125.
43. Mahmood 2004, 15.
44. Rose 1999, xv.
45. Michel Foucault. Quoted in Christiansen 2003, 152.
46. Christiansen 2003, 152.
47. Ibid., 155.

48. This is actually not a "verse" of the Qur'an, but a *hadith*. The narrator's assertion that these words are Qur'anic illustrates their sanctity.
49. Rose 1999, xx.
50. Mahmood 2004, 147.
51. Sabba Mahmood (2001), "Feminist Theory and the Egyptian Islamic Revival," *Cultural Anthropology* 16, 2: 215.
52. An American convert about to marry his third wife before consummating marriage with a second.
53. The imam had two wives.
54. Mahmood 2001, 217.
55. Qur'an 4:34, translation by Muhammad Asad.
56. Michael Walzer (1980), *Radical Principles: Reflections of an Unreconstructed Democrat*, New York: Basic Books, 55.
57. Dale F. Eickelman and James Piscatori (1996), *Muslim Politics*, Princeton: Princeton University Press, 44.
58. Al-Oraimi 2004,165.
59. Edward Shils (1997), *The Virtue of Civility: Selected Essays on Liberalism, Tradition, and Civil Society*, ed. Steven Grosby, Indianapolis: Liberty Fund, 58, 59.
60. Ibid., 45.
61. Saba Mahmood (1996), "Interview with Talal Asad: Modern Power and the Reconfiguration of Religious Traditions," *SEHR Contested Polities* 5, 1 (February 27), http://www.stanford.edu/group/SHR/5-1/text/asad.html (accessed 10 June 2006)

CHAPTER 5

1. See, for example, the volume by Mario Diani and Doug McAdam eds., (2003), *Social Movements and Networks: Relational Approaches to Collective Action*, Oxford: Oxford University Press.
2. For instance, Samuel H. Barnes and Max Kaase (1979), *Political Action*, Beverly Hills: Sage Publications.
3. Asef Bayat (2000), "Social Movements, Activism and Social Development in the Middle East," paper no. 3 (November), Geneva: UNRISD Publications.
4. Asef Bayat (1998), *Street Politics: Poor People's Movement in Iran*. Cairo: American University of Cairo Press.
5. Diane Singerman (1995), *Avenues of Participation: Family, Politics, and Networks in Urban Quarters of Cairo*, Princeton: Princeton University Press.
6. Janine A. Clark (2004), *Islam, Charity and Activism: Middle-Class Networks and Social Welfare in Egypt, Jordan, and Yemen*, Bloomington: Indiana University Press.
7. Guilain Denoeux (1993), *Urban Unrest in the Middle East: A Comparative Study of Informal Networks in Egypt, Iran, and Lebanon*, Albany: State University of New York Press.

8. Sangeetha Purushothaman (1997), *The Empowerment of Women in India: Grassroots Women's Networks and the State,* India: Sage India Publications.

9. David A. Snow and Robert D. Benford (1992), "Master Frames and Cycles of Protest," in *Frontiers in Social Movement Theory,* ed. A.D. Morris and C. M. Mueller. New Haven: Yale University Press, 135, 136.

10. Mario Diani (2003), "Introduction: Social Movements, Contentious Actions, and Social Networks: 'From Metaphor to Substance?' " in Mario Diani and Doug McAdam, eds., 6.

11. Ibid., 6, 7.

12. Ibid., 7.

13. See, for example, Maryjane Osa 2003, in Mario Diani and Doug McAdam eds.

14. Refer to Manlio Cinalli (2004), "Horizontal Networks vs. Vertical Networks within Multi-Organisation Alliances: A Comparative Study on the Unemployment and Asylum Issue-Fields in Britain," European Political Communication Working Paper Series, Issue 8/04.

15. Robert B. Cunningham and Yasin Sarayrah (1994), "Taming Wasta to achieve Development," *Arab Studies Quarterly* 16, 3: 29–41.

16. Karen Thomas (2002), "Gulf Businesswomen strike back!" AME Info. Middle East Finance and Economy, http://www.ameinfo.com/16669.html (accessed 13 December 2004).

17. Hadeel Qazzaz (2005), "No . . . WASTA, Favoratism & Nepotism," Aman's 2nd Annual Conference, Ramallah (March 28), "http://www.aman-palestine.org/English/Conf/wastaConf.htm

18. Hendrik Van der Meulen (1997), "The Role of Tribal and Kinship Ties in the Politics of the United Arab Emirates," PhD diss., Fletcher School of Law and Diplomacy, 101.

19. Ibid.

20. Ibid., 101, 102.

21. Cunningham and Sarayrah 1994.

22. For more on practical and strategic goals, see Maxine Molyneux (1985), "Mobilization without Emancipation? Women's Interests, the State, and Revolution in Nicaragua," in *Feminist Studies* 11, 2 (summer): 227–254.

23. They existed to essentially keep the children off the streets away from danger and to provide very basic skills and an Islamic education. It started off in the desert and the children had nothing to sit on except the sand.

24. See for example, Bert Klandermans (1997), *The Social Psychology of Protest,* Oxford: Blackwell.

25. Mara Loveman (1998), "High Risk Collective Action: Defending Human Rights in Chile, Uruguay, and Argentina," *American Journal of Sociology* vol. 104, no. 2: 480.

26. Doug McAdam (1992), "Gender as a Mediator of the Activist Experience: The Case of Freedom Summer," *The American Journal of Sociology* 97, 5 (March): 1211–1240.

27. Loveman 1998, 492.
28. In 2003 reportedly 73 abandoned babies were taken in and 107 in 2004. See UAE Interact, "UAE Best GCC State in Social Security Aid," (September 18, 2005) http://www.uaeinteract.com/news/default.asp?ID=277 (accessed 20 March 2006).
29. For a few examples, Article 70 states "No criticism shall be made against the Head of State or Rulers of the Emirates," Article 76, "No article blemishing the president of an Arab, Islamic or any other friendly state will be published," and Article 81, "It is prohibited to publish news that causes harm to the national currency, or causes damage to the national economy."
30. Still, only few newspapers in Europe and North America covered the issue until another report was issued in 2004.
31. At that time, however, participants of two other networks gave me the go ahead to interview on the topic.
32. All the families in the village in which she lived were in squalid conditions. Several persons occupied tiny rooms in shacks one could only enter by stooping through openings covered by carpets for doors.
33. Many, definitely not all, of those in prostitution in the UAE have been forced to out of practical circumstances. One interviewee was pushed into prostitution before reaching puberty by some women supposedly giving her shelter. She knew no other way to survive, and after running away from such "houses" numerous times was eventually found so sick she was near death. Every year many women in such circumstances die.
34. The names have been changed.
35. Charles Tilly (1998), "Contentious Conversations," *Social Research* 65, 3: 501.
36. In most cases, nonlocal women married to locals are not granted citizenship until after several years, as in one case, eighteen years. Divorcees rarely have citizenship, which means no rights to custody of children from the marriage to the local or housing or welfare. However, in 2005 a new law was passed that has allowed nonlocal women married to locals, divorced from locals, or widowers previously married to locals, access to welfare provisions.
37. When I first saw workers carrying out their duties in temperatures above 45 degrees Celsius, and queried how they could be required to, the typical reply I got was that the workers were used to such conditions and could handle it. Beginning 1 July 2006 the Ministry of Labor made a four-hour midday break (12:30 p.m. to 4:30 p.m.) mandatory for outdoor laborers during July and August.
38. Salaries for expatriates range from DH400 per month for domestic or agricultural workers to DH600 per month for construction workers to much higher salaries for highly skilled and white-collar employees.
39. One of the accidents was covered by the BBC, which, however, reported only a fraction of the number reported in the field at over 200 deaths.

40. Marilyn Carr, Martha Chen, and Renana Jhabvala eds., (1996), *Speaking Out: Women's Economic Empowerment in South Asia,* London: IT Publications, 215.

41. Peter Loizos (1996), "How Ernest Gellner got Mugged on the Streets of London, or: Civil Society, the Media and the Quality of Life," in *Civil Society: Challenging Western Models,* ed. Chris Hann and Elisabeth Dunn, London: Routledge, 51.

42. See, for example, Abdullah An-Na'im. 2002. "Religion and global Civil Society: Inherent Incompatibility or Synergy and Interdependence?" in *Global Civil Society.* Oxford: Oxford University Press, ed. M. Glasius, M. Kaldor and H. Anheier. 55–74.

43. Quintan Wiktorowicz (2000), "The Salafi Movement in Jordan," *International Journal of Middle East Studies,* vol. 32, no. 2 (May): 220.

44. Roger V. Gould (2005), "Why do Networks Matter? Rationalist and Structuralist Interpretations," in Mario Diani and Doug McAdam, eds., 236.

45. See for example, www.softskey.com

46. www.softskey.com

47. Margaret Somers, cited in Florence Passy (2003), "Social Networks Matter. But How?" in Mario Diani and Doug McAdam, eds., 24.

48. Passy 2003, 24.

49. Michael W. Foley and Bob Edwards (1996), "The Paradox of Civil Society," *Journal of Democracy* 7, 3 (July): 49.

50. See findings on Salafis in Jordan Wiktorowicz 2000, 236.

51. From June to November 2005 many children were rescued bringing the total number of those repatriated to 295 in November. See the Pakistani based newspaper reports on the third wave of children repatriated: Ali Waqar, "64 Jockeys Back Home," *Daily Times* (November 26, 2005) http://www.dailytimes.com.pk/default.asp?page=2005%5C11%5C26%5Cstory_26-11-2005_pg7_9 (accessed 2 December 2005). The issue of child camel jockeying has been pursued by Amnesty International, Anti-Slavery International and Pakistani human rights activist Ansar Burney, among others.

52. Remonda Kleinberg and Janine A. Clark eds., (2000), *Economic Liberalization, Democratization and Civil Society in the Developing World,* Houndmills: Macmillan Press, 295, 296; and Wiktorowicz 2000, 236.

53. Wanda Krause (2004), "The Role and Example of Chilean and Argentinean Mothers in Democratisation," *Development in Practice* 14, 3 (April): 366–380.

54. Osa 2003, 78, 79.

55. Kleinberg and Clark 2000, 296.

56. Wiktorowicz 2000, 237.

57. Farida Shaheed (1994), "Controlled or Autonomous: Identity and the Experience of the Network Women Living under Muslim Laws," *Signs* 19, 4: 997–1019.

58. Boutheina Cheriet (1997), "Fundamentalism and Women's Rights: Lessons from the City of Women," in *Muslim Women and the Politics of Participation: Implementing the Beiging Platform,* ed. Mahnz Afkhami and Erika Friedl, U.S.: Library of Congress, 17.
59. Robert D. Putnam (2001), *Bowling Alone: The Collapse and Revival of American Community,* New York: Touchstone.
60. Ibid., 23.
61. Edward Shils (1997), *The Virtue of Civility: Selected Essays on Liberalism, Tradition, and Civil Society,* ed. Steven Grosby, Indianapolis: Liberty Fund, 340.

CHAPTER 6

1. Nikolas Rose (1999), *Governing the Soul: The Shaping of the Private Self,* 2nd ed. London: Free Association Books, xxiii.
2. Abdulkhaleq Abdulla (2000), *The Arab Gulf States: Old Approaches and New Realities,* Emirates Center for Strategic Studies and Research: Abu Dhabi, 8.

BIBLIOGRAPHY

Abdo, Nahla. 1994. "Nationalism and Feminism: Palestinian Women and the Intifada—No Going Back?" In *Gender and National Identity: Women and Politics in Muslim Societies,* edited by Valentine M. Moghadam. London: Zed Books, 215–227.

Abdul Majeed, Razan Hamdi. 2000. "Modernity and Social Problems: Case of Dubai." M.Phil. diss., University of Exeter.

Abdulhadi, Rabab. 1998. "The Palestinian Women's Autonomous Movement: Emergence, Dynamics, and Challenges." *Gender & Society* 12:649–673.

Abdulla, Abdulkhaleq. 2000. *The Arab Gulf States: Old Approaches and New Realities.* Abu Dhabi: Emirates Center for Strategic Studies and Research

Abdulla, Abdulkhaleq; Taha Hussein Hassan; and Rashid Mohamed Rashid. 1995. *Al-Mujtama' al-madani wal-tahawwal al-dimuqrati fi al-imarat al-'arabiyya al-mutahida* [Civil Society and Democratic Change in the UAE], prefaced by Saad Eddin Ibrahim. Cairo: Ibn Khaldoun Centre for Development Studies.

Abdullah, Aaisha Ahmed. 2002. *Al-mara' wa idarat al-'amal al-ahli fi dawlat al-imarat al-'arabiyya al-mutahida: Dirasa mukarana bayna gamayyat al-nahda al-nissaya bi dubai wa jamayat wa reyayat al-ubhath bi dubai* [Women and Voluntary Work Administration in the UAE: A Comparative Study between the Women's Association in Dubai and the Guidance and Welfare of Juvenile Delinquency in Dubai]. M.A. thesis, Cairo University School of Political Science and Economics.

Abdullah, Lootah-Hessah. 1999. "Unveiling the Mask: Representation of Women on Dubai (United Arab Emirates) Television." Ph.D. diss., Ohio State University.

Abu-Lughod, Leila. 1989. "Zones of Theory in the Anthropology of the Arab World." *Annual Review in Anthropology* 18:267–306.

Ackerly, Brooke. 1997. "What's in a Design? The Effects of NGO Programme Delivery Choices on Women's Empowerment in Bangladesh." In *Getting Institutions Right for Women in Development,* edited by Anne Marie Goetz. London: Zed Books, 140–158.

Afsaruddin, Asma, ed. 1999. *Hermeneutics and Honor: Negotiating Female "Public" Space in Islamic/ate Societies.* Cambridge, MA: Harvard Center for Middle Eastern Studies.

Afshar, Haleh. 1994. *Why Fundamentalism? Iranian Women and Their Support of Islam.* Heslington, York: University of York.

Ahmed, Leila. 1982. "Western Ethnocentrism and Perceptions of the Harem." *Feminist Studies* 8, 3: 521–534.

———. 1992. *Women and Gender in Islam: Historical Roots of a Modern Debate.* New Haven, CT: Yale University Press.

al-Abed, Ibrahim. 2001. "The Historical Background and Constitutional Basis for the Federation." In *United Arab Emirates: A New Perspective,* edited by Peter Hellyer and Ibrahim al-Abed. Bookcraft, UK: Trident Press, 121–144.

al-Ali, Nadje. 2000. *Secularism, Gender and the State in the Middle East: The Egyptian Women's Movement.* Cambridge, UK: Cambridge University Press.

———. 2003. "Gender and Civil Society in the Middle East." *International Feminist Journal of Politics* 5, 2 (August): 216–232.

———. 2005. "Gender and Civil Society in the Middle East." In *Gender and Civil Society: Transcending Boundaries,* edited by Jude Howell and Diane Mulligan. London: Routledge, 101–116.

al-Alkim, Hassan H. 2000. "The United Arab Emirates and Subregional Powers." In *A Century in Thirty Years: Shaykh Zayed and the United Arab Emirates,* edited by Joseph A. Kechichian. Washington, D.C. Middle East Policy Council, 169–198.

al-Awadhi, Badria Abdullah. 2005. "Women in the Gulf and Globalization: Challenges and Opportunities." In *The Gulf Challenges of the Future.* Abu Dhabi: Emirates Center for Strategic Studies and Research, 127–133.

al-Azmina Al-Arabiya. http://www.alazmina.info/ (accessed 3 July 2006).

al-Fahim, Mohammed. 1995. *From Rags to Riches: A Story of Abu Dhabi.* London: London Centre of Arab Studies.

al-Hajji, Saad Ahmed. 2000. *Al-Jam'iyyat al-nisaa'iyya al-ojtima'iyya bedu w'al-majlis al-ta'awun ledu wa al-khaleej al-'arabiyya* [Women's Social Associations in GCC Countries]. Kuwait: Published by author.

al-Hamed, Mowza bint Mohammed bin Butti. 2002. *Zayed: The Millennial Legend.* Dubai, UAE: Bin Dasmal.

al-Jandali, Bassma. "Man Confesses to Striking Match That Set Wife Ablaze." *Gulf News* (December 7, 2004) http://search.gulfnews.com/articles/04/07/12/125969.html. (accessed 25 December 2006).

al-Jandali, Bassma. "Women Proved Their Competence in All Fields—Manal." *Gulf News* (November 26 2002). http://www.gulfnews.com/Articles/news.asp?ArticleID=69538. accessed 13 December 2004).

al-Mughni, Haya. 1993. *Women in Kuwait: The Politics of Gender.* London: Saqi Books.

———. 1996. "Women's Organizations in Kuwait." *Middle East Report* 26:32–35.

———. 1997. "From Gender Equality to Female Subjugation: The Changing Agendas of Women's Groups in Kuwait." In *Organizing Women: Formal and Informal Women's Groups in the Middle East,* edited by Dawn Chatty and Annika Rabo. Oxford: Berg, 195–209.

———. 2001. "Women's Organisations in Kuwait." In *Women and Power in the Middle East*, edited by Suad Joseph and Susan Slyomovics. Pennsylvania: University of Pennsylvania Press, 176–182.

al-Mughni, Haya, and Mary Ann Tétreault. 2000. "Citizenship, Gender, and Politics of Quasi States." In *Gender and Citizenship in the Middle East*, edited by Suad Joseph. Syracuse, NY: Syracuse University Press, 237–260.

———. 2005. "Political Actors without the Franchise: Women and Politics in Kuwait." In *Monarchies and Nations: Globalisation and Identity in the Arab States of the Gulf*, edited by Paul Dresch and James Piscatori. London: I. B. Tauris, 203–221.

al-Murr, Mohammad. 1997. *Amal wataniyah: Maqalat fi hubb al-imarat* [National Hopes: Essays in the Love of the Emirates]. Sharjah, UAE: Dar al-Khalij.

al-Naboodah, Hassan M. 2000. "From a Traditional Society to a Modern State." In *A Century in Thirty Years: Shaykh Zayed and the United Arab Emirates*, edited by Joseph A. Kechichian. Washington, D.C.: Middle East Policy Council.

al-Oraimi, Suaad Zayed. 2004. "Gender and Development: The Role of Women in the Formal Economic and Political Spheres in the United Arab Emirates." Ph.D. diss., American University of Washington.

al-Qasimi, Hind Abdul Aziz. 1993. *Al-Mara' fi al-imarat: Tahadiat al-ta'leem wa'l 'amal wa itikhath al-qarar* [Women in the Emirates: Challenges for Education, Work, and Decision-Making]. M.A. thesis. Cairo: Ain Shams University. Published by the Association of Sociologists, Sharjah, UAE.

———. 1998. *Al-Thabit w'al-mutaghayrah fi thaqafat al mar'ah fi al-imarat* [The Constant and the Variable in the Women's Culture in the Emirates]. Sharjah, UAE: Sociologists' Association.

al-Qasimi, Sultan bin Muhammad. 1999. *Power Struggles and Trade in the Gulf*. Forest Row: University of Exeter Press.

al-Sabah, Suad M. 1983. *Development Planning in an Oil Economy and the Role of the Woman: The Case of Kuwait*. London: Eastlords Publishing.

al-Sayegh, Fatma. 2000. "Diversity in Unity: Political Institutions and Civil Society." In *A Century in Thirty Years: Shaykh Zayed and the United Arab Emirates*, edited by Joseph A. Kechichian. Washington, D.C.: Middle East Policy Council.

al-Sayyid, Mustapha K. 1993. "A Civil Society in Egypt?" *Middle East Journal* 47, 2 (Spring): 227–242.

al-Shamsi, Maytha, and Abdallah Coulon. 2001. *Al-adwar al-mutaghayrah lil-mar'ah fi dawlat al-imarat al-'arabiyya al-mutahida* [Women in the UAE and Personal Status Disputes]. Cairo: Published by author.

Alwani, Taha Jabir. 1996. *Islah al-fikr al-islami bayna al-qudrat wa al-'aqabat: Waraqat 'amal* [The Reform of Islamic Thought between Capabilities and Obstacles]. The Islamization of Knowledge Series, no. 10. Herndon, VA: International Institute of Islamic Thought.

al-Zaabi, Nora. 1993. *Ta'akhur sin al-zawaj wa'atharuh al-ijtima'iyya: Dirasah 'ala mujtama' al-imarat al-'arabiyya al-mutahida* [The Rising

Marriage Age and Its Social Effect: A Study on UAE Society]. Dubai, UAE: Women's Renaissance Association in Dubai.

al-Zekri, Mohamad A. K. 1998. "Folk Beliefs of Arab Women of Dubai Prior to Oil Discovery in 1966." M.Phil. diss., University of Exeter.

Ammar, Nawal H. and Leila S. Lababidy. 1999. "Women's Grassroots Movements and Democratization in Egypt." In *Democratization and Women's Grassroots Movements,* edited by Jill M. Bystydzienski and Joti Sekhon. Bloomington, IN: Indiana University Press, 150–172.

Amnesty International. "Stop Violence against Women." http://web.amnesty.org/actforwomen/qtr-221205-background-eng (accessed 7 April 2006).

Amnesty International. 1997. "United Arab Emirates: Imprisonment and Flogging for Marriage across Faiths—the Case of Elie Dib Ghaleb." http://web.amnesty.org/library/Index/ENGMDE250031997?open&of =ENG-ARE (accessed 7 April 2006).

Amnesty International. 2005. "United Arab Emirates: Covering Events from January–December 2004." http://web.amnesty.org/report2005/are-summary-eng (accessed 27 April 2006).

Anderson, Lisa. 1987. "The State in the Middle East and North Africa." *Comparative Politics* 20, 1: 1–18.

Anheier, Helmut. 2003. "Movement Development and Organizational Networks: The Role of 'Single Members' in the German Nazi Party,1925–30." In *Social Movements and Networks: Relational Approaches to Collective Action,* edited by Mario Diani and Doug McAdam. Oxford: Oxford University Press, 49–74.

an-Na'im, Abdullah. 2002. "Religion and global Civil Society: Inherent Incompatibility or Synergy and Interdependence?" In *Global Civil Society,* edited by M. Glasius, M. Kaldor and H. Anheier. Oxford: Oxford University Press, 55–73.

Antonius, Rachad and Qusay Samak. 1987. "Civil Society at the Pan-Arab Level? The Role of Non-Governmental Organizations." In *Arab Nationalism and the Future of the Arab World,* edited by Hani A. Faris. Boston, MA: Association of Arab-American University Graduates.

Antoun, Richard T. 1989. *Muslim Preacher in the Modern World.* Princeton, NJ: Princeton University Press.

———. 2000. "Civil Society, Tribal Process, and Change in Jordan: An Anthropological View," *International Journal of Middle East Studies* 32, 4 (November).

APS Review's Gas Market *Trends* 52, 4.

Arab Studies Journal. 1998. 6, 1 (Spring).

Arruda, Nancy. 2000. *The Politics in Popular Urban Women's Organizing: Empowerment and Women's Organizations in Rio's Favelas.* M.A. thesis. Guelph: University of Guelph.

Asad, Talal. 1975. "Two European Images of Non-European Rule." In *Anthropology and the Colonial Encounter,* edited by T. Asad. London: Ithaca Press, 103–118.

————. 1986. *The Idea of an Anthropology of Islam*. Washington, D.C.: Georgetown University Center for Contemporary Arab Studies.

Ayubi, Nazih N. 1999. *Over-stating the Arab State: Politics and Society in the Middle East*. London: I. B. Tauris.

Badran, Hoda. 2001. *A Working Framework for Arab Voluntary Organizations2001–2005*. Cairo: Alliance for Arab Women.

Badran, Margot. 1994. "Gender Activism: Feminists and Islamists in Egypt." In *Identity Politics and Women*, edited by Valentine M. Moghadam. Boulder, CO: Westview Press.

Barnes, Samuel H., and Max Kaase. 1979. *Political Action*. Beverly Hills, CA: Sage Publications.

Barry Andrew, Thomas Osborne, and Nikolas Rose, eds. 1996. *Foucault and Political Reason: Liberalism, Neo-liberalism and Rationalities of Government*. Chicago. University of Chicago Press.

Batliwala, Srilatha. 1993. "Empowerment of Women in South Asia: Concepts and Practices." Columbo, Sri Lanka: Asian-South Pacific Bureau of Adult Education.

Bayat, Asef. 1998. *Street Politics: Poor People's Movement in Iran*. Cairo: American University of Cairo Press.

————. 2000. "Social Movements, Activism and Social Development in the Middle East." Paper No. 3 (November), Geneva: UNRISD Publications.

Beblawi, Hazem. 1987. "The Rentier State in the Arab World." In *The Rentier State*, edited by Hazem Beblawi and Giacomo Luciani. New York: Croom Helm.

Bellin, Eva. 2005. "Coercive Institutions and Coercive Leaders." In *Authoritarianism in the Middle East: Regimes and Resistance*, edited by Marsha Pripstein Posusney and Michele Penner Angrist. Boulder, CO: Lynne Rienner.

Bergdall, Terry and Frank Powell. 1998. "Grassroots Empowerment in Ethiopian Villages." In *Beyond Prince and Merchant: Citizen Participation and the Rise of Civil Society*, edited by John Burbidge. New York: Pact.

Béteille, André. 1999. "Citizenship, State and Civil Society." *Economic and Political Weekly* 34, 36 (September 4): 2588–2591.

Bewley, Aisha. "The Murabitun of North African and Andalusia," http://bewley.virtualave.net/tashfincont.html (accessed 7 February 2008).

Boddy, Janice. 1989. *Wombs and Alien Spirits: Women, Men, and the Zar Cult in Northern Sudan*. Madison, WI: University of Wisconsin Press.

Bookman, Ann and Sandra Morgen, eds. 1988. *Women and the Politics of Empowerment*. Philadelphia, PA: Temple University Press.

Boserup, Ester. 1970. *Women's Role in Economic Development*. London: George Allen and Unwin.

Bothwell, Robert. 1998. "Indicators of a Healthy Civil Society." In *Beyond Prince and Merchant: Citizen Participation and the Rise of Civil Society*, edited by John Burbidge. New York: Pact.

Bowen, John R. 1993. *Muslims through Discourse: Religion and Ritual in Gayo Society*. Princeton, NJ: Princeton University Press.

Brand, Laurie A. 1998. *Women, the State, and Political Liberalization: Middle Eastern and North African Experiences.* New York: Columbia University Press.

Brenner, Suzanne. 1996. "Reconstructing Self and Society: Javenese Muslim Women and 'the Veil'." *American Ethnologist* 23, 4 (November): 673–697.

Bristol-Rhys, Jane. 2005. "In the Other's Words: Histiography of the UAE." Paper presented at the American Anthropological Association Meeting (November).

Bromley, Simon. 1994. *Rethinking Middle East Politics.* Austin,TX: University of Texas Press.

Brooks, Adrienne A. R. 2002. "Women in the Emirati Military: Spearhead of Change." *Military Review* 82, 2 (March/April): 103–104.

Brown, Andrea M. 1999. "Democratisation in Tanzania: Women's Associations and the Potential for Empowerment." Ph.D. diss.,: University of Toronto.

Brown, Wendy. 1995. "Finding the Man in the State." In *States of Inquiry: Power and Freedom in Late Modernity.* Princeton: Princeton University Press.

Bryant, Christopher G. A. 1994. "A Further Comment on Kumar's Civil Society." *The British Journal of Sociology* 45, 3 (September): 497–499.

Brynen, Rex, Bahgat Korany, and Paul Noble. 1995. "Introduction: Theoretical Perspectives on Arab Liberalization and Democratization." In *Political Liberalization and Democratization in the Arab World, Volume 1 Theoretical Perspectives,* edited by Bahgat Korany, Rex Brynen, and Paul Noble. Boulder, CO: Lynne Rienner Publishers.

Butler, Judith. 1992. "Contingent Foundations: Feminism and the Question of 'Postmodernism'." In *Feminists Theorize the Political,* edited by Judith Butler and Joan W. Scott. London: Routledge.

Butt, Gerald. 2001. "Oil and Gas in the UAE." In *United Arab Emirates: A New Perspective,* edited by Peter Hellyer and Ibrahim al-Abed. Bookcraft, UK: Trident Press.

Bystydzienski, Jill M. 1992. *Women Transforming Politics: Worldwide Strategies for Empowerment,* edited by Jill. M. Bystydzienski. Bloomington, IN: Indiana University Press.

Cahoone, Lawrence E. 2002. *Civil Society: The Conservative Meaning of Liberal Politics.* Malden, MA: Blackwell.

Carapico, Sheila. 1996. "Yemen between Civility and Civil War." In *Civil Society in the Middle East,* edited by Richard Norton, vol. 2. Leiden: Brill.

———. 1998. *Civil Society in Yemen: The Political Economy of Activism in Modern Arabia.* Cambridge: Cambridge University Press.

Carothers, Thomas. 1999. "Civil Society: Think Again," *Foreign Policy* 117: 18–24.

———. 1999. *Aiding Democracy Abroad: The Learning Curve.* Washington, D.C.: Carnegie Endowment for International Peace.

Carr, Marilyn, Martha Chen, and Renana Jhabvala, eds. 1996. *Speaking Out: Women's Economic Empowerment in South Asia.* London: IT Publications.

Centre for Civil Society. "Report on Activities for2002–05." London School of Economics and Political Science. http://www.lse.ac.uk/collections/CCS/pdf/CCS_Report_on_Activities_2002-5.pdf (accessed 24 June 2006).

Charrad, Mounira M. 2001. "State and Gender in the Maghrib." In *Women and Power in the Middle East,* edited by Suad Joseph and Susan Slyomovics. Philadelphia: University of Pennsylvania Press.

Chaudhry, Kiren Aziz. 1994. "Economic Liberalization and the Lineages of the Rentier State." *Comparative Politics* 27, 1: 1–25.

———. 1997. *The Price of Wealth.* New York: Ithaca University Press.

Cheriet, Boutheina. 1997. "Fundamentalism and Women's Rights: Lessons from the City of Women." In *Muslim Women and the Politics of Participation: Implementing the Beging Platform,* edited by Mahnz Afkhami and Erika Friedl. U.S.: Library of Congress.

Cherifati-Merabtine, Doria. 1994. "Algeria at a Crossroads: National Liberation, Islamization and Women." In *Identity Politics and Women,* edited by Valentine M. Moghadam. Boulder, CO: Westview Press.

Christiansen, Connie Carøe. 2003. "Women's Islamic Activism: Between Self Practices and Social Reform Efforts." In *Modernizing Islam: Religion in the Public Sphere in Europe and the Middle East,* edited by John L. Esposito and Françoit Burgat. New Brunswick: Rutgers University Press.

Cinalli, Manlio. 2004. "Horizontal Networks vs. Vertical Networks within Multi-Organisation Alliances: A Comparative Study on the Unemployment and Asylum Issue-Fields in Britain." *European Political Communication Working Paper Series,* 8, 4.

Clark, Janine A. 1994. "Islamic Social-Welfare Organizations and the Legitimacy of the State in Egypt: Democratization or Islamization From Below?" Ph.D. diss., University of Toronto.

———. 2004. *Islam, Charity and Activism: Middle-Class Networks and Social Welfare in Egypt, Jordan, and Yemen.* Bloomington, IN: Indiana University Press.

Clark, Janine A., and Remonda Bensabat Kleinberg, eds. 2000. "Conclusions: Politics of Democratization—the Force of Civil Society." In *Economic Liberalization, Democratization and Civil Society in the Developing World.* New York: Macmillan Press.

Clark, John. 1997. "Petro-Politics in Congo," *Journal of Democracy* 8, 3: 62–76.

Codrai, Ronald. 2001. *Faces of the Emirates: An Arabian Album. A Collection of Mid-20th Century Photographs.* Dubai: Motivate Publishing.

Cohen, Jean and Andrew Arato. 1992. *Civil Society and Political Theory.* Cambridge: MIT Press.

Crystal, Jill. 1990. *Oil and Politics in the Gulf: Rulers and Merchants in Kuwait and Qatar.* New York: Cambridge University Press.

———. 1992. *Kuwait: The Transformation of an Oil State.* Boulder, CO: Westview Press.

———. 1995. "Civil Society in the Arab Gulf States." In *Toward Civil Society in the Middle East? A Primer,* edited by Jillian Schwedler. Boulder, CO: Lynne Rienner Publishers.

———. 1996. "Civil Society in the Arabian Gulf." In *Civil Society in the Middle East,* edited by Augustus Richard Norton, vol. 2. Leiden: Brill.

Cruikshank, Barbara. 1999. *The Will to Empower: Democratic Citizens and Other Subjects.* Ithaca, NY: Cornell University Press.

Cunningham, Robert B., and Yasin Sarayrah. 1994. "Taming Wasta to achieve Development." *Arab Studies Quarterly* 16, 3: 29–41.

Curtis, Shaun. 2001. "Globalization, Countertrade and Privatization in the Arabian Gulf." Ph.D. diss., University of Toronto.

Davidson, Christopher M. 2006. "The Emirates of Abu Dhabi and Dubai: Contrasting Roles in the International System." Paper presented to conference on "The Global Gulf," Institute of Arab and Islamic Studies, University of Exeter (July).

———. 2005. *The United Arab Emirates: A Study in Survival.* Boulder,CO: Lynne Rienner Publishers.

Dawson, Elsa L. 1999. "Gender: Assessing the impact." In *Gender Works: Oxfam Experience in Policy and Practice,* edited by Fenella Porter, Ines Smyth, and Caroline Sweetman: London: Oxfam.

Dean, Mitchell. 1999. *Governmentality: Power and Rule in Modern Society.* London: Sage.

Denoeux, Guilain. 1993. *Urban Unrest in the Middle East: A Comparative Study of Informal Networks in Egypt, Iran, and Lebanon.* Albany, NY: State University of New York Press.

Diamond, Larry J. 1994. "Rethinking Civil Society: Toward Democratic Consolidation." *Journal of Democracy* 5, 3: 4–17.

Diamond, Larry, Juan Linz, and Seymour Martin Lipset, eds. 1988. "Introduction: Roots of Failure, Seeds of Hope." In *Democracy in Developing Countries: Africa.* Boulder, CO: Lynne Rienner Publishers.

Diani, Mario. 1995. *Green Networks: A Structural Analysis of the Italian Environmental Movement.* Edinburgh: Edinburgh University Press.

———. 2003. "Introduction: Social Movements, Contentious Actions, and Social Networks: 'From Metaphor to Substance?'" In *Social Movements and Networks: Relational Approaches to Collective Action,* edited by Mario Diani and Doug McAdam. Oxford: Oxford University Press.

Doumato, Eleanor Abdella. 2000. *Getting God's Ear: Women, Islam, and Healing in Saudi Arabia and the Gulf.* New York: Columbia University Press.

Dresch, Paul. 2005. "Debates on Marriage and Nationality in the United Arab Emirates." In *Monarchies and Nations: Globalisation and Identity in the Arab States of the Gulf,* edited by Paul Dresch and James Piscatori. London: I.B. Tauris,

Dresch, Paul and James Piscatori, eds. 2005. *Monarchies and Nations: Globalisation and Identity in the Arab States of the Gulf.* London: I.B. Tauris.

Edwards, Bob and Michael W. Foley. 1998. "Beyond Tocqueville: Civil Society and Social Capital in Comparative Perspective," *American Behavioral Scientist* 42, 2 (September): 5–20.

Edwards, Bob, Michael W. Foley, and Mario Diani, eds. 2001. *Beyond Tocqueville: Civil Society and the Social Capital Debate in Comparative Perspective*. New England: University Press of New England.

Eickelman, Dale F., and James Piscatori. 1996. *Muslim Politics*. Princeton, NJ: Princeton University Press.

Einhorn, Barbara and Charlie Sever. 2005. "Gender, Civil Society and Women's Movements in Central and Eastern Europe." In *Gender and Civil Society: Transcending Boundaries*, edited by Jude Howell and Diane Mulligan. London: Routledge.

Elshtain, Jean Bethke. 1981. *Public Man, Private Woman: Women in Social and Political Thought*. Princeton, NJ: Princeton University Press.

Enloe, Cynthia. 1989. *Bananas, Beaches and Bases: Making Feminist Sense of International Politics*. London: Pandora.

———. 1993. *The Morning After: Sexual Politics at the End of the Cold War*. Berkeley, CA: California University Press.

Entelis, John P. 1996. "Civil Society and the Authoritarian Temptation in Algerian Politics: Islamic Democracy vs. the Centralized State." In *Civil Society in the Middle East*, edited by Augustus Richard Norton, vol. 2. Leiden: Brill.

Epps, John. 1997. "Core Values of Civil Society." In *Beyond Prince and the Merchant: Citizen Participation and the Rise of Civil Society*, edited by John Burbidge. New York: Pact Publications.

Ewing, Katherine P. 1988. "Introduction: Ambiguity and *Shari'at*: A Perspective on the Problem of Moral Principles in Tension." In *Shari'at and Ambiguity in South Asian Islam*, edited by Katherine P. Ewing. Berkeley, CA: University of California Press.

Fakhro, Munira Ahmed. 2005. "The Changing Role of Women in the Gulf Region." In *The Gulf Challenges of the Future*. Abu Dhabi: Emirates Center for Strategic Studies and Research.

Fatton, Robert, Jr. 1992. *Predatory Rule: State and Civil Society in Africa*. Boulder, CO: Lynne Rienner Publishers.

Ferguson James. 1994. *The Anti-Politics Machine: Development, "Depoliticization," and Bureaucratic Power in Lesotho*. Minneapolis: University of Minnesota Press.

Ferguson, James and Akhil Gupta. 2002. "Spatializing States: Toward an Ethnography of Neoliberal Governmentality." *American Ethnologist* 29, 4: 981–1002.

Fernea, Elizabeth Warnock. 1998. *In Search of Islamic Feminism: One Woman's Global Journey*. New York: Doubleday.

Ferree, Myra Marx and David A. Merrill. 2000. "Hot Movements, Cold Cognition: Thinking about Social Movements in Gendered Frames." *Contemporary Sociology* 29, 3 (May): 454–462.

Finn, Melissa. 2005. "Media, Security, and Semiotics: A Theoretical and Qualitative Approach." M.A. thesis. University of Calgary.

Foley, Michael W., and Bob Edwards. 1996. "The Paradox of Civil Society." *Journal of Democracy* 7, 3 (July): 38–52.

Ford Foundation. 1990. *Annual Report, 1989.* New York: Ford Foundation.

Foucault, Michel. 1980. *The History of Sexuality: Volume One.* New York: Vintage.

———. 1991. "Governmentality." In *The Foucault Effect: Studies in Governmentality,* edited by Graham Burchell, Colin Gordon, and Peter Miller. Chicago: Chicago University Press.

Freedom House. 2005. "Freedom in the World Country Ratings: United Arab Emirates." http://www.freedomhouse.org/template.cfm?page=22&year=2005&country=6856 (accessed 23 June 2006).

Fukuyama, Francis. 1999. "Social Capital and Civil Society." Paper presented to IMP Conference on Second Generation Reforms.

Gause, Gregory F., III. 1991. *Oil Monarchies: Domestic and Security Challenges in the Arab Gulf States.* New York: Council on Foreign Relations Press.

Gellner, Ernest. 1996. *Conditions of Liberty: Civil Society and its Rivals.* London: Penguin Books.

Ghabra, Shafeeq. 1991. "Voluntary Associations in Kuwait: The Foundation of a New System?" *Middle East Journal* 45: 199–215.

Ghanem, Shihab M. A. 1992. *Industrialization in the United Arab Emirates.* Aldershot: Avebury.

Ghannouchi, Rached. 1999. *Muqarabat fi al-ʿilmaniyya w'al-mujtamʿ al-madani* [Papers on Secularism and Civil Society]. London: Maghreb Center for Research and Translation.

Ghubash, Mouza. 1999. *Al-Teknolojiyya wa tanmiyyat al-marʾah al-rifiyya w'al-badawiyya bi dawlat al-imarat* [Technology and the Development of Rural and Bedouin Women in the Emirates (1971–1998)]. Dubai, UAE: Reading for All Publishing.

———. 1997. "Social Development in the United Arab Emirates." In *Perspectives on the United Arab Emirates,* edited by Edmund Ghareeb and Ibrahim al-Abed. London: Trident Press.

Glasius, Marlies. 2005. "Who is the Real Civil Society? Women's Groups versus Pro-Family Groups at the International Criminal Court Negotiations." In *Gender and Civil Society,* edited by Jude Howell and Diane Mulligan. London: Routledge.

Glavanis-Grantham, Kathy. 1996. "The Women's Movement, Feminism and the National Struggle in Palestine: Unresolved Contradictions." In *Women and Politics in the Third World,* edited by Haleh Afshar. New York: Routledge.

Göle, Nilüfer. 1994. "Towards an Autonomization of Politics and Civil Society in Turkey." In *Politics in the Third Turkish Republic,* edited by Metin Heper. Boulder,CO: Westview Press.

Goody, Jack. 1996. "Civil Society in an Extra-European Perspective." In *Civil Society: Challenging Western Models,* edited by Chris Hann and Elizabeth Dunn. London: Routledge.

Gould Roger V. 1991. "Multiple Networks and Mobilization in the Paris Commune, 1871." *American Sociological Review* 14: 27–54.

———. 2005. "Why do Networks Matter? Rationalist and Structuralist Interpretations." In *Social Movements and Networks: Relational Approaches to Collective Action,* edited by Mario Diani and Doug McAdam. Oxford: Oxford University Press.

Gouldner, Alvin A. 1971. *Coming Crisis of Western Sociology.* London: Heinemann Educational Books.

Graz, Liesl. 1990. *The Turbulent Gulf.* London: I.B. Tauris.

Guazzone, Laura. 1995. "Islamism and Islamists in the Contemporary Arab World." In *The Islamist Dilemma: The Political Role of Islamist Movements in the Contemporary Arab World,* edited by Laura Guazzone. Berkshire, UK: Ithaca Press.

Hafez, Sherine. 2003. *The Terms of Empowerment: Islamic Women Activists in Egypt.* Cairo Papers in Social Science 24, 4. Cairo: American University of Cairo Press.

Hale, Sondra. 1997. *Gender Politics in Sudan: Islamism, Socialism, and the State.* Boulder,CO: Westview Press.

Hann, Chris and Elizabeth Dunn, eds. 1996. *Civil Society: Challenging Western Models.* London: Routledge.

Hasso, Frances S. 1998. "The Women's Front: Nationalism, Feminism, and Modernity in Palestine." *Gender & Society* 12: 441–465.

Hatem, Mervat F. 1985. "Conservative Patriarchal Modernization in the Arabian Gulf." *Contemporary Marxism* no. 11 (Fall): 96–109.

———. 1992. "Economic and Political Liberation in Egypt and the Demise of State Feminism," *International Journal of Middle East Studies* 24: 231–51.

———. 1993. "Toward the Development of Post-Islamist and Post Nationalist Feminist Discourses in the Middle East." In *Arab Women, Old Boundaries, New Frontiers,* edited by Judith Tucker. Bloomington, IN: Indiana University Press.

———. 1995. "Liberalization, Gender, and the State." In *Political Liberalization and Democratization in the Arab World, Volume 1 Theoretical Perspectives,* edited by Bahgat Korany, Rex Brynen, and Paul Noble. Boulder,CO: Lynne Rienner Publishers.

Haynes, Jeff. 2000. *Democracy and Civil Society in the Third World: Politics and New Political Movements.* Cambridge: Polity Press.

Heard-Bey, Frauke. 2001. "The Tribal Society of the UAE and its Traditional Economy." In *United Arab Emirates: A New Perspective,* edited by Peter Hellyer and Ibrahim al-Abed. Bookcraft, UK: Trident Press.

Hefner, Robert W. 1998. *Democratic Civility: The History and Cross-Cultural Possibility of a Modern Political Ideal.* New Brunswick: Transaction.

Henderson, Edward. 1988. *This Strange Eventful History: Memoirs of Earlier Days in the UAE and Oman.* Dubai: UAE.

Herb, Michael. 1999. *All in the Family: Absolutism, Revolution, and Democracy in The Middle Eastern Monarchies,* edited by Shahrough Akhavi. New York: University of New York Press.

———. 2002. "Democratization in the Arab World? Emirs and Parliaments in the Gulf." *Journal of Democracy* 13, 4 (October): 41–47.

———. 2002. "Do Rents Cause Authoritarianism?" Paper presented at the Middle East Studies Association Annual Meeting (November).

Hindess, Barry. 1997. *Discourses of Power: From Hobbes to Foucault.* Oxford: Blackwell.

———. 2004. "Liberalism—What's in a Name?" In *Global Governmentality: Governing International Spaces,* edited by Wendy Larner and William Walters. London: Routledge.

Hirschmann, David. 1998. "Civil Society in South Africa: Learning from Gender Themes." *World Development* 26, 2 (February): 227–238.

Howell, Jude and Diane Mulligan, eds. 2005. *Gender and Civil Society: Transcending Boundaries.* London: Routledge.

Huntington, Samuel. 1991. *The Third Wave: Democratization in the Late Twentieth Century.* Norman: University of Oklahoma Press.

Hurreiz, Sayyid H. 2002. *Folklore and Folklife in the United Arab Emirates.* London: RoutledgeCurzon.

Hvidt, Martin. 2006. "Governance in Dubai: The Emergence of Political and Economic Ties between the Public and Private Sector." Centre for Contemporary Middle East Studies, University of Denmark. Working Paper No. 6 (June).

Hyden, Goran. 1990. "Reciprocity and Governance in Africa." In *The Failure of the Centralized State,* edited by James S. Wunsch and Dele Olowu. Boulder, CO: Westview Press.

Ibrahim, Saad Eddin. 1998. "Populism, Islam, and Civil Society in the Arab World." In *Beyond Prince and Merchant: Citizen Participation and the Rise of Civil Society,* edited by John Burbidge. New York: Pact.

———, ed. 1996. *Egypt, Islam and Democracy: Twelve Critical Essays.* Cairo: American University Press.

IMF Issues Brief (2000–2003). 2003. "Globalization: Threat or Opprtunity?":1–9.

Ismail, Salwa. 1994. "The Civil Society Concept and the Middle East: Questions of Meaning and Relevance." Paper presented at the Canadian Political Science Association Annual Meeting. Calgary: University of Calgary.

———. 2003. *Rethinking Islamist Politics.* London: IB Tauris.

Ismail, Tareq Y. 2001. *Middle East Politics Today? Government and Civil Society.* Gainesville, FL: University Press of Florida.

Jad, Islah. 1995. "Claiming Feminism, Claiming Nationalism: Women's Activism in the Occupied Territories." In *Women's Movements in Global Perspective,* edited by Amrita Basu. Boulder, CO: Westview Press.

Johns, Anthony. 1975. "Islam in Southeast Asia: Reflections and New Directions." *Indonesia* 19: 33–55.

Joseph, Suad. 1997. "The Reproduction of Political Process among Women Activists in Lebanon: 'Shopkeepers' and Feminists." In *Organizing Women: Formal and Informal Women's Groups in the Middle East,* edited by Dawn Chatty and Annika Rabo. Oxford: Berg.

———. 2001. "Women and Politics in the Middle East." In *Women and Power in the Middle East*, edited by Suad Joseph and Susan Slyomovics. Pennsylvania: University of Pennsylvania Press.

Joseph, Suad and Joe Stork. 1993. "Gender and Civil Society: An Interview with Suad Joseph." *Middle East Report* 183 (July): 22–26.

Kamrava, Mehran. 1998. *Democracy in the Balance: Culture and Society in the Middle East*. New York: Chatham House.

Kanafani, Aida Sami. 1983. *Aesthetics and Ritual in the United Arab Emirates: The Anthropology of Food and Personal Adornment among Arabian Women*. Lebanon: American University of Beirut.

Kandil, Amani.1995. *Civil Society in the Arab World*. Cairo: Civicus.

———, ed. 1997. *Dalil awwali lil-jam'iyyat al-ahliyya al-'arabiyya* [An Initial Guide to the Arabic Civil Associations]. Cairo: Second Conference for Arabic Civil Organizations.

———, ed. 1999. *Al-mar'ah fi al-munazzamat al-ahliyya al-arabiyya* [Women in Arabic Civil Organizations: A group of researchers]. Cairo: Dar al-Mustaqbel al-Arabi.

———. 1999. "Women and Civil Society." In *Civil Society at the Millenium*. Civicus. West Hartford, CT: Kumarian Press.

———. 2001. "Women and Philanthropy in Egypt." In *Women, Philanthropy, and Civil Society*, edited by Kathleen D. McCarthy. Bloomington, IN: Indiana University Press.

Kandiyoti, Deniz. 1991. "Women, Islam and the State." *Middle East Report* 21: 9–14.

———, ed. 1996. *Gendering the Middle East: Emerging Perspectives*. London: I.B. Tauris Publishers.

———. 2001. "The Politics of Gender and the Conundrums of Citizenship." In *Women and Power in the Middle East*, edited by Suad Joseph and Susan Slyomovics. Pennsylvania: University of Pennsylvania Press

Karam, Azza 1998. *Women, Islamisms and the State: Contemporary Feminisms in Egypt*. New York: St. Martin's Press.

———. 2000. "Democrats without Democracy: Challenges to Women in Politics in the Arab World." In *International Perspectives on Gender and Democratisation*, edited by Shirin M. Rai. New York: St. Martin's Press.

Kazim, Aqil. 2000. *The United Arab Emirates A.D. 600 to the Present: A Socio-Discursive Transformation of the Arabian Gulf*. Dubai: Gulfbook Center.

Keane, John. 1988. *Democracy and Civil Society*. London: Verso Publishers.

Khalifa, Ali Mohammed. 1979. *The United Arab Emirates: Unity in Fragmentation*. London: Croom Helm.

Khatib, Maha K. 1994. "Beyond the Mysterious and Exotic: Women of the Emirates (And I) Assess Their Lives and Society." Ph.D. diss., Brown University.

Khoury, Philip S., and Joseph Kostiner. 1990. "Introduction: Tribes and Complexities of State Formation in the Middle East". In *Tribes and State Formation in the Middle East*, edited by Philip S. Khoury and Joseph Kostiner. Berkeley, CA: University of California Press.

Klandermans, Bert. 1997. *The Social Psychology of Protest.* Oxford: Blackwell.

Kleinberg, Remonda and Janine A. Clark, eds. 2000. *Economic Liberalization, Democratization and Civil Society in the Developing World.* Houndmills, UK: Macmillan Press.

Knight, Andy W. 2000. "State-Society Complexes and the New Multilateralism: Creating Space for Hierarchic Governance." In *Global Institutions and Local Empowerment: Competing Theoretical Perspectives,* edited by Kendall Stiles. Houndmills, UK: Macmillan Press.

Krause, Wanda C. 2004, "Civil Society in the Democratization Process: A Case Study on Cairo Islamic Women's and Secular Feminist Organizations." *Global Development Studies* 3, 3–4 (Winter 2003-Spring 2004):221–250.

———. 2004. "The Role and Example of Chilean and Argentinean Mothers in Democratisation." *Development in Practice* 14, 3 (April):366–380.

Kumar, Krishan. 1993. "Civil Society: An Inquiry into the Usefulness of an Historical Term." *British Journal of Sociology* 44, 3 (September): 375–395.

Lapidus, Ira. 1975. "The Separation of State and Religion in the Development of Early Islamic Society." *International Journal of Middle East Studies* 6, 4 (October): 363–365.

Lewis, David. 2001. "On the Difficulty of Studying 'Civil Society': Reflections on NGOs, State and Democracy in Bangladesh." Paper presented at South Asian Anthropologists Group Annual Meeting (September 13-14). University College, London.

Lienhardt, Peter. 2001. *Shaikhdoms of Eastern Arabia,* edited by Ahmed al-Shahi. New York: Palgrave.

Loizos, Peter. 1996. "How Ernest Gellner got Mugged on the Streets of London, or: Civil Society, the Media and the Quality of Life." In *Civil Society: Challenging Western Models,* edited by Chris Hann and Elisabeth Dunn. London: Routledge.

Looney, Robert E. 1997. "Diminishing Returns and Policy Options in a Rentier State: Economic Reform and Regime Legitimacy in Saudi Arabia." *Political Crossroads* 5, 1–2: 31–50.

———. 2001. "Saudi Arabia: Measures of Transition from a Rentier State." In *Iran, Iraq, and the Arab Gulf States,* edited by Joseph Kechichian. New York: Palgrave.

Loveman, Mara. 1998. "High Risk Collective Action: Defending Human Rights in Chile, Uruguay, and Argentina." *American Journal of Sociology* 104, 2: 477–525.

Lovenduski, Joni. 2005. *State Feminism and Political Representation.* Cambridge, MA: Cambridge University Press.

Luciani, Giacomo. 1987. "Allocation vs. Production States: A Theoretical Framework." In *Nation, State and Integration in the Arab World - Volume II: The Rentier State,* edited by Beblawi. London: Croom Helm.

———. 1990. "Allocation vs. Production States: A Theoretical Framework." In *The Arab State,* edited by Giacomo Luciani. Berkeley, CA: University of California Press.

Lukens-Bull, Ronald A. 1996. "Metaphorical Aspects of Indonesian Islamic

Discourse about Development." In *Intellectual Development in Indonesian Islam*. Tempe, AZ : ASU Program for Southeast Asian Studies Monograph Series.

————. 1999. "Between Text and Practice: Considerations in the Anthropological Study of Islam." *Marburg Journal of Religion* 4, 2 (December): 3–13.

Macleod, Arlene Elowe. 1991. *Accommodating Protest: Working Women, the New Veiling, and Change in Cairo*. New York: Columbia University Press.

Mahdavy, Hussein. 1970. "The Patterns and Problems of Economic Development in Rentier States: The Case of Iran." In *Studies in Economic History of the Middle East*, edited by A. Cook. London: Oxford University.

Mahmood, Saba. 1996. "Interview with Talal Asad: Modern Power and the Reconfiguration of Religious Traditions." *SEHR Contested Polities* 5, 1 (February 27), http://www.stanford.edu/group/SHR/5-1/text/asad.html (accessed 10 June 2006).

————. 2001. "Feminist Theory and the Egyptian Islamic Revival." *Cultural Anthropology* 16, 2: 202–236.

————. 2004. *Politics of Piety: The Islamic Revival and the Feminist Subject*. Princeton, NJ: Princeton University Press.

Mahmoud, Mohamed. 1999. *Al-Mar'ah fi dawlat al-imarat al-'arabiyya al-mutahida markazha al-qanuni fi zil al-qawaneen al-Nafidha wa qada' al-naqd fi al-imarat* [Woman in the State of the UAE : Her Legal Status under Effective Statutes and according to the Higher Court of the Emirates]. Al-Ain, UAE: UAE University Press.

McAdam, Doug. 1982. *Political Process and the Development of Black Insurgency,1930–1970*. Chicago: University of Chicago Press.

————. 1986. "Recruitment to High-Risk Activism: The Case of Freedom Summer." *American Journal of Sociology* 92, 1: 64–90.

————. 1992. "Gender as a Mediator of the Activist Experience: The Case of Freedom Summer." *American Journal of Sociology* 97, 5 (March): 1211–1240.

Mercado, Marta. 1999. "Power to Do: and to Make Money." In *Women and Power: Fighting Patriarchies and Poverty*. edited by Janet Gabriel Townsend, Emma Zapata, Joanna Rowlands, Pilar Alberti, and Marta Mercado. London: Zed Books.

Migdal, Joel S. 1988. *Strong Societies and Weak States: State-Society Relations and State Capabilities in the Third World*. Princeton, NJ: Princeton University Press.

Mitchell, Timothy. 1991. "The Limits of the State: Beyond Statist Approaches and Their Critics," *American Political Science Review* 85, 1: 77–96.

Moghadam, Valentine M. 1992. "Development and Women's Emancipation: Is there a Connection?" *Development and Change* 23: 215–255.

————. 1993. *Modernizing Women: Gender and Social Change in the Middle East*. Boulder, CO: Lynne Rienner Publishers.

————. 1998. *Women, Work and Economic Reform in the Middle East and North Africa*. Boulder, CO: Lynne Rienner Publishers.

Mohanty, Chandra. 1991. "Under Western Eyes: Feminist Scholarship and Colonial Discourses." In *Third World Women and the Politics of Feminism,* edited by C. Mohanty, Anna Russo, and Lourdes Torres. Bloomington, IN: Indiana University Press.

Molyneux, Maxine. 1985. "Mobilization without Emancipation? Women's Interests, the State, and Revolution in Nicaragua." In *Feminist Studies* 11, 2 (Summer): 227–254.

Moussalli, Ahmad. 1995. "Muslim Fundamentalist Discourses." In *Civil Society in the Middle East,* vol. 1, edited by Richard Norton. Leiden: E.J. Brill Publishers.

Naidoo, Kumi and Rajesh Tandon. 1999. "The Promise of Civil Society." In *Civil Society at the Millenium.* Civicus. Connecticut: Kumarian Press.

Navaro-Yashin, Yael. 2002. *Faces of the State: Secularism and Public Life in Turkey,* Princeton,NJ: Princeton University Press.

Neocleous, Mark. 1995. "From Civil Society to the Social." *The British Journal of Sociology* 46, 3 (September): 395–408.

Norton, Augustus Richard. 1993. "The Future of Civil Society in the Middle East." *Middle East Journal* 47, 2: 205–216.

———, ed. 1995. *Civil Society in the Middle East,* vol. 1. Leiden: Brill Publishers.

———, ed. 1996. *Civil Society in the Middle East,* vol. 2. Leiden: Brill Publishers.

Nyrop, Richard F., ed. 1985. *Persian Gulf States: Country Studies.* Washington D.C.: U.S. Government Printing Office.

Oberschall, Anthony. 1993. *Social Movements: Ideologies, Interests, and Identities.* New Brunswick: Transaction.

O'Donnell, Guillermo, Philippe C. Schmitter, and Laurence Whitehead, eds. 1986. *Transitions from Authoritarian Rule: Prospects for Democracy.* Baltimore, MD: John Hopkins University Press.

Okin, Susan Moller. 1979. *Women in Western Political Thought.* Princeton: Princeton, NJ University Press.

Okruhlik, Gwenn. 1999. "Rentier Wealth, Unruly Law, and the Rise of Opposition: The Political Economy of Rentier States." *Comparative Politics* 31, 3 (April): 295–315.

Ong, Aihwa.1988. "Colonialism and Modernity: Feminist Representations of Women in Non-Western Societies." *Inscriptions* 3/4 (October): 79–93.

Opp, Karl-Dieter and Christiane Gern. 1993. "Dissident Groups, Personal Networks, and Spontaneous Cooperation. The East German Revolution of 1989." *American Sociological Review* 58: 659–680.

Osa, Maryjane. 2003. "Networks in Opposition: Linking Organizations through Activists in the Polish People's Republic." In *Social Movements and Networks: Relational Approaches to Collective Action,* edited by Mario Diani and Doug McAdam. Oxford: Oxford University Press.

Ouis, Pernilla. 2002. *Power, Person, and Place: Tradition, Modernity, and Environment in the United Arab Emirates.* Ph.D. diss., Lund University. Lund: Studentliteratur.

Owen, Roger. 2000. *State, Power and Politics in the Making of the Modern Middle East,* 2nd ed. London: Routledge.

Paider, Parvin. 1995. *Women and the Political Process in Twentieth-Century Iran.* Cambridge, MA: Cambridge University Press.

Parpart, Jane L., and Marianne H. Marchand. 1995. "Exploding the Canon: An Introduction/Conclusion." In *Feminism/Postmodernism/Development,* edited by Marianne H. Marchand and Jane L. Parpart. New York: Routledge.

Passy, Florence. 2003. "Social Networks Matter. But How?" In *Social Movements and Networks: Relational Approaches to Collective Action,* edited by Mario Diani and Doug McAdam. Oxford: Oxford University Press.

Pateman, Carole. 1989. *The Disorder of Women: Democracy, Feminism and Political Theory.* Stanford, CA: Polity Press.

Peck, Malcolm. 1986. *The United Arab Emirates: A Venture in Unity.* Boulder, CO: Westview Press.

———. 2001. "Formation and Evolution of the Federation and its Institutions. In *United Arab Emirates: A New Perspective,* edited by Peter Hellyer and Ibrahim al-Abed. Bookcraft, UK: Trident Press.

Peterson, J. E. 1989. "The Political Status of Women in the Arab Gulf States. *Middle East Journal* 43: 34–50.

———. 1989. *The Arab Gulf States: Steps toward Political Participation.* New York: Praeger.

Phillips, Anne. 2002, "Does Feminism Need a Conception of Civil Society?" In *Alternative Conceptions of Civil Society,* edited by Kymlicka W. Chambers. Princeton, NJ: Princeton University Press.

Purushothaman, Sangeetha. 1997. *The Empowerment of Women in India: Grassroots Women's Networks and the State.* India: Sage India Publications.

Putnam, Robert D. 1995. "Bowling Alone: America's Declining Social Capital." *Journal of Democracy* 6, 1 (January): 65–78.

———. 2000. *Bowling Alone: The Collapse and Revival of American Community.* New York: Touchstone.

Qazzaz, Hadeel. 2005. "No . . . WASTA, Favoratism & Nepotism." Aman's 2nd Annual Conference, Ramallah (March 28). http://www.aman-palestine.org/English/Conf/wastaConf.htm (accessed 24 May 2006).

Qur'an 24:30. Translation by T.B. Irving.

Qur'an 4:34. Translation by Muhammad Asad.

Rabo, Annika. 1996. "Gender, state and civil society in Jordan and Syria." In *Civil Society: Challenging Western Models,* edited by Chris Hann and Elizabeth Dunn. London: Routledge.

———. 1997. *Organizing Women: Formal and Informal Women's Groups in the Middle East.* Oxford: Berg.

Ramazani, Nesta. 1985. "Arab Women in the Gulf." *The Middle East Journal* 39, 2 (Spring): 258–275.

Raudvere, Catharina. 2003. "Knowledge in Trust: Sufi Women in Istanbul." *Social Compass* 50, 1: 23–34.

Ritter, Gretchen and Nicole Mellow. 2000. "The State of Gender Studies in

Political Science." *Annals of the American Academy of Political and Social Science* 571 (September): 121–134.

Rizvi, Asad S. N. 1993. "From Tents to High Rise: Economic Development of the United Arab Emirates." *Middle Eastern Studies* 29, 4 (October): 664–678.

Rizzo, Helen Mary. 2000. "Islam, Democracy and the Status of Women: The Case of Kuwait." Ph.D. diss., Ohio State University.

Rose, Nikolas. 1996. "Governing 'Advanced' Liberal Democracies." In *Foucault and Political Reason: Liberalism, Neo-Liberalism and Rationalities of Governmentality,* edited by Andrew Barry, Thomas Osborne, and Nikolas Rose. Chicago: University of Chicago Press.

———. 1999. *Governing the Soul: The Shaping of the Private Self.* 2nd ed. London: Free Association Books.

Ross, Michael L. 2001. "Does Oil Hinder Democracy?" *World Politics* 53 (April): 325–61.

Rowlands, Jo. 1998. "A Word of the Times, but What Does it Mean? Empowerment in the Discourse and Practice of Development." In *Women and Empowerment: Illustrations from the Third World,* edited by Haleh Afshar. New York: St. Martin's Press.

Roy, Oliver. 1998. "Has Islamism a Future in Afghanistan?" In *Fundamentalism Reborn? Afghanistan and the Taliban,* edited by William Maley. New York: New York University Press.

Rugh, William A. 2000. "Leadership in the UAE: Past, Present and Future." In *A Century in Thirty Years: Shaykh Zayed and the United Arab Emirates,* edited by Joseph A. Kechichian. Washington: Middle East Policy Council.

———. 1997. "The United Arab Emirates: What are the Sources of its Stability?" *Middle East Policy* 5, 3 (September): 14–25.

Russel, Sharon Stanton. 1990. "Migration and Political Integration in the Arab World." In *The Arab State,* edited by Giacomo Luciani. London: Routledge.

Sabban, Rima 1996. "Broken Spaces; Bounded Realities: Foreign Female Domestic Workers in the UAE." Ph.D. diss., The American University, Washington.

Sadowski, Yahya. 1993. "The New Orientalism and the Democracy Debate." *Middle East Report* 183: 14–21.

Salmennlemi, Suvi. 2003. "Renegotiating Citizenship: Gender and Civil Society in Contemporary Russia." Paper presented at Gender and Power in the New Europe, the 5th European Feminist Research Conference (August 20-21), Lund: Lund University, Sweden.

Salvatore, Armando and Dale F. Eickelman, eds. 2004. *Public Islam and the Common Good.* Brill: Leiden.

Said, Edward. 1978. *Orientalism.* New York: Vintage.

Schmitter, Philippe. 1974. "Still the Century of Corporatism." *Review of Politics* 36, 1 (January): 85–131.

Scott, Joan Wallach. 1988. *Gender and the Politics of History.* New York: Columbia Press.

Seikaly, May. 1997. "Bahraini Women in Formal and Informal Groups: The Politics of Identification." In *Organizing Women: Formal and Informal Women's Groups in the Middle East*, edited by Dawn Chatty and Annika Rabo. Oxford: Berg.

Seligman, Adam B. 1992. *The Idea of Civil Society*. New York: The Free Press.

Shaheed, Farida. 1994. "Controlled or Autonomous: Identity and the Experience of the Network Women Living under Muslim Laws." *Signs* 19, 4: 997–1019.

Sharma, Aradhana. 2006. "Crossbreeding Institutions, Breeding Struggle: Women's Empowerment, Neoliberal Governmentality, and State (Re)Formation in India." *Cultural Anthropology* 21, 1: 60–95.

Shihab, Mohamed. 2001. "Economic Development in the UAE." In *United Arab Emirates: A New Perspective*, edited by Peter Hellyer and Ibrahim al-Abed. Bookcraft, UK: Trident Press.

Shils, Edward. 1992. "The Virtue of Civil Society." *Government and Opposition* 26, 1 (Winter): 3–20.

———. 1997. *The Virtue of Civility: Selected Essays on Liberalism, Tradition, and Civil Society*, edited by Steven Grosby. Indianapolis: Liberty Fund.

Sidaway, James D. 2005. "Geographies of Postdevelopment." Paper presented to the Inaugural Nordic Geographers Meetings, Lund (May 10–14), 13.

Singerman, Diane 1995. *Avenues of Participation: Family, Politics, and Networks in Urban Quarters of Cairo*. Princeton, NJ: Princeton University Press.

Site Institute. "Al-Qaeda in the United Arab Emirates and Oman Issues Ultimatum to the U.A.E. to Remove Jews and Christians from the Country within 10 Days." *The Search for International Terrorist Entities* (August 3, 2005) http://sitcinstitute.biz/bin/printerfriendly/pf.cgi (accessed 9 July 2006).

Skocpol, Theda. 1984. "Bringing the State Back In: Current Research." In *Bringing the State Back In*, edited by Peter Evans, Dietrich Ruschemeyer, and Theda Skocpoll. Cambridge, MA: Cambridge University Press.

Snow, David A., and Robert D. Benford. 1992. "Master Frames and Cycles of Protest." In *Frontiers in Social Movement Theory*, edited by A.D. Morris and C. M. Mueller. New Haven, CT: Yale University Press.

Soffan, Linda Usra. 1980. *The Women of the United Arab Emirates*. London: Croom Helm.

Sullivan, Denis J. 1994. *Private Voluntary Organizations in Egypt: Islamic Development, Private Initiative, and State Control*. Gainesville, FL: University Press of Florida.

Tamimi, Azzam, ed. 2000. *Islam and Secularism in the Middle East*. New York: New York University Press.

Tapper, Richard. 1990. "Anthropologists, Historians, and Tribespeople on Tribe and State Formation in the Middle East." In *Tribes and State Formation in the Middle East*, edited by Philip S. Khoury and Joseph Kostiner. Berkeley, CA: University of California Press.

Taussig, Michael. 1992. "Maleficium: State Fetishism." In *The Nervous System*, edited by Emily Apter and William Pietz. New York: Routledge.

Tétreault, Mary Ann. 1993. "Civil Society in Kuwait: Protected Spaces and Women's Rights." *Middle East Journal* 47: 275–291.

———. 1995. "Patterns of Culture and Democratization in Kuwait." *Studies in Comparative National Development* 30: 26–45.

Tétreault, Mary Ann and Haya al-Mughni. 1995. "Modernization and its Discontents: State and Gender in Kuwait." *Middle East Journal* 49: 403–417.

———. 1996. "Gender, Citizenship and Nationalism in Kuwait." *British Journal of Middle Eastern Studies* 22: 64–80.

Thomas, Karen. 2002. "Gulf Businesswomen strike back!" AME Info. Middle East Finance and Economy. http://www.ameinfo.com/16669.html (accessed 13 December 2004).

Thompson, Eric Vincent. 1999. "Democracy, Authoritarianism & Islam: Jordanian and Arab States." Ph.D. diss., University of Virginia.

Tilly, Charles. 1998. "Contentious Conversations." *Social Research* 65, 3: 491–510.

Toprak, Binnaz. 1996. "Civil Society in Turkey." In *Civil Society in the Middle East*, edited by Richard Norton, vol. 2. Leiden: Brill.

Townsend, Janet Gabriel et al. 1999. "Empowerment Matters: Understanding Power." In *Women and Empowerment: Illustrations from the Third World*, edited by Haleh Afshar. Houndmills: Macmillan Press.

Townsend, Janet Gabriel, Emma Zapata, Joanna Rowlands, Pilar Alberti, and Marta Mercado, eds. 1999. *Women and Power: Fighting Patriarchies and Poverty*. London: Zed Books.

Troxel, James P. 1998. "The Recovery of Civic Engagement in America." In *Beyond Prince and Merchant: Citizen Participation and the Rise of Civil Society*, edited by John Burbidge. New York: Pact.

UAE Interact, "UAE Best GCC State in Social Security Aid." September 18, 2005. http://www.uaeinteract.com/news/default.asp?ID=277 (accessed 20 March 2006).

"UAE Women." www.uaewomen.net (accessed 28 October 2005).

Ulph, Stephen. 2005. "New Qaeda Threats to the UAE." *The Jamestown Foundation. Terrorism Focus* 2, 15 (August 5): 5–6.

———. 2006. "Declassified Document Outlines History of al-Qaeda Threat to the UAE," *The Jamestown Foundation. Terrorism Focus* 3, 11 (March 21): 2-3.

UN Economic and Social Commission for Western Asia. 2003. *Report by the Arab Women's Center 2003*. New York: United Nations.

Van der Meulen, Hendrik. 1997. "The Role of Tribal and Kinship Ties in the Politics of the United Arab Emirates. Ph.D. diss., Fletcher School of Law and Diplomacy.

Vandewalle, Dirk. 1998. *Libya since Independence: Oil and State-Building*. Ithaca: Cornell University Press.

Walzer, Michael. 1980. *Radical Principles: Reflections of an Unreconstructed Democrat*. New York: Basic Books.

Waterbury, John. 1997. "From Social Contract to Extraction Contracts: The Political Economy of Authoritarianism and Democracy." In *Islam, Democracy and the State in North Africa*, edited by John P. Entelis. Bloomington: Indiana University Press.

Waylen, Georgina. 1994. "Women and Democratization: Conceptualizing Gender Relations in Transition Politics." *World Politics* 46: 327–354.

Werner, Cynthia Ann. 1997. "Women and the Art of Household Networking in Rural Kazakstan," *Islamic Quarterly: A Review of Islamic Culture* xli, 1 (first quarter): 54–67.

White, Gordan. 1994. "Civil Society, Democratization, and Development: Clearing the Analytical Ground." *Democratization* 1, 3 (Autumn): 375–390.

Wikan, Unni. 1991. *Behind the Veil in Arabia: Women in Oman*. Chicago: University of Chicago Press.

Wikipedia Encyclopedia. Economy of the United Arab Emirates. http://en .wikipedia.org/wiki/Economy_of_the_United_Arab_Emirates (accessed 12 February 2005).

Wiktorowicz, Quintan. 1999. "The Limits of Democracy in the Middle East: The Case of Jordan." *Middle East Journal* 53, 4 (Autumn): 606–620.

———. 2000. "The Salafi Movement in Jordan." *International Journal of Middle East Studies* 32, 2 (May): 219–240.

Wodak, Ruth and Michael Meyer. 2001. *Methods of Critical Discourse Analysis*. London: Sage.

"Women in the UAE." *Arab Women Connect*, www.awc.org.jo/english/uae/ downloads/WOMEN%20IN%20THE%20UAE.doc *(accessed 3 November 2003)*.

"Women in UAE." http://www.uaeforever.com/Women/ (accessed 3 November 2003).

"Women's Developing Role in the UAE." http://sjw.hct.ac.ae/html/ students/noorah/personal6.htm (accessed 9 November 2003). "Women Living under Muslim Laws." http://www.wluml.org (accessed 17 September 2006).

Woodward, Mark. 1988. "The *Slametan*: Textual Knowledge and Ritual Performance in Central Javanese Islam." *History of Religions* 28, 1: 54–89.

Word Reference Com: World Dictionary. http://www.wordreference.com/ definition/tolerance (accessed 5 May 2006).

World Pipelines. 2006. "Regional Briefing: UAE." Palladian Publications. http://www.worldpipelines.com/Pipelines/WP_regional_report_Sept04 .htm (accessed 15 June 2006).

Yamani, Mai. 1997. "Health Education, Gender and the Security of the Gulf in the Twenty-first Century." In *Gulf Security in the Twenty-First Century*, edited by David E. Long and Christian Koch. Abu Dhabi: Emirates Center for Strategic Studies and Research.

———. 2000. *Changed Identities: The Challenge of the New Generation in Saudi Arabia*. London: Royal Institute of International Affairs, 115.

Zubaida, Sami. 1992. "Islam, the State and Democracy." *Middle East Report* 179 (November-December): 2–10.

GOVERNMENT DOCUMENTS

CIA World Factbook. 2002. United Arab Emirates. http://www.odci.gov/ cia/publications/factbook/geos/tc.html (accessed 23 April 2004).

CIA World Factbook. 2005. United Arab Emirates. http://www.cia .gov/cia/publications/factbook/geos/ae.html (accessed 23 June 2006).

Government.ae. 2006. "Oil and Gas." http://www.government.ae/gov/ en/biz/industry/oil.jsp (accessed 15 June 2006).

Library of Congress Country Studies: United Arab Emirates. 1993. http://lcweb2.loc.gov/cgi-bin/query/r?frd/cstdy:@field(DOCID+ae0033 (accessed 12 February 2005).

The Emirates Center for Strategic Studies and Research. http://www .ecssr.ac.ae/system.htm (accessed 12 February 2005).

U.S. Central Intelligence Agency. UT Library Online. 2005. http:// www.lib.utexas.edu/maps/united_arab_emirates.html (accessed 14 June 2006).

U.S. Department of State Human Rights Reports for 2000. February 2001. "The 57th Commission on Human Rights." http://www.humanrights-usa .net/reports/unitedarabemirates.html 2003. (accessed 16 November 2003).

U.S. Department of State. 2005. "United Arab Emirates: Country Reports on Human Rights Practices 2004." http://www.state.gov/g/drl/rls/ hrrpt/2004/41734.htm (accessed 23 June 2006).

U.S. Department of State. 2006. "United Arab Emirates: Country Reports on Human Rights Practices 2005." Released by the Bureau of Democracy, Human Rights, and Labor (March 8). http://www.state.gov/g/drl/ rls/hrrpt/2005/61701.htm (accessed 23 June 2006).

UAE Interact: The Official Website for the Ministry of Information and Culture in the UAE. 2002. "Sheikha Fatima Hails Zayed's Support for Women's Issues." (July 2). http://www.uaetravelguide.com/news/?ID= 200 (accessed 12 May 2003).

United Arab Emirates Zayed Centre for Coordination and Follow-up. 2000. *Feminine Issues in the United Arab Emirates: Perspectives of a Visionary Leader.* Dubai: Zayed Centre.

"Women in UAE." http://www.uae.gov.ae/Government/Women.htm (accessed 3 November 2003).

NEWSPAPER ARTICLES

al-Jandali, Bassma. "Women Proved Their Competence in All Fields-Manal." *Gulf News* (November 26, 2002) http://www.gulfnews.com/Articles/ news.asp?ArticleID=69538 (accessed 13 December 2004).

al-Jandali, Bassma. "Man Confesses to Striking Match that Set Wife Ablaze", *Gulf News* (December 7, 2004) http://search.gulfnews.com/articles/04/07/12/125969.html (accessed 25 December 2006).

Bisset, Susan. "Emirate Prince Ousted in Women's Rights Row," *Daily Telegraph* (June 15, 2003) www.telegraph.co.uk/news/main.jhtml?xml=/news/2003/06/15 (accessed 9 September 2005).

Georgia, Lydia. "UAE first lady calls for dialogue." http://www.metimes.com/2K2/issue2002–14/women/uae_first_lady.htm (accessed 14 December 2004).

Gulf News. "Sheikha Fatima Urges Women to Join Council." (March 10, 2002) http://www.gulf-news.com/Articles/news.asp?ArticleID=64620 (accessed 14 December 2004).

Gulf News. "Fatima Sees Promising Future for UAE Women." (November. 8, 2002) http://www.gulf-news.com/Articles/news.asp?ArticleID=67882m (accessed 13 December 2004).

Gulf News. "Woman Gets Divorce after Three Years of Wrangling." http://www.gulf-news.com/Articles/news.asp?ArticleID 67962 (accessed 2 February 2005).

Gulf News. "Women in Theater 'Enrich Literary Scene." http://www.sharjah-y welcome.com/News/Archives/2000/April/wk5/womensclub.htm (accessed 13 December 2004).

Gulf News. "Women will enrich FNC says Hind." (December 1, 2002) http://www.gulf-news.com/Articles/news.asp?ArticleID=70782 (accessed 13 December 2004).

Kanafani, Samar. "Child-raising Should Come First: Sheikha Fatima Gives Her View of a Woman's Place." *Daily Star*, http://www.lebanonwire.com/news/02021816DS.htm (accessed 14 December 2004).

Shaghouri, Tahseen. "Expats Employing Illegals will be Deported." *Gulf News* (April 24, 2003) http://gulfnews.com/Articles/news.asp?ArticleID–85414 (accessed 2 May 2003).

The Independent (*Online Edition*). "Migrants and the Middle East: Welcome to the Other Side of Dubai." (March 28, 2006) http://news.independent.co.uk/world/middle_east/article354070.ece (accessed 28 March 2006).

Waqar, Ali. "64 Jockeys Back Home." *Daily Times* (November 26, 2005) http://www.dailytimes.com.pk/default.asp?page=2005%5C11%5C26%5Cstory_26-11-2005_pg7_9 (accessed 2 December 2005).

———. "Divorce Survey to Begin Soon." *Gulf News* (November 12, 2002) http://www.gulf-news.com/Articles/news.asp?ArticleID=68212 (accessed 2 February 2003).

BLOGS

shabakat wa muntadayat al-mass (Diamond Blogs and Network) www.almassuae.com

muntada jeeran (the Neighbors' Blog) www.boy123.jeeran.com/alenawiah/

muntada shumou' (The Blog of the Candles) www.shm03.uae

UAE Community Blog, "LG: Life's Not Fair," (April 27, 2006) http://
  uaecommunity.blogspot.com/2006/04/lg-lifes-not-good.html (accessed
  27 April 2006).

INDEX